Handbook of
Product Cost Estimating
and Pricing

Thomas S. Dudick
Consultant to Ernst & Young

PRENTICE HALL
BUSINESS & PROFESSIONAL DIVISION
Englewood Cliffs, New Jersey 07632

Library of Congress Cataloging-in-Publication Data

Dudick, Thomas S.
  Handbook of product cost estimating and pricing/Thomas S. Dudick.
    p. cm.
  Includes index.
  ISBN 0–13–372780–7
  1. Pricing. 2. Prices. 3. Costs, Industrial—Estimates.
I. Title.
HF5416.5.D84   1991
658.8′16—dc20   90-7373
                                                    CIP

Prentice-Hall International (UK) Limited, *London*
Prentice-Hall of Australia, Pty. Limited, *Sydney*
Prentice-Hall Canada Inc., *Toronto*
Prentice-Hall Hispanoamericana, S.A., *Mexico*
Prentice-Hall of India Private Limited, *New Delhi*
Prentice-Hall of Japan, Inc., *Tokyo*
Simon & Schuster Asia Pte. Ltd., *Singapore*
Editora Prentice-Hall do Brasil Ltda., *Rio de Janeiro*

Printed in the United States of America

10 9 8 7 6 5 4 3

ISBN 0-13-372780-7

PRENTICE HALL
BUSINESS & PROFESSIONAL DIVISION
A division of Simon & Schuster
Englewood Cliffs, New Jersey 07632

*Dedicated to
Michael, Christopher,
Colin and Caitlin Dudick*

ABOUT THE AUTHOR

Thomas S. Dudick is consultant to Ernst & Young in cost systems, product costing, pricing, manufacturing cost and operating controls. He has served as budget director, plant controller and internal consultant for GTE-Sylvania, Allen B. DuMont Laboratories and Raytheon Company.

His educational background includes a B.S. Degree from New York University and an MBA degree from Boston University. He has been guest lecturer at Boston University, Loyola College, and Harvard Business School. In Beijing, China, he participated in a seminar given to key industrial executives from all parts of China.

Mr. Dudick is author of *Cost Controls for Industry*, Dudick on Manufacturing Cost Controls (Prentice-Hall), *Profile for Profitability*, *How to Improve Profitability Through More Effective Business Planning and Cost Accounting Desk Reference Book*. He co-authored *Inventory Control for the Financial Executive* and was Editor-in-Chief of the *Handbook for Business Planning and Budgeting for the Executive with Profit Responsibility*. His articles have been published in numerous professional and trade association journals.

Foreword

We often talk about improving productivity and maintaining quality as the key issue in the renewal of American manufacturing. We see technology as the backbone of this renewal and point, with no shortage of pride, to the ways technology has contributed to an improved competitive posture for U.S. industry, both at home and abroad. Yet our successes (and our failures) in these vital areas of operations improvement depend on more than the new technologies we adopt, important as they may be. Already the winners in the process of renewal are distinguishing themselves from the losers because they understand this fact. They are attacking operations improvement across the entire spectrum of organizational activity, from strategic planning to the organization of people to effective performance measurement.

This book addresses one of the fundamental issues underlying operations improvement for competitive advantage—product cost estimating and pricing. Its twenty-two chapters and dozens of exhibits argue convincingly for renewed efforts to improve product cost estimating, not only for use as a guide to pricing, as Thomas Dudick's preface states, but [also] as a means for determining profitability of the various products. Executives with profit responsibilities will want to consider the chapter on the role of fixed and variable costs in product costing and pricing. They will find valuable insights in the separate chapters on the differences between cost-based pricing for commercial and government customers, the relationship of product costs to pricing and real-world problems in cost estimating and pricing. A case study of profit planning, profits and pricing gives detailed analyses of cost estimates in relation to profits. A final chapter provides "ten commandments" for more realistic costing and pricing.

Thomas Dudick has done an admirable job in treating this difficult but vital subject. His many years' experience in cost accounting and product pricing, much of it as a consultant with Ernst & Young, lend weight and credibility to each topic addressed by the book. With *Handbook of Product Cost Estimating and Pricing*, he has added significantly to the literature and knowledge within the field.

John G. D. Carden
Vice Chairman
Management Consulting
Ernst & Young

80 Firing Line Topics

It should be apparent to every executive with profit responsibility that costing procedures in many, if not most, companies must be greatly improved before product costs can play their proper role in pricing products for sale. Product cost estimating must be improved not only for use as a guide to pricing but as a means for determining profitability of the various products. The purpose of this book is to point the way toward accomplishing these ends.

The book covers the following 80 topics in the various chapters.

1. What was ElectroComp, Inc. doing wrong that its 888 circuit board was not selling while 864 and 892 were selling well? See chapter 1.

2. If you are using only one plantwide overhead rate, based on either direct labor or machine hours, your product costs are probably incorrect. See Exhibits 1.2 and 1.3 for a suggested quick test to determine how many rates are needed.

3. If your company purchases products for resale and you do not use a material-related overhead rate, you are probably overstating the profitability of the resale products and understating the profitability of your manufactured products. See chapter 1.

4. The same principle applies to contractors who receive government-furnished material. Do not forget that you are incurring material handling costs such as receiving, incoming inspection, and storage. If you do not

use a material-related overhead rate to cover these costs, you are penalizing other contracts.

5. In the event that a contract (government or otherwise) is cancelled, you will need a material-related overhead rate to support your request for reimbursement of material handling costs incurred. See chapter 1.

6. An appliance manufacturer could not understand why some of his products showed such a low gross profit. A study revealed that the material content ranged from a high of 80% of prime cost to a low of 58%. Departmental overhead rates based on direct labor were being used because this was a labor-paced operation. As a result, products with a high material and low labor content were being subsidized by products with a high labor and low material content. See Exhibit 1.4.

7. Material-related overhead rates should not always be expressed in terms of dollars. There are times when weight or size provide a better base. See chapter 1.

8. Before using a plantwide percentage for production reject allowances, make certain that the variations of rejections are not great. See Exhibit 1.6, which shows that reject percentages in this company ranged from a high of 17% to a low of 3%. Using the plantwide average of 9%, which the company did, would understate the allowance for some products and overstate others.

9. Sewing Notions, Inc. used a plantwide percentage of manufacturing cost to provide for tooling costs. Much to the company's surprise, the actual tooling costs for one of their products was three and a half times greater than the amount allocated through use of the percentage. It's all right to use the percentage if most of the tooling costs are small; but look for the ones whose tool costs are large and deal with them separately. See chapter 1.

10. Many, if not most, companies use a production line approach in allocating selling, general, and administrative (SG&A) because they use percent of sales or percent of cost of sales as the base for distributing these non-manufacturing costs. These one-size-fits-all methods can greatly distort product line profitability, as shown in Exhibit 2.1.

11. Exhibit 2.2 lists seven large SG&A expenses in three market segments and explains why they vary from one market segment to another.

12. A company manufacturing sunglasses and combs learned how the one-size-fits-all method of allocating SG&A can distort costs of the smaller product line, which in this case was the combs. See chapter 2.

13. Exhibits 3.1 through 3.5 explain a five-step method for developing machine hour rates. Exhibit 3.4 shows how five rates can be expanded by adding differential rates to the five basic rates.

14. Exhibit 3.7 shows how a wire drawing company interpolates the cost of a nonstandard draw.

15. Many books on the subject of breaking down overhead into its fixed and variable segments recommend the use of scatter charts. Exhibit 4.3 shows the ideal pattern of a scatter chart as depicted in many books. Exhibit 4.4 shows the more likely real-world pattern, which recognizes that some overhead expenses lead changes in volume, and others lag.

16. See chapter 4 for a discussion of other methods used in the determination of fixed and variable costs.

17. Among the available methods for breaking down the overhead into its fixed and variable segments, the writer favors analysis of an experienced level of activity in which the determination of what is fixed and what is variable is resolved by consulting the various department heads with responsibility for controlling the expenses. See chapter 4.

18. Exhibit 4.6 illustrates how Runzheimer International projects fixed and operating (variable) costs for 10 selected automobile models. The American and Canadian Automobile Associations rely on these figures, as does the Internal Revenue Service, which establishes the per-mile rates for income tax purposes.

19. Exhibit 4.7 shows how the fixed and variable data presented to a manufacturer of filler assemblies and heat exchangers facilitated the adjustment of the selling price of one of the four products.

20. Exhibit 4.8 shows the impact of mix changes on profit before fixed costs, profit after fixed costs, and the break-even point.

21. Intracompany transfer pricing can create problems in pricing the end products correctly. See Exhibits 5.1 and 5.2.

22. Exhibit 5.3 shows the break-even point for Plant 3 prior to revision and after revision to illustrate the impact on the break-even point if the entire transfer price had not been treated as a variable cost.

23. Chapter 6 provides an overview of differences in classifying costs for customized and standardized products. See "Differences in Cost Classification." Subsequent chapters will provide illustrative examples.

24. If your company manufactures customized products, do you continually monitor the size of the Request for Quotation (RFQ) backlog? If not, you should. See chapter 6.

25. Do you monitor the number of elapsed days from date of receipt of the RFQ to date of completion? If not, you should. See chapter 6.

26. If your company manufactures highly engineered products, are you aware of the number of possible inspections that add materially to product cost? If not, see Exhibit 7.1.

27. Are you aware of the material versus conversion cost differences in your products if you make a wide range of sizes? If not, see Exhibit 7.2 for an illustrative example of how one company realized that material-related overhead had to be calculated separately from the conversion-related overhead.

28. Does your company utilize a feedback procedure to compare RFQ cost estimates with the resulting profit? If not, see Exhibit 7.3.

29. If the comparison of cost estimates with profit shows that the profit is too low, check the detail behind the cost estimate as shown in Exhibit 7.4.

30. Is your classification of costs used in developing the annual financial plan consistent with the classifications used when charging costs to the contract(s)? If not, read the section titled "Forecasting Direct Labor and Overhead Rates" in chapter 8.

31. Any changes that are made in the make/buy policy must be taken into account when preparing cost estimates. If this is not done, the material/conversion cost relationship may not be consistent with the breakdown in the annual financial plan from which overhead costing rates were developed. See chapter 8.

32. In the case of contracts, auditors are likely to review transfer prices more closely if purchases are made from other units within the company. The purpose is to prevent overcharging.

33. In establishing overhead rates, do you base these on practical capacity? If not, large variances will occur. This could lead to suspicion that the large variances may be due to other contracts (or to commercial products being produced). See the section titled "Available versus Practical Capacity" in chapter 8.

34. The defense department favors the use of learning curves as a basis for costing products. See the section, "The Learning Curve as a Guide to Costing and Pricing" in chapter 8.

35. If your contracts include product development with follow-on production of these products, see Exhibit 8.4.

36. Do you regularly prepare Estimate to Complete analyses of the contracts in process? Such analyses can be very helpful in tracking progress in the work being performed. This not only tracks cumulative costs but the status of profits as well. If the profit appears to be falling short of goals, it could be an indication that quoted prices were too low. See Exhibit 9.1.

37. If you have long-term contracts for commercial products, see Exhibit 9.2. These are actual figures taken from a contract to build industrial equipment.

38. Exhibit 9.3 tracks the Estimate to Complete costs through work-in-process and into finished goods.

39. Chapter 10 shows how overhead costs are integrated from development of the overhead costing rates to preparation of job cost estimates, flexible budgets, and break-even analyses. Chapter 21 discusses integrating the cost system and its role in product costing and pricing.

40. Is your costing of standardized products computerized? If not, chapter 11 should be helpful, particularly for integrating the cost system with computer aided manufacturing (CAM). Exhibit 11.3 shows how manufacturing process sheets are structured to arrive at the material, direct labor, and overhead costs for the various levels. See also Exhibits 11.4, 11.5, and 11.6.

41. How good is your annual financial plan? Good financial plans require realistic sales forecasts—a topic which is discussed in chapter 21. Since Stereo, Inc., which is discussed in chapter 12, did base its financial plan on good sales forecasts, it was selected for analysis of profitability of the individual products. See Exhibit 12.4.

42. Exhibit 12.6 shows how Stereo, Inc. used its profit plan to single out products for redesign to meet competitive prices.

43. Does your company periodically test the impact of changes in the economy on costs and prices? See Exhibit 12.7.

44. Markup factors in many, if not most, companies are attained by applying a single percentage to the total product cost. See chapter 13, which discusses different types of markup factors.

45. Do you monitor return on investment (equity) as well as return on sales? See Exhibits 13.7 through 13.9. The figures are significant because the decade of the 1970s shows the impact of two recessions, a period of high inflation, and government price controls.

46. What is wrong with using a single markup factor on total manufacturing cost? See Exhibit 13.11.

47. The marketplace does not permit a price increase every time the price index makes an upward move. The price of first-class postage, for example, increased only 11 times in 56 years. See Exhibit 14.2.

48. Prices can even decline, as was the case with television set manufacturing from 1947 through 1957, during which time the average size of the picture doubled. The growing volume, coupled with design improvements, more than offset the inflation rate. See Exhibit 14.6.

49. During the high inflationary decade of the 1970s, the price index for television sets remained close to the 1967 price index of 100% while the index of total goods and services rose from about 120% to almost 250%. See Exhibit 14.5.

50. If your company has long-term contracts, it would be wise to provide for surcharges to recover the additional costs incurred because of increases in the inflation rate. Estimate to Complete reports, discussed in chapter 9, should also monitor the impact of inflation on the Cost to Complete estimates.

51. How do you cope with customers who do not provide adequate information in their RFQ? Read how one general manager handled this problem in chapter 15.

52. Some customers, instead of including the specifications of the product they want, will say "similar to" or "same as." Chapter 15 tells what the risks are.

53. Read how you can ease into a price increase in chapter 15.

54. Is your company one of the many that rarely checks the estimated costs in RFQs with the actuals? Feedback is one way to improve accuracy. Review the format referred to earlier in Exhibits 7.3 and 7.4.

55. Take precautions when using marginal pricing. Chapter 15 explains why.

56. If your company manufactures equipment and also makes on-site installations of that equipment, read the section titled "Estimating Costs for Systems Installation" in Chapter 15.

57. Companies that start with a basic price plus adders to take care of various options may not have made the best choice. Chapter 15 tells why.

58. Chapter 1 discussed the need for a material-related overhead rate when costing purchases for resale. Chapter 15 calls attention to the desirability of comparing the percentage return on sales with the percentage return on investment, inasmuch as there is virtually no investment required for resale purchases except finished goods inventory. See chapter 15.

59. If cost estimates and suggested prices are too high, the cause could be poorly maintained equipment. Exhibit 15.2 lists defects in 19 of the 36 machines in a division of a well-known company.

60. Product life cycles are assumed by many to follow a standard pattern, as shown in Figure 16.1. Exhibit 16.2 shows that there are numerous different patterns that must be taken into account when projecting potential profitability.

61. Product costs and prices can vary widely in different stages of the product life cycle. See Exhibit 16.4.

62. Exhibits 16.5 and 16.6 show the financial results of two companies in the early stages of growth. Note in the former exhibit that it took five years for the new operation to get out of a loss position, and in the latter, six years. This is typical in many companies.

63. Chapter 13 dealt with the increased costs of just-in-time (JIT) inventory deliveries to suppliers. Chapter 17 deals with JIT from the viewpoint of the purchaser. See Exhibits 17.1 through 17.3.

64. Salespeople are often unaware of the extra costs incurred in providing just-in-time inventory delivery. Others who are aware are reluctant to press for a higher price. One company made the sales department more profit conscious by breaking down the internal income statement to show the profit performance for Manufacturing separately from Marketing. See Exhibit 17.4.

65. Reluctance on the part of some cost estimators to adapt to change could result in unwarranted price reductions. See "Cost Estimating in Transition" in chapter 18.

66. Chapter 18 discusses how a dominant product can distort costs of other products.

67. To find out how to slot new additions into a family of similar products to ensure consistency in costing, see Exhibit 18. See also Exhibit 19.3, which illustrates a pricing matrix for the same family of products.

68. For the case histories of three companies whose product pricing was incorrect because of costing deficiencies, see chapter 19.

69. Pricing a premium product to show a greater dollar profit is not enough: it must show a greater *percentage* profit than the standard product of the same type. See "Premium Pricing" in chapter 19.

70. Under what conditions is it proper to cut prices? See "Marginal Pricing" in chapter 19.

71. When pricing a new product, how can the required volume to meet competitive prices be determined? See "Break-even Test for Pricing" in chapter 19.

72. Doral Electronics established selling prices for its replacement parts that yielded an 18% profit, with which management was pleased. Overlooked, however, was the inventory carrying cost of the replacement parts, which alone amounted to 23.8% of the inventory value. See chapter 19.

73. See Exhibit 19.6 for a suggested format for monitoring the success ratio of price quotations.

74. Read "Monitoring the Backlog of Orders" in chapter 20 to see how size of the backlog of orders can affect pricing.

75. Companies with development and follow-on production contracts should monitor the backlog of both. The Ethcos Company realized the importance of doing so only after its backlog of production work dropped precipitously, thus increasing product costs. See the section titled "Balancing Development and Production Contracts" in chapter 20, as well as Exhibit 20.4.

76. Many customers, in obtaining bids for the low-value C and D items, are not likely to put as much emphasis on price as they would on the higher-cost A or B items. Keep in mind that the customer C and D items might be A and B items to the supplying company. See "Customer-related Pricing Strategy" in chapter 20.

77. To whom should the cost estimator report? See also "Qualifying Cost Estimators by Type of Products" in chapter 20.

78. Read the section titled "Why Sales and Accounting Coordination is Important" in chapter 20 to find out how these two functions in one company changed an adverserial relationship to a more cooperative team approach.

79. How internal and external factors can affect pricing. See chapter 20.

80. Read the "Ten Commandments" in Chapter 22 which can be used as a frame of reference to provide more realistic product costs and prices.

Contents

CHAPTER 16

The Product Life Cycle: Its Impact on Product Cost Estimating and Pricing, 199

CHAPTER 17

Increased Product Costs Due to JIT are Often Overlooked, 215

CHAPTER 18

Various Formats for Estimating Product Costs, 229

CHAPTER 1

Correcting Product Cost Deficiencies

Many managers are surprisingly naive on the subject of product costing and its relationship to pricing products for sale. They believe that scrupulously calculated costs are used for setting selling prices. Nothing could be further from the truth. Product costs in most companies must be improved before they can play a larger role in setting prices. The focus of this chapter, therefore, will be directed to typical product costing deficiencies related to calculation of manufacturing costs.

OVERHEAD-RELATED PRODUCT COSTING DEFICIENCIES

S. Paul Garner, in *Evolution of Cost Accounting to 1925* (University of Alabama, 1976), mentions that John Whitmore, in one of his articles written as far back as 1906, recommended the use of machine hour rates in allocating overhead costs in machine-paced operations.

Now, near the twilight of the twentieth century, many companies are still using direct labor as the vehicle for allocating overhead to machine-paced operations. Use of direct labor as an allocation base for products that are produced on automatic equipment may result in erroneous product costs. ElectroComp, Inc. (name disguised) is a case in point. This company produces three types of circuit boards, which are processed on automated equipment. One of these, CB-888, requires some additional operations that must be performed manually rather than by machine. By using direct labor as the overhead allocation base, this additional direct labor would penalize CB-888 by charging an excessive amount of machine-related overhead to it.

This is illustrated in Exhibit 1.1. The upper third of this exhibit lists the direct labor requirements for making the three boards. It also shows the machine time required for the operations that are performed automatically.

The middle section of the exhibit shows the percentage of direct labor and the percentage of machine time for each of the three boards. Note that the direct labor percentage for CB-888 is 56%, while the remaining 44% is split between the other two. The same breakdown by machine hours shows close to a one-third distribution for each of the three.

The bottom third of the exhibit shows the dollar impact of overhead distribution based on both direct labor and on machine time. A comparison of the two shows how greatly the overhead for CB-888 is overstated because of the additional direct labor required for CB-888. This is evidenced by the $133.32 for CB-888 when direct labor is used as the allocation base, compared with only $86.49 when the overhead allocation is made by machine hours. The

EXHIBIT 1.1

**CIRCUIT BOARDS
DIRECT LABOR VERSUS MACHINE HOURS**

Circuit Board Number	Direct Labor Cost per 100	Machine Hours per 100
Direct Labor Cost versus Machine Hours		
CB-864	$ 23.70	.1261
CB-888	66.66	.1502
CB-892	28.86	.1378
	$119.22	.4141
Percentage Breakdown of Direct Labor and Machine Time		
CB-864	20%	30%
CB-888	56%	36%
CB-892	24%	34%
	100%	100%
Overhead Cost Breakdown by Both Methods		
CB-864	$ 47.40	$ 72.57
CB-888	133.32	86.49
CB-892	57.72	79.38
	$238.44	$238.44

additional direct labor cost must, of course, be included in the cost of CB-888. It would carry with it only the labor-related overhead.

Labor-Paced Operations

There are many companies whose operations are substantially labor paced and will remain so in the foreseeable future. But even in labor-paced operations, product costs are frequently flawed because of arbitrariness in the assignment of overhead to the individual products. FluorLamp, Inc. (name disguised) is a case in point.

FluorLamp, a small manufacturer of specialty fluorescent fixtures, will continue to use direct labor as a base because of the highly customized nature of this company's products. The company had been using a single plantwide overhead rate until the plant manager was advised that certain of the products were being overcosted and others undercosted. The large fluorescent fixtures, for example, are made of heavier-gauge steel and therefore require the use of heavy presses, while the smaller fixtures are fabricated in the medium and light press section.

The addition of a louver to some fixtures requires the use of what the company identifies as accessory equipment. If the fixture is to be suspended rather than attached flush with the ceiling, this equipment is also used to cut the suspension tubing to length and thread it at both ends.

In view of these differences in type of equipment, a test calculation was made for two different fixtures. The objective was to compare the metal shop cost of the two fixtures by using the single overall metal shop rate; and then to recost the two fixtures by taking into account the operating cost differences of the three metal shop sections. In the interest of simplicity in making the test calculation, only two major costs were considered: (1) depreciation plus maintenance; and (2) rent-equivalent cost.

Exhibit 1.2 illustrates how the basic figures were accumulated to make this test. Note that the monthly cost of depreciation plus maintenance is 3.3 times as much per operator for the heavy presses than the medium and light presses ($139 divided by $42). For the rent-equivalent costs, the cost per operator for the heavy presses is 2.4 times greater than the medium and light presses $833 divided by $344).

Exhibit 1.3 shows the cost calculation for the two fixtures based on individual metal shop rates and also on an overall basis in which the costs per operator for the two expenses are averaged out. Note that the cost of fixture A based on individual shop metal rates is $317 for depreciation plus maintenance and $1,838 for rent-equivalent costs. This compares with $198 and $1,098,

EXHIBIT 1.2

BREAKDOWN OF METAL SHOP EQUIPMENT BY TWO MAJOR ITEMS OF COST

		Monthly Cost of Major Items		Monthly Cost per Operator	
	Normal Complement of Operators	*Depreciation + Maintenance*	*Rent-Equivalent Cost*	*Depreciation + Maintenance*	*Rent-Equivalent Cost*
Heavy Presses					
2 Press Brakes	3	368	2,100	123	700
3 95–150-Ton Presses	3	438	2,700	146	900
4 250-Ton Presses	6	858	5,200	143	866
9	12	1,664	10,000	139	833
Medium and Light Presses					
8 50-Ton Presses	8	348	2,600	44	325
6 Versons	4	183	1,500	46	375
9 25-Ton Presses	6	232	2,100	39	350
23	18	763	6,200	42	344
Accessory Equipment					
6 Bench Presses	2	28		14	
6 Spot Welders	6	162		27	
5 Shears	5	262		52	
3 Threaders and Cutoffs	2	52		26	
20	15	504	300	35	20
Total Metal Shop	45	2,931	16,500	66	366

EXHIBIT 1.3

APPLICATION OF TWO MAJOR COSTS TO LIGHT FIXTURES A AND B BASED ON THREE RATES

	Number of Operators	*Depreciation + Maintenance*	*Rent Equivalent Costs*
Light Fixture A			
Heavy Presses	2	$278 (2 × $139)	$1,666 (2 × $833)
Medium and Light Presses	$\frac{1}{2}$	21 ($\frac{1}{2}$ × $42)	172 ($\frac{1}{2}$ × 344)
Accessory Equipment	$\frac{1}{2}$	18 ($\frac{1}{2}$ × $35)	—
Total Fixture A	3	$317	$1,838
Light Fixture B			
Heavy Presses	—	—	—
Medium and Light Presses	2	84 (2 × $42)	688 (2 × $344)
Accessory Equipment	—	—	—
Total Fixture B	2	$ 84	$ 688

APPLICATION OF TWO MAJOR COSTS TO LIGHT FIXTURES A AND B BASED ON ONE OVERALL RATE

Light Fixture A	3	$198 (3 × $66)	$1,098 (3 × $366)
Light Fixture B	2	$132 (2 × $66)	$ 732 (2 × $366)

Note: The overall metal shop rates of $66 and $366 are shown on the last line of Exhibit 1.2.

respectively, when the overall metal shop costs are averaged. For fixture B, the equivalent costs on an individual basis are $84 for depreciation plus maintenance and $688 for rent-equivalent costs. This compares with $132 and $732 when averaged.

The manufacture of fluorescent fixtures is not limited to metal shop work. The fixtures, on leaving the metal shop, call for painting and assembly. Both painting and assembly will require their own individual rates.

The painting production center should use its own overhead rate because the painting operations and associated overhead costs are quite different from the metal shop and assembly operations. The overhead costing rate will be based on direct labor because the fixtures are sprayed manually.

The assembly cost center must also use its own overhead rate, which will reflect the lower overhead expenses related to assembly work. As in metal shop work and painting, the labor requirements will vary with the type of fixture. A fixture with four lamps will require substantially more wiring labor than a two-lamp fixture. Bathroom fixtures with an outlet for plugging in a shaver or electric toothbrush will require more wiring than a similar fixture not having such an outlet.

The plant manager noted that variations in product cost in the metal shop, which accounted for the bulk of the plant overhead, were great enough to convince him that he was losing money on the large fixtures, which were being underpriced. He noted further that the orders for the smaller fixtures had been tailing off, probably because they were being overpriced. Chapter 3 will focus on the development of overhead costing rates for a plant with both labor-paced and machine-paced operations.

Product Line Versus Functional Costing Rates

Some companies use a product line overhead rate when several product types are made under the same roof. An example of this would be a television set manufacturer who also made auto radios in the same facility. One such manufacturer of both TV sets and auto radios was using a labor-based overhead rate of 125% for auto radios which had been reduced to 115%, only to find that the lower rate was not competitive. The sales manager proposed a further reduction to 100%. The rate used for TV sets was 140% of direct labor. There was no problem in meeting competitive prices with the 140% rate because the TV market was new and sets could be sold as quickly as they could be produced.

A new general manager who had entered the picture about this time felt uncomfortable with the arbitrariness of merely dropping costing rates to meet competitive prices. He felt that he should have more detailed information as to the true cost of manufacturing both the TV sets and auto radios. A study of the manufacturing operation revealed that both television sets and auto radios were processed in three production cost centers: fabrication, where metal parts for both products were stamped from sheet steel; plating, where the metal parts were degreased and then finished with a cadmium plating; and assembly, which involved the use of simple tools for soldering, turning screws, riveting, and inserting components. The breakdown of effort for both products, expressed as percentages of total direct labor, was as follows:

BREAKDOWN OF DIRECT LABOR

	Televisions	Radios
Fabrication	8%	16%
Plating	17	19
Assembly	75	65
Total	100%	100%

Fabrication and plating, because of high equipment depreciation, maintenance, and other machine-related costs, are both high cost overhead centers. Assembly, on the other hand, is a relatively low overhead center because simple tools rather than high-cost equipment were used. A good deal of the assembly overhead varied with direct labor because both TV and auto radios were labor-paced operations at that time. The foregoing table shows that the manufacture of TV sets required 25% of its labor effort in fabrication and plating, both of which were higher cost areas. Auto radios, on the other hand, required 35% of the effort in fabrication and plating. This indicated that the radios should have had the higher of the two product line rates rather than the lower. The reason for this difference is that the TV sets used a wood cabinet which was purchased. The "cabinet" of the auto radio was fabricated from steel. The general manager, on reviewing these figures, expressed the desire to cost the products through the use of departmental (functional) overhead rates rather than product line rates. He felt that with the constantly changing design of these two products, he would have more reliable product cost information through a breakdown of the overhead costs by function.

Some writers recommend the reorganization of factories into manufacturing cells wherein all the operations required to make the complete product would be self-contained. They further recommend that the total pool of overhead be divided by the units produced to arrive at an overhead cost per unit. This is cited as an advantage because it eliminates the inaccuracies attributed to incorrect overhead allocations. This approach has the advantage of simplicity and would be valid if such splintering of the factory into individual cells did not require additional investment in equipment and overhead support labor to merely simplify an overhead allocation problem.

Material-Related Overhead Rates

Many of the writers and speakers who predict that machine hours and units of product will displace direct labor as an allocation base for overhead fail to recognize that material-related overhead can be a significant factor which should be allocated on material content of the product. Examples include (1) companies that, in addition to manufacturing their own products, also purchase finished products from other manufacturers for resale; (2) defense and nondefense contracts subject to contract cancellation; and (3) companies whose product line has wide differences in material content.

Products Purchased for Resale. The knitwear division of a large company purchased a number of products from another manufacturer and resold them to its own customers. These products incurred such material-related overhead as purchasing, receiving, incoming inspection, and repacking. Since the company did not utilize a material-based overhead rate, the purchases for resale were being subsidized by the products of the company's own manufacture. A separate material-related overhead rate was therefore developed. The rate was calculated by dividing the total material-related overhead by the total cost of all material purchased. If, for example, the material-related overhead amounted to $10 million and the total material purchases were $100 million, the material overhead rate would be 10% of the cost of all material purchases. When this 10% figure was added to purchases for resale, management recognized that products purchased for resale were not as profitable as originally perceived. It also became obvious that internally manufactured products were subsidizing the purchases for resale.

Defense Contractors. The government has been known to cancel contracts when an order has been only partially completed. When the material-related overhead is part of the labor and/or machine hour rate, the company would have no basis for claiming full reimbursement of the material-related overhead costs. As in the case of the company that purchased some of its products for resale, a material-related overhead rate is necessary to support recovery of such costs.

Products with a Wide Range of Material Content. This can be illustrated by an appliance manufacturer whose product line material content ranged from a high of 80% of prime cost (material plus direct labor) to a low of 58%. The direct labor, on the other hand, ranged from a low of 20% to a high of 42% of prime cost (see Exhibit 1.4). As was the case in the preceding two examples, the material-related overhead costs were being recovered through labor-based overhead rates. As a result, products with a high material content and low labor were being undercosted. Conversely, products with a high labor and low material content were being overcosted.

Material-based overhead rates cannot be applied on the one-size-fits-all concept any more than in the case of labor-based or machine hour-based rates. In the assembly of military fighter planes, for example, which require approximately 75,000 parts, a different percentage of the dollar value of material would be applied to the purchased engine than would be applied to the smaller purchased items.

When the materials are somewhat homogeneous—copper sheet and steel sheet, for example—a separate percentage for each, based on dollar value of material, would penalize the copper and understate the steel because copper is so much more expensive than steel. A more appropriate method for applying

EXHIBIT 1.4

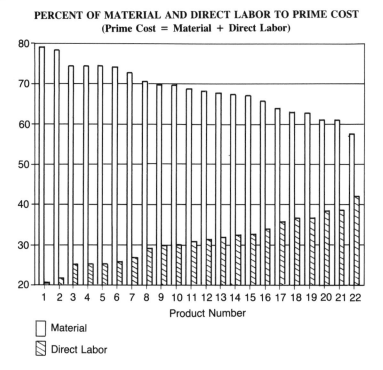

PERCENT OF MATERIAL AND DIRECT LABOR TO PRIME COST
(Prime Cost = Material + Direct Labor)

material overhead in this case would be on a per-pound basis. The rate would calculated by dividing the total annual material overhead cost by the number of pounds handled of either copper or steel.

Material overhead rates serve their purpose well in costing a homogeneous group of products, but serious inequities can result if two products of differing characteristics are produced within the same facility. An example would be the manufacture of low-volume oscilloscopes under the same roof with a high-volume production line product such as computer terminals.

The material-related costs for the low-volume product being produced at the rate of 100 per day would be greater per unit, while the high-volume product being produced at 10 times the quantity would require less effort per unit. Ordering quantities for the computer terminals would be larger. In fact, blanket orders would be placed with suppliers with releases scheduled for just-in-time delivery. Large items, such as CRTs, could be scheduled for daily delivery. Instead of carrying large inventories, the CRTs would be hung on conveyors at the receiving dock and transported to the production lines at speeds matching the production rate. This would eliminate the need for large storage areas in the warehouse as well as time-consuming handling and paperwork.

The oscilloscopes were highly customized to government specifications. Although only 100 were produced daily, the wide variation in specs was equivalent to producing at least 10 different products requiring much more material-related effort on a per-unit basis than the computer terminals. This must be taken into account when applying the material-related overhead.

Packing Costs on a Per-Unit Basis

This method usually works well in an operation where many small parts are produced and sold in large quantities. One metal stamping company which produces thousands of varieties of low-priced stampings used this method for a number of years. Per-unit costs were calculated to differentiate for variations in size of the parts and in fragility of certain items. Shaped parts required specialized packing with the use of dividers to prevent crushing. Silver-plated parts had to be packed with camphor granules to prevent tarnishing. Flat parts, on the other hand, were packed in larger containers at lower cost.

To cover the many remaining items which were merely bagged and stapled, a token charge of five cents per thousand was used to cover packing. Even though the five cent per thousand charge appeared to be miniscule, it was found that the use of this amount put some of the items in a loss position. One of the products in this category was wire cuts. The operation was highly automated. Wire was fed through cutting dies and cut in lengths of $\frac{1}{8}''$ to $\frac{1}{2}''$. A typical order of this type would contain as many as 500,000 cuts. In checking the operation it was found that these parts were being measured out on a counting scale, poured into a three-cent bag, and stapled in a matter of two minutes. The seemingly small charge of five cents per thousand amounted to one-third of the selling price. Even though the packing charge appeared to be a token amount, it was enough to throw these items into a loss position. The company corrected this by further categorizing items of this type and developing a unit charge by category.

Impact of Production Rejects on Product Costs

Japanese quality circles and zero defect programs notwithstanding, production rejects will continue as a cost to be dealt with in most companies. The manufacture of CRTs provides a good example of unavoidable rejects. Since the manufacture of CRTs requires the use of a glass bulb and a meticulous process in applying a screen to the face plate, it is unlikely that a zero defects goal will ever be attained. The obvious objective should be the minimization of defects and recognition that the lower the defect rate the lower the cost and therefore the greater the profitability.

Exhibit 1.5 illustrates this point through the use of a hypothetical example in which the cost per CRT is shown for two levels of rejects at the seal-in stage of production.

EXHIBIT 1.5

CRTs Sealed In	1,000	1,000
Rejections	500	800
% Rejected	50%	80%
Net Good CRTs	500	200
Cost per Good	$2.00	$5.00

Note that rejections increased by 60%, from 500 to 800, while the cost per unit increased by 150% from $2.00 to $5.00. Although this example is hypothetical, it points out how an increased number of rejects can have a high multiplier impact on product costs and profitability. Arbitrariness is discussed next to show how the use of overall percentage allowances for rejects can distort individual product costs.

Arbitrariness in Accounting for Production Rejects

A common practice in many companies is the use of an overall percentage to provide for production losses. This was the case at Pylon Corp. (name disguised).

In developing product cost estimates, the estimator used an overall figure of 10% for all products. In reviewing the information that was available in the production control department, the author found that a weekly rejection report, shown in Exhibit 1.6, was regularly prepared for management review. The part number rejected, as well as the final product in which it is used, is shown on the report. The week's scheduled production is included so that a comparison can be made with the number of rejects. The percentages in the last column indicate that the rejection percentages can range from a low of 3% (part 198) to 17% (part 498). Although the 10% figure used by the estimator was close to the 9% shown in the exhibit, this overall percentage would overstate the cost of six of the parts and understate the cost of parts 673 and 498. The individual part number reject rates should have been used rather than a single overall rate.

EXHIBIT 1.6

WEEKLY REJECTION REPORT

Part Number	Used on Product Number	Scheduled Production	Number of Rejects	Percent Rejected
603	78396	300	19	6
301	69842	150	9	6
673	39461	75	8	11
498	21312	890	150	17
306	14398	250	14	6
403	31982	600	32	5
106	21699	300	25	8
198	14443	250	8	3
		2,815	265	9

This report is prepared at the close of business on Tuesday of each week and issued Wednesday morning. In a weekly meeting on Wednesday, the quality control manager and production foremen, as well as the plant manager, discuss the causes of rejects and remedies for reducing the rejections. When appropriate, other parties are called in. The purchasing agent or production control supervisor might be called in for discussion of the quality of parts or other materials being purchased—while the stockroom supervisor might be questioned as to defects originating from improper handling or storage. In view of the cost estimating problems the company was having, a recommendation was made to include the estimator on the distribution list for this report. The plant manager expressed surprise that the estimator had not requested this report some time ago.

Certain products, microwave tubes for example, once assembled, cannot be taken apart for repair—the tube is considered a loss. One manufacturer of microwave tubes utilizes a weekly report in which the number of rejects are enumerated for each assembly operation, as illustrated in Exhibit 1.7. At operation 1, 100 units are assumed to have been started with one rejected, leaving only 99 potentially good tubes. Operation 2 shows 99 starts with one rejected. Operation 3, with 98 starts because two had already been rejected, results in three rejects or the equivalent of 96.9% good units compared with the number started at that operation (95 ÷ 98 = 96.9%). Operation 4 follows the same pattern.

EXHIBIT 1.7

WEEKLY SCRAP REPORT
(Units Scrapped)

Assembly Operations	Number of Starts	Good Units	Percent Good to Starts	Cumulative Percent Good	Rejects
1	100	99	99.0%	99%	1
2	99	98	98.9%	98%	1
3	98	95	96.9%	95%	3
4	95	75	78.9%	75%	20

The cumulative percent good shows the cumulative effect of total losses at each assembly operation as they relate to the 100 units that were started at operation 1. Note that the cumulative percent good (75% at operation 4) compares with the 75 good units shown in the good units column. The reason that these two columns agree is that they are both based on the original 100 started at assembly operation 1 with no new orders added into the system.

In actual practice, new orders received are continuously fed into the system; hence each addition of orders will alter the relationship of the figures in the various operations. The figures in Exhibit 1.8 are more typical because they recognize the variations of production through the operations.

Making Allowances for Material Utilization

In PlastiComp (name disguised), a company that does injection, compression, and transfer molding, it was found that product cost estimates prepared by the accounting department were based on 90% utilization of material for all molding operations. A check of powder consumption records maintained by the molding department (see Exhibit 1.9) showed that the utilization of material in the 800 and 200 Stokes presses was far less than the 90% figure used in product cost

EXHIBIT 1.8

WEEKLY SCRAP REPORT
(Units Scrapped)

Assembly Operations	Number of Starts	Good Units	Percent Good to Starts	Cumulative Percent Good	Rejects
1	145	145	100.0%	100.0%	—
2	140	134	95.7%	95.7%	6
3	42	41	97.6%	93.4%	1
4	41	36	87.8%	82.0%	5

Cumulative percent good calculated as follows: 100.0% in operation 1 multiplied by 95.7% in operation 2 = 95.7%; 95.7% in operation 2 multiplied by 97.6% in operation 3 = 93.4%; 93.4% in operation 3 multiplied by 87.8% in operation 4 = 82.0%.

estimates. Based on the figures in this exhibit, the product costs of the components made in these presses were being undercosted and therefore underpriced.

When this was brought to the attention of the general manager, his comment was: "No wonder the salespeople are pushing these items. We're undercosting the material in our quotes so we're below the competition in our pricing." Here again is another instance in which the information was available but not used.

Garment Fashioners, Inc. (name disguised) makes men's garments. The material used on some of the garments is sent out to be sponged when the cloth must be preshrunk. The company used an overall allowance of 1% for the yardage lost because of such shrinkage. Since all material is not sent out for sponging (preshrinking), the use of an overall 1% allowance understated the yardage losses of the preshrunk material and overstated the loss of material that was not sent out for preshrinking. A study showed that the yardage loss allowance for preshrunk material should have been 3% rather than using 1% for all material.

Tooling Costs

Tooling can be substantially higher for some products than for others. Nonetheless, cost systems in many companies include tooling in a pool that is allocated arbitrarily. Sewing Notions, Inc. (name disguised) is a case in point. This manufacturer followed the practice of allocating tooling as a percentage of the total manufacturing cost of each product—until an operations review disclosed that the actual tooling costs for their grommet Plier Kits were three and a half times greater than the amount allocated by use of the straight percentage.

Exhibit 1.10 illustrates the costing procedures for maintenance and repair of tooling. The report is titled "Production History" because the tool (die) maintenance costs are measured and applied to product costs as so much per

EXHIBIT 1.9

MATERIAL UTILIZATION REPORT
Plastic Molding

Press Type	Hours Running Time	Total Net Production	Total Theoretical Production	Percent Efficiency	Powder Consumption		Percent Utilized
					Actual Number Powder Used	Theoretical Number Powder Used	
Rotary	7,343	13,705,000	14,761,094	93%	221,690	203,891	92%
741 Stokes	5,585	4,421,683	4,695,061	94%	82,900	73,795	89%
800 Stokes	3,392	845,455	951,848	89%	11,040	7,445	67%
200 Stokes	1,492	801,347	808,097	99%	3,410	2,223	65%

1,000 pieces produced. The part number and material used to make the part are shown in the upper right-hand side of the report. Below this is the standard production per hour as well as the standard maintenance cost per 1,000 parts. The detail for arriving at the actual die maintenance hours per 1,000 pieces is recorded for each month and cumulatively at month end. This report not only provides valuable information for control purposes but can be helpful for cost-estimating purposes. Since die maintenance can be one of the largest single overhead items in a metal stamping operation, it is a report that every estimator should have available.

EXHIBIT 1.10

PRODUCTION HISTORY

Part Number	28-34634
Material	.020 × .500 Brass
Standards:	
Production per Hour	11,500
Die Maintenance per 1,000 Parts	.035

Month	Production	Press Hours	Production per Hour	Die Maintenance Hours	Die Maintenance Hours per Thousand
January	13,642,425	1,204	11,331	491	.036
February	10,186,243	973	10,469	413	.040
Year to Date	23,828,668	2,177	10,946	904	.380
March					
Year to Date					
April					
Year to Date					

Distortions in Actual Product Cost Due to Ideal Standards

Companies that value their inventories at ideal standards will often find it difficult to ascertain the actual cost per unit when ending inventories are higher than beginning inventories. Because the large inventory increase is valued at ideal standards that assume a very high degree of efficiency, the actual cost is over-stated by the change in inventory measured by the difference between ideal standards and realistic standards. This is illustrated in Exhibit 1.11, which compares the actual cost of a product when ideal standards are used and when more realistic standards are used. Note in the first column that inventories have risen from $3,923 to $24,713—an increase of $20,790. The second column, which is based on realistic standards that more closely approximate reasonably attainable actual costs, shows a rise from $4,904 to $30,891, an increase of $25,987.

EXHIBIT 1.11

IMPACT OF IDEAL STANDARDS ON ACTUAL PRODUCT COSTS

	Ideal Standards	*Realistic Standards*
Beginning Inventory	$ 3,923	$ 4,904
Subassemblies Transferred In	25,159	25,159
Fabricated Parts Transferred In	5,649	5,649
Total Available	$34,731	$35,712
Less Ending Inventory	24,713	30,891
Total Cost of Production	$10,018	4,821
Total Units Completed	81	81
Cost per Unit	$123.68	$ 59.52

The $5,197 difference between the two ending inventories results in a higher cost of production in the first column of the exhibit. As a result, the production cost for 81 units shown in the first column is $10,018, or $123.68 per unit. The second column, based on the more realistic standards, shows a total production cost of $4,821, or $59.52 per unit—less than half the unit cost indicated in the first column.

While some proponents of standard cost accounting frown on what they refer to as "loose" standards, keep in mind that management demands realistic product costs. Government auditors look with suspicion on costs that are subject to wide fluctuations because of large variances from standard. Their responsibility for auditing costs of the contractor requires them to ensure that the government is not absorbing variances which are truly chargeable to services performed for other than government business.

Impact of Variance Apportionment on Product Costs

When actual costs are developed from a standard cost system, it is important that the variances from standard be apportioned properly when transfers of components or subassemblies are made to the next stage of production. The transfer of variances can be based on input into the receiving cost center or on the basis of usage.

Using the input method means that the entire variance applicable to the transferred units will be charged to the current period's cost of production. The usage method, on the other hand, would charge only the portion of the variance applicable to the units actually consumed.

Exhibit 1.12 illustrates a case in which variances on subassemblies and on fabricated parts transferred for assembly were charged to the current period's cost of production in their entirety (see the column titled "Apportionment of Variance by Input"). The second column, "Apportionment of Variance by Usage," charges to production cost only the portion of the variance applicable to the fabricated parts and subassemblies that were actually used in the current month.

EXHIBIT 1.12

IMPACT OF VARIANCE APPORTIONMENT INPUT VERSUS USAGE

	Apportionment of Variance by Input		Apportionment of Variance by Usage	
Beginning Inventory at Standard Cost		$ 387		$ 387
Subassemblies Issued to Final				
Assembly	$17,620		$17,520	
Variance on Subassemblies	4,008	21,628	535	18,155
Fabricated Parts Issued to Final				
Assembly	$20,797		$20,797	
Variance on Fabricated Parts	2,040	22,837	216	21,013
Total Available		$44,852		$39,555
Less Ending Inventory at Standard				
Cost		30,948		30,948
Current Month's Cost of Production		$13,904		$ 8,607
Good Units Produced		24		24
Total Cost per Unit		$579.33		$358.62
Variance per Unit		$252.00		$ 31.29

Note in the first column that the total variance charged to production on the basis of input amounts to $6,048 ($4,008 plus $2,040). The variance based on usage (second column) is only $751 ($535 plus $216), representing only the portion consumed in production. This difference of $5,297 reduces the current month's cost of production from $13,904 in the first column to $8,607 in the second column.

Note that the total cost per unit, based on input, is $579.33, of which $252.00 represents variance. But when the apportionment is made on the basis of usage, the total unit cost is reduced to $358.62, of which only $31.29 represents variance. Such large differences usually occur at the beginning of a new production run when inventory buildup occurs more rapidly than production of finished products. However, as production increases and in-process transfers more closely approximate usage, the amount of difference between input and usage diminishes.

This can be seen in Exhibit 1.13. The exhibit shows seven stages in the production run in which the number of units increases from 24 to 933. As the run progresses, the variance based on input drops from a high of $252.00 per unit to $4.58. In the next column, showing the variances apportioned on the basis of usage, the variance per unit starts with $31.29 and ends up with $7.76 per unit. The last column, which represents the difference between the input and usage methods, shows a steady decline in this difference.

EXHIBIT 1.13

IMPACT OF VARIANCE APPORTIONMENT AT SEVEN STAGES OF PRODUCTION

| | | Variance per Unit | | |
Inventory Buildup or Reduction	Units of Output	Based on Input	Based on Usage	Difference
Buildup	24	$252.00	$ 31.29	$220.71
Buildup	45	185.13	121.58	63.55
Relatively Stable	66	13.18	74.22	61.04
Relatively Stable	125	− 2.23	21.76	23.99
Relatively Stable	160	38.79	20.23	18.56
Relatively Stable	726	1.41	6.58	5.17
Reduction	933	4.58	7.76	3.18

SUMMARY

This chapter provided a range of examples of product costing deficiencies inherent in the cost systems of far too many companies—*Fortune* 500 companies included. For example, FlourLamp, Inc., which was discussed early in the chapter, found it was incorrectly pricing its lighting fixtures because of improper product cost estimating. Later chapters will provide other examples.

There are similar weaknesses in allocating nonmanufacturing expenses such as selling, general, and administrative (SG&A) costs—the bridge between manufacturing costs and selling prices. SG&A in some companies exceeds the manufacturing cost. For this reason, a separate chapter is warranted to point out what improvements are needed in the practices followed in distributing SG&A costs to product lines and market segments.

CHAPTER 2

Better Allocation of SG&A for Improved Market Segment Pricing

In recent years, selling, general, and administrative expenses (SG&A) have been rising as a percentage of manufacturing cost (cost of sales). In some cosmetic and pharmaceutical companies, the percentage of SG&A has even exceeded the manufacturing cost. Chapter 1 gave some examples in which incorrect allocation of manufacturing overhead resulted in product costs that in some cases exceeded and in others fell short of competitive selling prices. If improper allocation of manufacturing overhead can so badly distort product costs, imagine the multiplier effect if SG&A is also improperly allocated.[1]

To better allocate nonmanufacturing costs, companies are developing more precise measures of their SG&A expenses. Many, however, continue to rely on production line methods for allocating SG&A costs. I have observed this many times in the course of my work with several hundred clients. It can be found in every industry and in companies that are well managed in other respects.

In organizations that take a production line approach to SG&A, the controller typically uses the percent-of-sales, cost-of-sales, or some other arbitrary method of allocation. When percent of sales, one of the most common methods, is used, the corporate accounting department simply divides the total corporate sales revenue into the total companywide SG&A expense and applies the resulting percentage to all product lines. If, for example, the company's SG&A

---

[1] This chapter has been adapted from: Thomas S. Dudick, "Why SG&A Doesn't Always Work," *Harvard Business Review* (January–February 1987). (Copyright by the President and Fellows of Harvard College.)

cost is 10% of its sales revenue, then that is the percentage charged to each product line based on its sales. Under the cost-of-sales method, each product line is charged an SG&A amount based on its share of manufacturing cost (materials, direct labor, and factory overhead).

Although the use of such standardized, across-the-board methods simplifies SG&A cost accounting for company accountants working under the pressure of meeting financial reporting deadlines, these arbitrary measures can distort the profitability of a company's different product lines and market segments. Profits can be inflated and losses understated using broadbrush SG&A accounting methods. While a variety of distortions are possible, there are several ways of correcting for them.

MATERIAL COST DISTORTIONS

When a company's raw material costs vary greatly among its product lines, severe distortions in SG&A costs can result if accountants use conventional percent-of-sales or cost-of-sales methods of allocation.

The president of a sewing notions company had been puzzled by the profit performance of his woolen goods line. Although his woolen goods sales had been steadily increasing, the line showed a loss. Because wool had a higher material cost than the company's other products, it had a low gross margin. The president discovered that the profit for the woolen goods line was being penalized because the company' use of the percent-of-sales allocation formula meant that wool's high materials cost resulted in an overstatement of its SG&A charges.

It was suggested that the company use a conversion cost ratio, which would eliminate profit distortions caused by differences in raw material costs. To construct the conversion ratio, the total direct factory labor and overhead were added together and divided into the total SG&A expense. The resulting conversion cost ratio was used to allocate SG&A costs to each product line based on each line's direct factory labor and overhead. Now the woolen goods line showed a profit, while the other lines showed reduced net income.

Although a conversion cost ratio is usually an improvement over the percent-of-sales method, it too has built-in distortions and therefore should be used with caution. If a company has certain product lines with a big percentage of finished components bought from vendors for resale, those lines will incur much lower conversion costs. Their SG&A charges would be understated and their profitability inflated.

Since any across-the-board measure—including a conversion ratio—can lead to distorted perceptions of profitability, the best solution is to develop a finely tuned allocation method that will give more precise measures of the SG&A costs incurred by each of a company's product lines. The following cases illustrate how a specific type of distortion can be avoided by using more accurate SG&A cost information.

PRODUCT LINE DISTORTIONS

Confronted with intensifying competition, the senior management of an electronics company decided to review its manufacturing and nonmanufacturing costs. As part of that review, it looked at how the company's accountants were calculating SG&A expenses for each of the corporation's major product lines.

Up to that time, the company's accounting staff had been using the percent-of-sales method for allocating SG&A expenses to each of the manufacturing divisions. Some division managers were dissatisfied with the result, among them the vice-president of the television division. He complained that his division's SG&A charge was inflated because his product line used high-cost finished components—picture tubes and cabinets.

The problem arose because these components had a high percentage of material content in the selling price. This inflated the division's SG&A allocation in comparison with other divisions whose material content was much lower as a percentage of sales. As Part A of Exhibit 2.1 shows, the television line had

EXHIBIT 2.1

HOW SG&A COST ALLOCATION METHODS AFFECT PRETAX PROFITS

Product Line	Part A: Conventional Percent-of-Sales Method		Part B: New Product-Specific Method	
	SG&A Charge as a Percentage of Total Corporate SG&A	Pretax Profit	SG&A Charge as a Percentage of Total Corporate SG&A	Pretax Profit
Television	24.0%	−3.9%	17.2%	−1.4%
Cathode-Ray Tubes	17.7%	5.4%	10.2%	9.1%
Phosphors	2.0%	16.5%	1.2%	20.0%
TV Components	27.9%	15.4%	28.4%	15.3%
Electronics	2.4%	7.4%	3.3%	4.5%
Fabricated Parts	6.0%	13.1%	2.6%	17.9%
Lighting Products	20.0%	22.0%	37.1%	14.5%
Total	100.0%		100.0%	

a pretax loss of 3.9% using the percent-of-sales method. Its share of total corporate SG&A was 24% during that period. To get a more accurate measure of each line's profit-and-loss performance, a specialist from marketing and another from manufacturing services developed a more precise SG&A allocation formula.

The marketing specialist pointed out that reliable information was readily available to break down the selling expense for each product line. Fully 90% of the selling cost consisted of payroll expenses. After the specialist identified which product lines were handled by the different salespeople, the annual payroll costs for each product line could be calculated. The remaining nonpayroll component, 10% of the cost, was allocated on the same basis as the other 90%. Warehousing costs could be allocated to each product line by counting the number of bays used to store each product. Percentage rates of space utilization could then be calculated by product line.

Advertising expenses would continue to be allocated on the traditional percent-of-sales basis because the company's advertising campaigns usually promoted the corporation and its entire product. Allocation of promotional costs posed no problem either because promotions were always carried out on an individual product line basis.

The manufacturing services specialist recommended that the corporate purchasing department charge each product line according to the amount of material it actually used. Formerly, corporate purchasing had consolidated the purchase of high-volume material used in all product lines. He further recommended that the industrial relations department charge each product line according to its percentage share of the total number of employees. Finally, he suggested that corporate accounting and data processing costs be parceled out to the various product lines on the following basis:

1. Payroll costs would be charged according to the number of employees in each division.

2. Customer billing costs would be allocated according to the number of invoices or invoice lines for each division. Availability of computers made this feasible.

3. Sales reports prepared by corporate staff would be allocated on the basis of the same ratio used to charge sales office overhead to each product line.

4. Internal auditing expenses would be charged to each product line by multiplying the number of auditor days spent in each division by the auditor's per diem fee.

The manufacturing services specialist also suggested that corporate quality control costs be divided according to the number of QC employees assigned to each division. Other corporate services that could not easily be charged to each product line could be allocated simply by dividing those costs by the number of product lines. Each line would absorb an equal amount of the costs on the assumption that these services were equally available to all divisions at any time.

Top management implemented the specialist's recommendations. The impact of the new method on the profit performance of each of the company's product lines can be seen in Part B of Exhibit 2.1.

The results confirmed what the vice-president in charge of the television division had long suspected: His division's financial performance had been depressed under the old SG&A allocation measure. The product-specific SG&A method reduced his division's share of corporate SG&A from 24% to 17.2% and his division's pretax loss from 3.9% to 1.4%. The new method also led to near doubling of the cathode-ray tube division's profit—from 5.4% to 9.1%.

MARKET SEGMENT DISTORTIONS

A company's cost accounting system may also fail to capture accurately the SG&A costs of selling to different market segments. A manufacturer of power cords, switches, sockets, and other electrical fixtures sold to three different market segments: original equipment manufacturers (OEM), retail outlets (replacement market), and building contractors (distributor market). More finely tuned SG&A cost information would give top management a better picture of the true profitability of the different market segments.

The controller requested managers in the different departments to calculate advertising, warehousing, selling, and other nonmanufacturing costs for the three market segments. Warehousing costs, for example, could be distributed according to the space used in serving the different market groups. The hours spent by the sales force in the field were also logged and allocated to the different market segments.

As Exhibit 2.2 shows, the new method for allocating SG&A revealed substantial disparities in costs among the three segments in most expense categories—disparities not caused by differences in the kinds of electrical products sold in each market.

Freight, packing, and warehousing costs, for example, were much lower for the OEM market than for the other two markets. The reason, the controller deduced, was that OEMs typically order in bulk. Packing and freight costs for

EXHIBIT 2.2

ITEMIZED SG&A COSTS BY MARKET SEGMENT

Itemized Expenses	OEM Market	Replacement Market	Distributor Market
Selling	3.1%	4.3%	4.4%
Warehousing	1.4%	2.7%	2.4%
Packing	1.7%	3.5%	2.5%
Advertising	1.8%	3.5%	3.2%
Bad Debts	0.1%	0.9%	0.3%
Freight	0.9%	2.0%	1.3%
Administration*	2.6%	2.3%	2.6%
Total	11.6%	19.2%	16.7%

* Administration includes any remaining costs after direct charges have been made to the manufacturing units. These include such services as payroll, billing, accounts payable, and any other charges that can be specifically identified.

the replacement market were much higher because orders placed by retail chains are usually smaller and more varied. The cost of selling to the OEM market was also lower because the company's salespeople did not have to call on OEM accounts as frequently as on accounts in the other two markets. What top management learned was that the OEM market was more profitable than had been assumed.

LOW-VOLUME DISTORTIONS

The percent-of-sales method for allocating SG&A costs can be especially troublesome when sales of one product line constitute a very small percentage of total sales. The CEO of a sunglasses manufacturing company decided to add a line of hair combs. Because demand for sunglasses is seasonal, he had excess capacity on his plastic molding machines. He would incur no additional selling costs because his salespeople could easily sell the comb line when calling on their sunglasses accounts.

The CEO told the controller to charge the comb line for its fair share of SG&A costs, and the controller did so using the percent-of-sales method. The marketing group had projected that combs would account for 15% of the company's $21.5 million in total revenue, and the controller used that percentage to calculate the comb line's share of SG&A. (The comb line's share of revenue was small because its unit price was much lower than that of the sunglasses line.)

The company's SG&A expense (excluding sales commissions) was assessed as a fixed monthly cost. Based on sales projections, total SG&A would amount to approximately $3.8 million a year, or 18% of total sales. The controller apportioned 15% of the monthly SG&A charge ($48,462) to combs and 85% ($274,620) to sunglasses.

The comb line's low share of total revenues led to erratic fluctuations in its profit performance. When sunglasses sales dipped during the off-season, its effect on the comb line's share of sales magnified—because of the comb line's smaller percentage of revenue. The SG&A cost for sunglasses varied no more than three percentage points, from 11% in April to 14% in June. In sharp contrast, the SG&A cost for combs swung from 21% in April to 13% in June.

As the controller explained to the CEO, the erratic profit performance of the comb line resulted from the magnified impact of the sharp change in sunglasses sales on the comb line's percentage of revenue. This caused combs to be overcharged for SG&A. More sales effort was required to sell sunglasses; advertising, promotion, and packaging costs were also higher for sunglasses.

The controller solved the problem by charging the comb line a flat 5% of total corporate SG&A. This reduced the variability in the comb line's SG&A from 7% of sales in April to 4% of sales in June. He explained that although month-to-month variation in profitability would still occur, the profit figures for combs would be more accurate and stable using the new, more realistic SG&A percentage figure.

When companies rely on undifferentiated, one-size-fits-all cost accounting methods without regard to important differences among product lines and markets, measures of profitability can become distorted. Since SG&A costs can vary widely among a company's products or markets, more precise methods for allocating SG&A will give management a more accurate reading of each product line's profit.

There is, however, an important caveat. Corporate controllers must decide how far to go in breaking down SG&A expenses. It may not pay, for example, to count the number of phone calls made or salesperson hours spent in the field per account when allocating selling costs to a product line. Too much refinement may impose unjustifiable record-keeping costs.

A good case can be made, however, that reasonably detailed allocations should be carried out since in most cases SG&A percentage breakdowns will need to be done only once during the year, when the annual financial plan is developed. With more accurate cost and profit measures, management can know which product lines and markets most deserve corporate resources and attention.

CHAPTER 3

Developing Machine Hour Rates for More Reliable Product Costing and Pricing

With the tremendous increase in foreign competition, U.S. manufacturing has been undergoing dramatic changes in the installation of more advanced automation. Unfortunately, improvements in manufacturing processes are not always followed by corresponding improvements in product costing practices. All too many highly automated companies still cling to the traditional practice of using direct labor as the basis for applying overhead to the product. To continue the use of direct labor as the allocation base can result in distorted product costs, particularly when the ratio of direct labor operators to machines varies from one product to another. Distorted product costs can produce serious judgment errors in pricing. Exhibit 1.1 in chapter 1 illustrates the degree of distortion that occurred when direct labor, rather than machine hours, was used to allocate overhead to three different circuit boards.

The general manager wondered why the CB-888 was selling so many fewer than the amount forecasted. The sales manager advised that a competitor had come out with an equivalent product that was selling for a good deal less and suggested a reduction to meet the competitor's price. It was not until a study was made that the inequity in product costs for the three circuit boards was disclosed. When the revised product costs were reviewed, the sales manager sheepishly admitted that the competitor's prices for the CB-864 and CB-892 were higher. The general manager then agreed to reduce the price of the CB-888 but insisted that the increase in the other two circuit boards should be high enough to offset the price reduction for the CB-888.

Misapplication of overhead costs is not the only factor to be taken into account when product costs are compared with competitive selling prices. In addition to the other costing deficiencies mentioned in chapter 1, markup factors for pricing should be reviewed. As automated operations increase, direct labor shrinks in relation to material and overhead cost, as was illustrated chapter 1, Exhibit 1.1.

Since the end purpose of business is to obtain an adequate return on investment, it follows that the markup factor to arrive at the selling price must recognize a return on the higher investment rather than being based on the traditional method of applying a single overall percentage factor to the manufacturing costs of the various products. This will be discussed at greater length in chapter 13. In view of the importance of sound product costing for better pricing, two case studies will be discussed.

CASE 3.1: MACHINE HOUR RATES FOR ELECTRONIC COMPONENTS

The company in this example has five basic production cost centers: compression molding, injection molding, staking, lining, and metal fabrication. Within these five basic centers are others that are sufficiently different to warrant a further breakdown. Rather than develop numerous subcenter overhead costing rates initially, the first step was to develop the rate for each of the five basic centers. Then, certain of the larger overhead costs that affect each subcenter differently were allocated to the subcenters to determine the differential machine hour rates. The differential rates were then added to the basic rates to arrive at the total machine hour rate for each of the subcenters. All of the five exhibits required to develop these rates are reviewed next.

Calculation of Machine Hours

Exhibit 3.1 lists vertically the major cost centers as well as the subcenters. Listed horizontally are the (a) number of available machines of each type; (b) number of shifts operated; (c) total available machine hours per day; (d) percentage utilization of the equipment; (e) net machine hours available per day; and (f) net machine hours available during a 21-day month.

Molding is segregated into two separate groups—compression molding and injection molding. Within injection molding, the 8-ounce and 12-ounce presses are combined because the products of these presses are very similar

EXHIBIT 3.1

CALCULATION OF MACHINE HOURS

Equipment	Machines Available for Production	Shifts	Machine Hours Available per Day	Percent Utilization of Equipment	Net Machine Hours Available per Day	Net Machine Hours Available per Month (21 Days)
Compression Molding						
Rotaries	16	3	384	75%	288	6,048
Stokes	9	3	216	81	176	3,696
Transfer Presses	8	3	192	63	121	2,541
Strauss	10	3	240	75	180	3,780
Total Compression Molding	43		1,032	75	765	16,065
Injection Molding						
4 Ounce	6	3	144	80%	115	2,415
8 & 12 Ounce	3	3	72	70	50	1,050
96 Ounce	1	3	24	60	14	294
Total Injection Molding	10		240		179	3,759
Staking						
Automatic Stakers	9	2	144			
Semiautomatic Stakers	4	2	64	70%	168	3,528
Hand Stakers	4	1	32			
Lining	6	1	48	75	36	756
Total Staking	23		288	71%	204	4,284
Metal Fabrication						
Z&H—9-ton Presses	18	1	144			
V&O—#0, #1, 25 ton, 50 ton	8	1	64			
Minster—22 ton	5	1	40			
Benchmaster—4 ton, B&J	3	1	24	28%	81	1,701
Brandeis—30 ton	1	1	8			
Henry & Wright—60 ton	1	1	8			
Pin Machines	9	2	144	86	124	2,604
Total Metal Fabrication	45		432	47%	205	4,305

and frequently interchangeable. The operator-to-machine ratio for these two machine types is the same.

The automatics, semiautomatics, and hand stakers have been combined under the heading "Staking" because of similarity in costs and interchangeability of many of the products processed. The remaining equipment has been identified as metal fabrication.

Overhead Breakdown by Major Cost Centers

The total average monthly overhead of $73,188 is listed by item of expense in Exhibit 3.2. Each of the items is allocated to the five production cost centers on the basis of seven allocation methods shown at the bottom of the exhibit. Direct charges, which account for 46% of the total, are represented by specific charges to a basic production cost center. For example, indirect labor of the production departments was considered a direct charge because the individuals represented by these costs are directly assigned to these cost centers. Maintenance is another such example. Here, historical records of maintenance costs have been used as a basis. Since manufacturing gas is specific to one cost center, it was treated as a direct charge. Fringe benefits were distributed on the basis of the amount of direct and indirect labor payroll. Indirect labor of the service departments, small tools, and power were allocated by the number of machine hours in each of the five production cost centers. Expenses treated as direct charges amounted to 46% of total overhead. This 46% plus the 24% allocated on machine hours add up to 70%. The remaining 30% was allocated on the basis of floor space, direct and indirect payroll, material consumed, and adjusted gross sales.

The listing of the various expenses was also broken down according to those expenses considered to be variable and those considered to be fixed. This facilitated the determination of marginal contribution profits of the various products, the break-even costs, and marginal pricing. The use of break-even costs for pricing and the marginal pricing concept will both be discussed in chapter 4.

Calculating the Basic Machine Hour Rates

The last line of totals in Exhibit 3.2 becomes the first line in Exhibit 3.3. From these figures is subtracted $31,388 in differential overhead made up of differential items such as maintenance, manufacturing gas, depreciation, mold maintenance, overhead transfer, occupancy, and warehousing costs. The total dif-

EXHIBIT 3.2

OVERHEAD BREAKDOWN BY MAJOR COST CENTER

	Total Plant	Compression Molding	Injection Molding	Staking	Lining	Metal Fabrication	Allocation Code
Indirect Labor—Production Depts.							
Variable Payroll	$ 3,992	$ 274	$ 136	$ 2,552	$ 638	$ 392	1
Fixed Payroll	1,757	502	431	660	164	—	1
Total Indirect Labor	$ 5,749	$ 776	$ 567	$ 3,212	$ 802	$ 392	
Indirect Labor—Service Depts.							
Variable Payroll	$ 3,928						
Fixed Payroll	10,006						
Total Indirect Labor	$13,934	$ 7,942	$ 1,811	$ 1,672	$ 418	$ 2,091	4 & 5
Engineering Charges							
Variable Payroll	$ 2,612	$ 1,489	$ 340	$ 313	$ 78	$ 392	1
Variable Nonpayroll Costs							
Maintenance	$ 8,620	$ 1,795	$ 1,500	$ 1,900	$ 125	$ 3,300	1
Small Tools	200	114	26	24	6	30	4
Manufacturing Gas	1,000	1,000					1
Supplies	1,400	350	364	350	42	294	1
Total Variable Nonpayroll	$11,220	$ 3,259	$ 1,890	$ 2,274	$ 173	$ 3,624	
Fixed Nonpayroll Costs							
Telephone & Telegraph	$ 550	$ 314	$ 71	$ 66	$ 16	$ 83	4
Computer Supplies	200	114	26	24	6	30	4
Power	2,000	1,140	260	240	60	300	4
Travel	550	314	71	66	16	83	4
Postage & Stationery	600	342	78	72	18	90	4
Water	125	63	62				7
Employee Insurance	700	231	105	252	42	70	3
Depreciation	7,200	2,808	1,512	1,584	216	1,080	1
Employee Service	85	28	13	31	5	8	3
Periodicals & Memberships	15	9	2	2		2	4

EXHIBIT 3.2 (cont'd)

OVERHEAD BREAKDOWN BY MAJOR COST CENTER

	Total Plant	Compression Molding	Injection Molding	Staking	Lining	Metal Fabrication	Allocation Code
Raw Material Losses	650	215	58	240	59	78	5
Mold Maintenance	4,818	4,818					1
Overhead Transfer	2,000		1,800	200			1
Professional Services	25	14	3	3	1	4	4
Occupancy	4,600	2,116	644	782	414	644	2
Discount Earned	(825)	(273)	(74)	(305)	(74)	(99)	5
New Equipment Design	1,260	403	164	478	76	139	6
Division Assessments	3,045	1,736	396	365	91	457	4
Warehouse Cost	3,150	1,040	283	1,165	284	378	5
Total Fixed Nonpayroll	$30,748	$15,432	$ 5,474	$ 5,265	$1,230	$ 3,347	
Payroll Fringe Benefits							
Variable	$ 6,930	$ 2,287	$ 1,039	$ 2,495	$ 416	$ 693	3
Fixed	1,995	658	299	718	120	200	3
Total Payroll Benefits	$ 8,925	$ 2,945	$ 1,338	$ 3,213	$ 536	$ 893	
Total Overhead	$73,188	$31,843	$11,420	$15,949	$3,237	$10,739	

ALLOCATION BREAKDOWN BY CODE

Code	Amount	%
1—Direct Charges	$33,399	46%
2—Floor Space	4,600	6
3—Direct & Indirect Payroll	9,710	13
4—Machine Hours	17,559	24
5—Material Consumed	6,535	9
6—Adjusted Gross Sales	1,260	2
7—Other	125	—
Total	$73,188	100%

ferential costs for each of the basic production cost centers is subtracted from the total overhead costs carried over from Exhibit 3.2 to arrive at basic overhead for each of the five cost centers. Dividing these figures by the machine hours, which were developed in Exhibit 3.1, we obtain the basic machine hour rate for each of the basic cost centers. Using injection molding for illustrative purposes, the total monthly overhead carried over from Exhibit 3.2 amounts to $11,420. Subtracting from this the differential overhead of $5,604 leaves $5,816. Dividing this figure by the total injection molding machine hours of 3,759 results in a basic machine hour rate for all the injection molding equipment of $1.55.

Calculating the Differential Machine Hour Rates

With the basic machine hour overhead costing rates now determined for each of the five cost centers, the next step is to distribute the differential overhead of $31,388 to the various types of equipment within each of the basic cost centers. The first line of Exhibit 3.4 shows the distribution of the $31,388 over the basic cost centers and the subcenters. Note that the total maintenance of $8,620 has been broken down to show $700 chargeable to the rotaries, $130 to the Stokes, $433 to the transfer presses, and $532 to the Strauss presses. The entire amount of manufacturing gas is charged only to the rotaries because gas is not used on any of the other equipment. Mold maintenance is likewise distributed to the machine types that incur mold maintenance costs. After each of the seven differential expenses were distributed to the appropriate machine types, the machine hour rates for the differential expenses were calculated by dividing the total differential costs for each of the machine types by the machine hours.

Summary of the Machine Hour Rates

Exhibit 3.5 becomes the consolidation schedule which combines the basic and differential machine hour rates, to which are added the direct labor costs per machine hour. The first three columns, which refer to overhead, add together the basic and differential rates to arrive at the total machine hour overhead costing rates. The direct labor column is added to determine the combined overhead and direct labor machine hour rates. The direct labor cost per machine hour was calculated by dividing operators' costs by the number of machines tended.

EXHIBIT 3.3

CALCULATING THE BASIC MACHINE HOUR RATE

	Total Plant	Compression Molding	Injection Molding	Staking	Lining	Metal Fabrication
(A)* Total Overhead	$73,188	$31,843	$11,420	$15,949	$3,237	$10,739
Less Differential Overhead						
Maintenance	$ 8,620	$ 1,795	$ 1,365	$ 2,000	$ 160	$ 3,300
Manufacturing Gas	1,000	1,000				
Depreciation	7,200	2,808	1,512	1,584	216	1,080
Mold Maintenance	4,818	4,818				
Overhead Transfer	2,000		1,800	200		
Occupancy	4,600	2,116	644	782	414	644
Warehousing Cost	3,150	1,040	283	1,165	284	378
Total Differential Overhead	$31,388	$13,577	$ 5,604	$ 5,731	$1,074	$ 5,402
Total Basic Overhead	$41,800	$18,266	$ 5,816	$10,218	$2,163	$ 5,337
(B) Total Machine Hours	28,413	16,065	3,759	3,528	756	4,305
Basic Machine Hour Rate	$ 1.47	$ 1.14	$ 1.55	$ 2.90	$2.86	$ 1.24

* (A) is from Exhibit 3.2.   (B) is from Exhibit 3.1.

EXHIBIT 3.4

CALCULATING THE DIFFERENTIAL MACHINE HOUR RATE

	Main-tenance	Manufac-turing Gas	Deprecia-tion	Mold Main-tenance	Overhead Transfer	Occupancy	Wholesale Cost	Total Differential Cost	Total Machine Hours	Differential Machine Hour Rate
Total Plant	$8,620	$1,000	$7,200	$4,818	$2,000	$4,600	$3,150	$31,388	28,502	$1.10
Total Compression										
Molding	1,795	1,000	2,808	4,818		2,116	1,040	13,577	16,065	.85
Rotaries	700	1,000	1,364	3,151		727	676	7,618	6,048	1.26
Stokes	130		344	368		296	42	1,180	3,696	.32
Transfer Press	433		392	726		741	187	2,479	2,541	.98
Strauss	532		708	573		352	135	2,300	3,780	.61
Total Injection										
Molding	1,365		1,512		1,800	644	283	5,604	3,759	1.49
4 Ounce	550		529		1,080	277	92	2,528	2,415	1.05
8 & 12 Ounce	550		519		540	251	81	1,941	1,050	1.85
96 Ounce	265		464		180	116	110	1,135	294	3.86
Total Staking	2,000		1,584		200	782	1,165	5,731	3,528	1.62
Total Lining	160		216			414	284	1,074	756	1.42
Total Metal Fabrication	3,300		1,080			644	378	5,402	4,305	1.25

EXHIBIT 3.5

SUMMARIZATION OF THE MACHINE HOUR RATES

	Overhead			Direct Labor	Combined Rate
	Basic Machine Hour Rate	Differential Machine Hour Rate	Total Machine Hour Rate	Per Machine Hour	Per Machine Hour
Compression Molding					
Rotaries	$1.14	$1.26	$2.40	$ .36	2.76
Stokes	1.14	.32	1.46	.19	1.65
Transfer Press 1	1.14	.98	2.12	.54	2.66
Transfer Press 2	1.14	.98	2.12	1.40	3.52
Strauss	1.14	.61	1.75	.25	2.00
Injection Molding					
4 Ounce	1.55	1.05	2.60	.45	3.05
8 & 12 Ounce	1.55	1.85	3.40	2.21	5.61
96 Ounce	1.55	3.86	5.41	2.30	7.71
Staking					
Automatic	2.90	1.62	4.52	1.40	5.92
Semiautomatic	2.90	1.62	4.52	2.10	6.62
Hand Staking	2.90	1.62	4.52	2.10	6.62
Lining	2.86	1.42	4.28	1.85	6.13
Metal Fabrication					
Pins	1.24	1.25	2.49	.26	2.75
Automatic	1.24	1.25	2.49	.39	2.88
Nonautomatic Metal	1.24	1.25	2.49	1.81	4.30

Merely to convert from a labor-based overhead rate to a machine hour basis does not guarantee that all is well in product costing. Many companies have converted to a machine hour basis but have not looked deeply enough into overhead and direct labor variations within the subcost centers.

Note, for example, that if the machine hour rates were calculated for only the five basic cost centers, the rate for injection molding would be $3.04 per machine hour for all equipment regardless of size ($11,420 from Exhibit 3.3 divided by 3,759 machine hours). However, when the machine hour rate is split between basic and differential, the basic rate is reduced to $1.55 per machine hour for all injection molding equipment. The differential rate varies within the subcost centers from a low of $1.05 per machine hour for the 4-ounce press to $3.86 for the 96-ounce press—the latter being three and two-thirds times greater than the former.

This demonstrates that greater accuracy can be obtained in developing machine hour rates when the differential overhead costs are accounted for separately. Availability of the differential machine hour costs by subcost centers is useful as an indicator of where breaks in the selling prices should occur.

CASE 3.2: HEAT TREATING AND DIE COSTS

Accounting for heat treating (annealing) and die costs in product costing is a source of confusion in many companies that fabricate products made of metal and wire. As a background for a better understanding of how these costs should be treated, a medium-size wire drawing operation has been selected as a case study. A brief description of the manufacturing operation is given; the problem of equitable distribution of heat treating and die costs is discussed; and the method of developing the hourly machine hour rates for labor and overhead is explained.

What Is Wire Drawing?

Wire drawing is a method of reducing ductile metals from a larger to a smaller diameter. This is accomplished by pulling the wire through a series of reducing dies. These are carboloy or diamond dies which contain a carbide compound or diamond stone with a contoured hole through the center. The die is housed in a circular steel disc about the size of the wheel on a child's roller skate. Dies are placed in the wire drawing machines in progressively smaller sizes so that the wire can be threaded and pulled through at the optimum speed required.

Each time the wire passes through a die, its diameter becomes smaller and smaller until the desired size is obtained. Wire may be hot-drawn or cold-drawn. When hot-drawn, it passes through a furnace before passing through the die. If cold-drawn, the wire will go through a series of dies without the prerequisite of heating. However, after a certain degree of reduction has been attained, heat treating is necessary before further reduction takes place, in order to bring about an equi-axed grain structure and to restore ductility. Each time the wire passes through a successive die, the tensile and yield strengths increase while elongation decreases.

Proper temper is imparted by scheduling heat treatment at strategic points so that the reduction which follows will be of sufficient degree to bring about the desired hardness or temper. These vary with the products for which the wire is to be used. Such products are quite numerous, among which are the following:

Fences	Resistor wire in toasters
Springs	Filaments in light bulbs
Cables	Base pins in cathode-ray tubes
Nails	Electrical conductive wire
Wire for screens and weaving	Sponge wire for cleaning

Costing Problems in Wire Drawing; Machine Hour Basis

Costing of the drawing of wire presents somewhat unique problems because standards cannot readily be set on all the operations, particularly when a large variety of wire is drawn in relatively small lots. For one thing, heat treating (annealing) necessarily does not lend itself to time study. The amount of heat treating cost to be applied to each type of wire cannot be determined through the customary multiplication of production by the standard allowance. Die costs, likewise, present problems in allocation because the use of a die of a particular size is not confined to a specific size or type of wire. The allocation of die costs to types of wire is further complicated because of the tendency of different materials to have different rates of wear on the dies. Another peculiarity is that, in wire drawing, no material is added after the initial drawing.

A further characteristic is that, contrary to the frequent practice of using direct labor as a base for applying overhead, wire drawing utilizes machine hours as a base. The number of machine hours is multiplied by the machine hour rate, which includes not only overhead but direct labor as well. However, the basis is not used blindly but with discretion and, as will be shown later, a separate machine hour rate is set for differing types of equipment. This is because operators of wire drawing machines act more as machine attendants than operators. Their work consists of loading the machine, threading the wire through the dies, and removing the finished spool. If a break occurs, they must rethread the wire. The time expended is such that they can easily attend two machines of a type in general use. Their effort does not vary with the pounds (or meters) of wire drawn but rather with the number of times they must load, unload, and rethread breaks in the wire.

In short, it is the number of hours that the wire drawing machine operates which varies in direct proportion to the amount of wire drawn. Direct labor is more in the nature of a fixed cost. Machine maintenance, die costs, depreciation, and the other items of overhead are, therefore, apportioned more equitably on a machine hour base than on a direct labor base.

Heat Treating Costs

Two costs accompanying wire drawing, mentioned previously, merit initial attention. For one, heat treating cost is difficult to assign to specific sizes of wire because a good deal of the annealing is done in a pot furnace, i.e., various sizes, some on spools, some in unspooled coils, are heaped into the annealing pot, which is sometimes half full and sometimes one-quarter or three-quarters full. Some wire is strand annealed, i.e., passed through furnace tubes in individual strands.

Although standards can be set on strand annealing, the pot annealing operation defies all attempts at time study and scientific allocation. For this reason, pot annealing costs are best treated as general overhead in the wire drawing operation and allocated to the machines on the basis of machine hours.

The resulting costs will not be widely at variance with fact, because there is good correlation between the cost of heat treating and the number of machine hours of drawing time. The greater the degree of reduction, the greater the number of machine hours required to make the reduction. This also means that more frequent heat treating is needed, because ductility must be restored more frequently, for the harder the wire the smaller the degree of reduction which can be made in each pass. More machine hours and more frequent heat treating will be required to draw hard wire to a given diameter, than softer wire.

It is recognized that the machine hour basis of allocating heat treating costs as part of overhead results in a small amount of distortion, in the cost of some types of wire which are sold as "soft," because this means that there is a heat treat operation without any further drawing or else there is a heat treat with only a small amount of subsequent drawing. However, to attempt to account for the cost of heat treating on each type of wire drawn would mean a prohibitive amount of clerical expense. Selling prices do not distinguish hard or soft.

Die Costs

The allocation of die costs to types of wire drawn presents a problem in a plant where numerous metals are used and where there is frequent interchange of types of wire on the various machines. Carboloy dies are generally used in drawing wire down to .020"; diamond dies are used for diameters under .020". As soon as a diamond die gets "out of round," it is ground down and used again for the next larger diameter. The procedure is repeated until the die is finally so large it can no longer be used.

Die wear will be affected by the temper and type of wire as well as by the type of lubricant used. Generally, hard wires will wear dies faster. However, certain soft materials will wear them out as fast as the hard materials. Also, some types of wire, like aluminum, nickel, chromium, and titanium, have oxides present which cause rapid wear. Using the correct lubricant for each type of wire will aid in reducing die wear. However, it is not practical to empty out the lubricant and refill with the right kind when the type of wire is changed frequently. For this reason, some all-purpose lubricant is ordinarily used.

In a large wire drawing operation where the volume of each type of wire drawn is large enough to warrant the use of specific machines for wires having similar properties, it would be possible to determine die costs by types of wire drawn with a high degree of accuracy. However, in a small operation there is no choice but to allocate die costs on the basis of the number of machine hours required to draw each type of wire and then to apply correction factors based on an engineering estimate.

Two Products and the Development of Rates

At this point we describe briefly the steps in drawing wire for two particular uses and comment on the costing of the wire so drawn. Wire to be used for base pins in CRTs and for sponge wire used in kitchen cleaning pads has been selected for this purpose.

The wire used for these two products is a special alloy consisting of nickel, chrome, and iron. For purposes of this illustration, it will be assumed that the wire is purchased at a diameter of .150″ and cold-drawn down to .051″, at which dimension it is ready to be cut into proper lengths for use as finished base pins. The cold-drawing is done in two steps, down to .100″ on the bull block and down to .051″ on the 6-7 Pass Vaughn, with heat treating following each drawing.

The same alloy is then used for drawing sponge wire. This is accomplished by drawing .051″ wire down to .020″ on the 6-7 Pass Vaughn and then putting the .020″ wire through a fine wire drawing unit called the CF-1. This machine draws the wire down to .0055″, at which point the wire is ready for sale.

Overhead is assigned to the various machines on the most appropriate basis to determine sound machine hour rates for each type. Maintenance records indicate the amount of maintenance required for each machine. Depreciation is likewise known for each kind of machine. All rent-equivalent or occupancy expenses, such as heat, light, building depreciation, taxes, and building maintenance, are allocated to the basis of floor space occupied. The expense of carboloy dies is allocated to the equipment used for drawing down to .020″, while the cost of diamond dies plus the cost of die maintenance is charged to the remaining drawing machines on the basis of machine hours. Indirect labor is charged to each machine on the basis of percentages estimated by the departmental supervisors, in cases where a machine hour allocation would not be equitable.

After all overhead is distributed to machines, the monthly machine hours at which it is anticipated that each machine will be operated are divided into the monthly overhead to obtain the overhead rate per machine hour. The resulting figures are as follows:

Bull Block	$2.50 per machine hour			
6-7 Pass Vaughn	4.50 ”	”	”	
12 Pass Vaughn	5.15 ”	”	”	
CF-1	3.50 ”	”	”	

Direct labor is determined for each machine on an hourly basis and then added to the hourly overhead rate to obtain a combined rate.

Calculations for direct labor are illustrated by the following example:

MACHINE LABOR RATES

	Hrly. D.L. Cost per Shift	No. Mach.	Hrly. D.L. Cost per Machine	Allowances	D.L. Cost per Mach. Hour
Bull Block	$1.32	1	$1.32	10%	$1.47
6-7 Pass Vaughn	1.37	1	1.37	10%	1.52
12 Pass Vaughn	1.37	3	.46	10%	.51
CF-1	1.37	3	.46	10%	.51

The overhead rate is then added and also the rates for heat treating. In the interest of simplicity, strand annealing, like pot annealing, is assumed to be in the nature of a general overhead item. The total direct labor in both these operations is added to arrive at a total and then divided by the total machine hours for all wire drawing machines. Using the aforementioned overhead and direct labor rates and assuming $0.35 for heat treating, the combined machine rates became as follows:

MACHINE LABOR AND OVERHEAD RATES

	Labor	Overhead	Heat Treat.	Total
Bull Block	$1.47	$2.50	$.35	$4.32
6-7 Pass Vaughn	1.52	4.50	.35	6.37
12 Pass Vaughn	.51	5.15	.35	6.01
CF-1	.51	3.50	.35	4.36

Wire Drawing Standards

We have now developed the means through which labor and overhead costs (including heat treating) are applied, i.e., as a rate per hour, depending on the type of machine used. Thus, if we know the machine types and times involved in particular kinds of wire, we are in a position to set product standards for labor and overhead from the machine rates. If we again take base pins for CRTs and sponge wire as examples, we find the following pounds per hour (very fine wire is measured in meters) convertible into hours per cwt.

MACHINE PRODUCTION RATES

	Wire Drawn		Lb. per	Conversion to
	from	*to*	*Hour*	*Hrs. per Cwt.*
Base Pins for CRTs				
Bull Block	.150″	.100″	400	.25
6-7 Pass Vaughn	.100″	.051″	200	.50
Additional Drawing to Get Sponge Wire				
6-7 Pass Vaughn	.051″	.020″	.50	2.00
CF-1	.020″	.0055″	.20	5.00

Thus it takes only combined use of machine cost rates and the production rates appearing in the last column of the two preceding tables, to give labor and overhead product standards costs, as follows:

LABOR AND OVERHEAD STANDARD DRAWING COSTS

	Size		Hours	Machine	Cost per	Cumulative
	from	*to*	*per Cwt.*	*Rate*	*Cwt.*	*Cost per Cwt.*
Base Pins for CRTs						
Bull Block	.150″	.100″	.25	$4.32	$ 1.08	$ 1.08
6-7 Pass Vaughn	.100″	.051″	.50	6.37	3.19	4.27
Additional Drawing to Get Sponge Wire						
6-7 Pass Vaughn	.051″	.020″	2.00	6.37	12.74	17.01
CF-1	.020″	.0055″	5.00	4.36	21.80	38.81

From the final column of this table it will be seen that the labor and overhead standard cost of wire drawn down to base pin thickness will be $4.27 per 100 pounds and that the two additional drawings needed for sponge wire bring the labor and overhead standard cost for that product to $38.81 per 100 pounds.

To these standards we need to add the cost of material. Since no material is added in the process of wire drawing, material costing is fairly easy, inasmuch as material in one pound of .150″ wire is exactly the same as in .020″, the only varying factor being the amount of shrinkage caused through snarling, breakage, and poor drawing because of worn dies or improper annealing.

Production Report: Source of Product Cost Estimates

Because the presence of the operator of each group of machines is required regardless of whether all or only one machine is in operation, direct labor is a fixed cost in wire drawing operations. Therefore, the problem of controlling direct labor variances is similar to the problem of keeping the fixed overhead costs under control. The principal accounting means for this control is a production report issued daily, weekly, and monthly. This is illustrated in Exhibit 3.6 and compares actual with standard production hours. The information is also accumulated from month to month, so the report can be compiled on a quarterly, semiannual, or even annual basis, if need be. The comparison of the actual production per hour with the standard production per hour furnishes the wire department foreman with a quick analysis of each day's operation and the estimator with product cost estimates.

EXHIBIT 3.6

DAILY PRODUCTION REPORT

Machine	Material	Size from	to	Production	Hrs.	Actual Prod. Hr.	Std. Prod. Hr.
Bull Block	A Nickel	.125″	.100″	10,300 lb.	26.5	388 lb.	370 lb.
″ ″	A Nickel	.250″	.194″	13,900 ″	35.0	397 ″	385 ″
6-7 Pass Vaughn	S Nickel	.100″	.040″	1,500 lb.	13.0	114 lb.	115 lb.
″ ″ ″	#4 Alloy	.100″	.051″	2,700 ″	14.0	193 ″	200 ″
″ ″ ″	*#4 Alloy	.030″	.020″	2,000 ″	21.5	93 ″	102 ″

* Nonstandard draw.

The Problem of the Nonstandard Draw

A concern with control and estimating may be illustrated by the following typical example. Let us assume that the foreman's schedule requires that he draw 2,000 pounds of .051″ wire down to .020″. Since the time standard for this operation is two hours per 100 pounds, the foreman's total allowance would be 40 hours. Let us assume that because of pressure to get out production, 0.30″ wire (intended for another purpose) is drawn down to .020″. Obviously, it takes fewer machine hours to draw wire down from .030″ than from .051″. The budget will, therefore, show a favorable variance, even though this non-standard operation is costlier. It is costlier because it requires almost the same setup time and the same amount of effort in loading and unloading, whether the draw is .051″ to .020″ or .030″ to .020″.

The problem resolves itself into two parts. The first is an analysis of each day's production, in such fashion as to highlight any nonstandard draws. The daily production report does this. Second, in the event that a nonstandard draw is made, the budget allowance should be based only on the degree of reduction which actually takes place. This presents a difficulty, because standards are not set on reductions which are uneconomical.

The last line in Exhibit 3.6 displays such a nonstandard draw. The problem as to how the variance can be measured when .030″ wire, rather than .051″, is drawn down to .020″ resolves itself into a problem of interpolation. (This is how the necessary standard figure of 102 pounds per hour was provided for the applicable line on Exhibit 3.6.) Probably the graphic method is the simplest way to arrive at the answer. The 6-7 Pass Vaughn utilizes seven dies, each die bringing about a 15% to 20% reduction in the wire being drawn. Since the percentage reduction for each die in a given machine is the same, logarithmic graph paper should be used in preference to the conventional scale, because equal percentage changes will show as a straight line. (On the conventional graph scales, equal percentage changes would result in a curved line, which would make interpolation less accurate.)

Exhibit 3.7 shows the cost of .051″ wire plotted at $4.27 and .020″ wire plotted at $17.01. By connecting these two points with a straight line and interpolating at .030″, we arrive at a cost of $10.75 for .030″ wire. Subtracting $10.75 from $17.01, we get $6.26 per 100 pounds as the allowable cost for drawing between .030″ and .020″. Since the rate for this machine is $6.37 per hour, we need only divide $6.26 by $6.37 to arrive at the allowable machine hours for drawing .030″ wire down to .020″. The result of the division is .98 machine hours per 100 pounds. The allowance for drawing 2,000 pounds, therefore, would be 19.6 hours.

The standard production per hour would be obtained by dividing 19.6 hours into 2,000 pounds, the production quantity involved, thus arriving at 102 pounds per hour as the allowance. This is the figure shown in the last column

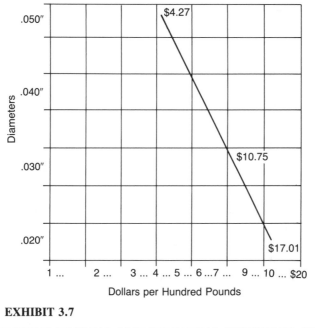

EXHIBIT 3.7

INTERPOLATION FOR COST OF DRAWING .030″ WIRE TO .020″

of the production report, asterisked to indicate a nonstandard draw. Highlighting nonstandard draws discloses uneconomical practices.

Linking Control and Product Cost Estimating

Wire drawing is an operation in which good control can be exercised through use of a single index, i.e., comparison of actual production per hour with standard production per hour. The reason that this single index will work effectively is that material, labor, and overhead are closely tied together. Material is put into process only once. Labor and overhead are closely tied together. Material is put into process only once. Labor and overhead are applied in a single rate.

An inspection of the production report on a particular day in which shrinkage was high in drawing nickel from .125″ to .100″, for example, will show that the production per hour was less than the standard allowance per hour. It would follow that labor and overhead costs would also be in excess of standard. (Incidentally, if the aforementioned .100″ wire were taken out of stock at a later time to be drawn further, the material cost would then be the accumulated material, labor, and overhead cost at the end of the .125″ to .100″ draw.)

It is true that exercise of control through comparison of actual production per unit of time with the standard allowance is fundamental to product costing in industry as a whole. However, it is especially applicable to wire drawing because of the correlation among material, labor, and overhead in the process. In the manufacture of products with many components, this correlation seldom exists to the same extent. One component might take a large amount of material, with very little labor, and might require a large automatic machine utilizing a great amount of overhead. Another component of the same product might require only a small amount of material with little overhead but a great deal of hand labor.

Wire drawing presents problems in the treatment of annealing and die costs, particularly in a low-volume operation. However, a good analytical approach such as the foregoing should produce reasonably good product cost estimates for more reliable pricing and profit measurement of individual products.

SUMMARY

Case 3.1 discussed development of machine hour rates for five stand-alone component manufacturing cost centers—each of which produces its own unique product line. It also dealt with the differentiation of machine hour rates to reflect cost differences within the basic cost centers. This cost delineation provides for more accuracy in product costing as a basis for realistic pricing. Many companies overlook the importance of this step.

Case 3.2 discussed products in which material enters only once—at the first drawing operation. It illustrated the use of machine hours from a different perspective. Recognizing that tooling and heat treating costs are frequently difficult to allocate accurately, this case study demonstrated how these were dealt with in a difficult situation.

CHAPTER 4

Role of Fixed and Variable Costs in Product Costing and Pricing

Exhibit 3.2 in chapter 3 segregated the fixed and variable overhead costs in the breakdown by the five basic production cost centers but did not reflect this breakdown in the machine hour costing rates. This step was omitted in the interest of simplifying the three exhibits that followed.

The breakdown of overhead into its fixed and variable segments is frequently determined by the accountant's perception of cost behavior for the individual expenses without consulting the various managers with responsibility for controlling these expenses. These arbitrary decisions raise serious questions as to the reliability of incremental pricing decisions, make/buy comparisons, break-even analyses, and profit volume projections, all of which can play an important part in product costing and pricing. This chapter, therefore, will discuss the six common methods used for identifying fixed and variable overhead. It will explain how the fixed and variable breakdown can be used to calculate profitability when the product mix changes. It will also show how a new price can be calculated to maintain a proper relationship with a similar product.

IDENTIFYING FIXED AND VARIABLE COSTS

The six common methods for identifying fixed and variable costs are: "eye-balling" the chart of accounts, scatter charts, regression analysis, low–high method, capacity method, and analysis of an experienced level.

Eyeballing the Chart of Accounts

Use of the word *eyeballing* may seem facetious. However, there are many companies that determine the cost behavior of overhead expenses in this manner. The typical eyeballer performs this operation from behind the desk without consulting the various managers who are far more qualified in making this determination. Some companies structure their chart of accounts to reflect fixed and variable expense breakdown.

In one such company electricity was considered to be entirely variable. When the company electrician was consulted, he disagreed. He explained that utility company charges include a demand charge, which covers the additional costs incurred by the utility in order to meet the peak loads. This portion could amount to as much as 25% of the total charge and should have been treated as a fixed charge. The same principle applies to other overhead costs such as the indirect support labor in the various departments, maintenance, and factory supplies. Consulting the various departmental managers ensures a more realistic breakdown of the fixed and variable expenses. An additional benefit in following this method is that the accountant will become far more familiar with the manufacturing operations.

Scatter Charts

While many books and articles recommend the use of the scatter chart method for identifying the fixed and variable costs, the author has found this method to be flawed because it assumes a theoretically stable operation. Another disadvantage of scatter charts is the voluminous amount of work required. As an example, a plant containing 25 departments with an average of 80 items in the chart of accounts would require 2,000 scatter charts to be drawn. This represents a tremendous clerical task which cannot be assigned to someone without some knowledge of charting and proper use of scales.

Exhibits 4.1 and 4.2 illustrate the problem. Note in the first exhibit that when the vertical scale is too spread out, it becomes difficult to fit a straight line to the plotted points because they do not fall in a stable pattern. However, if the vertical scale values were compressed, as in the second exhibit, a straight line can be fitted—but the values are now difficult to read because of over-compression. If the scales are not correctly selected, both vertically and horizontally, much trial-and-error charting would be necessary.

The scatter chart presents another problem in that some expenses can lead factory activity by as much as eight weeks, while other expenses lag. The production control department, for example, must place requisitions with the

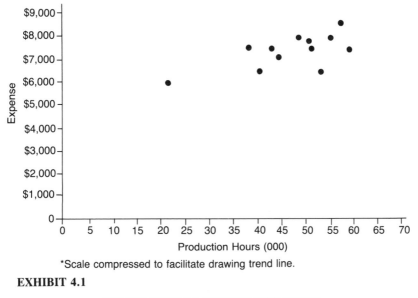

*Scale compressed to facilitate drawing trend line.

EXHIBIT 4.1

RELATIONSHIP OF EXPENSE TO VOLUME

purchasing department long before factory activity can increase. The purchasing department, in turn, must place orders several weeks in advance. The personnel department must review its seniority lists and recall employees from layoff. Quality control and shipping, on the other hand, lag activity in the factory.

This lead–lag effect can produce scatter patterns which are difficult to interpret. Exhibit 4.3 illustrates an ideal pattern in which the expense is directly related to the factory volume. Most scatter charts depicted in the literature illustrate this type of pattern. In actual practice, however, the lead pattern is more likely to correspond to the one shown in Exhibit 4.4. Since purchasing effort is likely to precede a rise in factory activity, it would be at a high level before activity in the factory reaches its high point. The opposite would be true of expenses that lag factory activity. These examples are illustrative of the shortcomings of the scatter chart method.

Regression Analysis

Regression analysis is a mathematical approach to the scatter chart in which a least squares line of variability is fitted by a mathematical formula. Although use of a computer would expedite the calculations, this method has the same disadvantage as the scatter chart plus the addition of another flaw if extreme items are present in the data. If, for example, there is an extreme item in one

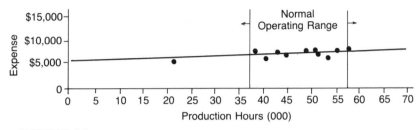

EXHIBIT 4.2

RELATIONSHIP OF EXPENSE TO VOLUME

of the periods at the beginning or end of the sequence of data, the extreme item is likely to tilt unduly the line of variability either upward or downward, causing both the fixed and variable costs to be incorrect.

Low–High Method

This method is a variation of the scatter chart. Instead of plotting expenses to multiple time periods, two experienced levels of activity within the normal activity range would be selected. Exhibit 4.5 shows the required steps in determining the fixed and variable costs by this method.

This method is simpler than the scatter chart method and requires far less work.

Capacity Method

This is a more sophisticated approach than those discussed earlier. In this method several capacity levels within the normal operating range are selected. For each of these levels, the various expenses are estimated. This has an advantage in that changes in amount of expense at any capacity level can be provided for rather than being determined by extrapolating from a straight line. If, for example, certain operations require some second (or third) shift work, this increase in overhead cost can be provided for at the appropriate capacity level, as follows:

Percent Capacity	65%	70%	75%	80%	85%
Plant Manager	$55,000	55,000	55,000	55,000	55,000
Foremen	$65,000	65,000	65,000	88,000	88,000
Supplies	$20,800	22,400	24,000	25,600	27,200

EXHIBIT 4.3

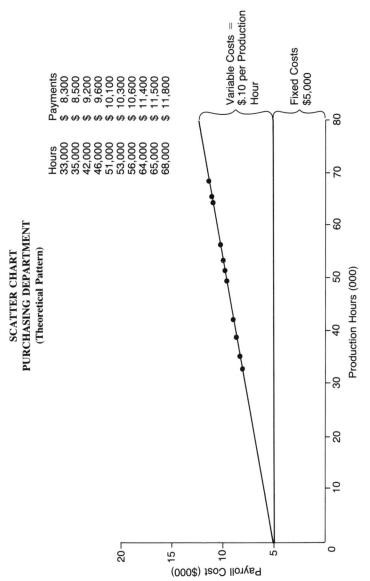

SCATTER CHART
PURCHASING DEPARTMENT
(Theoretical Pattern)

Hours	Payments
33,000	$ 8,300
35,000	$ 8,500
42,000	$ 9,200
46,000	$ 9,600
51,000	$ 10,100
53,000	$ 10,300
56,000	$ 10,600
64,000	$ 11,400
65,000	$ 11,500
68,000	$ 11,800

Variable Costs =
$.10 per Production
Hour

Fixed Costs
$5,000

Production Hours (000)

Payroll Cost ($000)

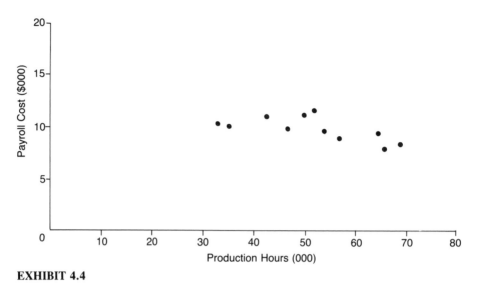

EXHIBIT 4.4

SCATTER CHART
PURCHASING DEPARTMENT
(Actual Pattern)

EXHIBIT 4.5

LOW-HIGH METHOD

	Low	High	Difference
Step 1			
Production Hours	700	1,400	700
Monthly Cost	$189	$238	$49

The $49 difference divided by 700 production hour difference shown in last column = $.07/hr.

Step 2

Variable cost for low and high volumes is determined by multiplying the low and high hours by $.07.

	Low	High
	$49	$98

Step 3

Fixed cost = Monthly cost in step 1 less variable cost:

	Low	High
Monthly Cost	$189	$238
Less Variable Cost	49	98
Fixed Cost	$140	$140

The plant manager's salary is shown as a completely fixed cost regardless of the percentage of capacity. The foremen, on the other hand, are increased when the capacity reaches 80%. Factory supplies have been considered to be completely variable because the incidence of cost relates directly to the activity in the plant.

The step method has merit because it provides for recognition of steps in the semivariable overhead costs. However, the determination of what the expenses will be at five, six, or more capacity levels will require substantially more effort to develop and use.

Analysis of an Experienced Level

A relatively simple method used in working with various department heads is to request them to break down their staff according to the cost behavior of the individual functions performed. Following is an example of such an approach:

Quality Control Breakdown of Fixed and Variable Labor Costs			
Job Categories	Total	Fixed	Variable
QC Engineers	3	2	1
Engineering Inspection	1	1	–
Quality Technician	1	1	–
Calibration	2	2	–
Test Audit	3	1	2
Administration	3	3	–
Total	13	10	3
Annual Payroll	$376,480	292,390	84,090

The parameters given to the quality control manager in the preceding example were to assume a range that would fluctuate between 15% to 20% above and below the normal level of operations. This method breaks down the semivariable expenses by individual employee into the fixed and variable segments. The eyeballing approach previously used in this company showed the quality control department as being 100% fixed. Eyeballing is obviously too arbitrary.

FIXED AND VARIABLE COSTS OF OPERATING A CAR

Exhibit 4.6 illustrates how variable and fixed costs are used in determining the annual cost of operating selected car models. These figures are relied on by

EXHIBIT 4.6

RUNZHEIMER PROJECTED FIXED AND OPERATING COSTS FOR SELECTED 1989 MODELS

Make and Model	Head Room	Leg Room	Luggage Capacity (Cu. Ft.)	Curb Weight (Lb.)	Overall Length	Drive Unit	Cyl.	Displace (Ltr.)	Annual Costs[2] Operating	Fixed	Total
Cadillac Deville	39.3"	42.4"	16.1	3,437	196.5"	FWD	8	4.5	$1,780	$7,101	$8,881
Chevrolet Caprice CL	38.5	42.2	20.9	3,654	212.2	RWD	8	5.0	1,860	4,594	6,454
Olds Cutlass Ciera	38.6	42.1	15.8	2,733	190.3	FWD	6	3.8	1,590	4,626	6,216
Chevrolet Celebrity	38.6	42.1	16.2	2,765	188.3	FWD	6	2.8	1,550	4,545	6,095
Ford Taurus L	38.3	41.7	17.0	2,887	188.4	FWD	6	3.0	1,520	4,436	5,956
Ford Tempo GL	37.5	41.5	12.9	2,585	177.0	FWD	4	2.3	1,420	4,080	5,500
Chevrolet Cavalier	38.6	42.2	13.6	2,363	174.3	FWD	4	2.0	1,300	4,120	5,420
Dodge Caravan	37.6	34.9	125.0	3,068	175.9	FWD	4	2.2	1,530	3,771	5,301
Plymouth Rel. Amer.	38.6	42.2	15.0	2,408	178.6	FWD	4	2.2	1,300	3,917	5,217
Ford Escort GL	37.9	41.5	16.4	2,222	166.9	FWD	4	1.9	1,320	3,730	5,050

[1] All four-door vehicles similarly equipped including automatic transmission, power steering, power disc brakes, air conditioning, tinted glass, AM-FM stereo, body side molding, cruise control, and left-hand remote control mirror.

[2] Costs include operating expenses (fuel, oil, maintenance, and tires), fixed expenses (insurance, depreciation, financing, taxes, and licensing), and are based on a 36-month/60,000 miles retention cycle.

Source: Runzheimer International, Rochester, Wisconsin.

the American and Canadian Automobile Associations—as well as the Internal Revenue Service, which depends on Runzheimer to establish national per-mile rates for U.S. taxpayers.

The variable costs include such items as fuel, oil, maintenance, and tires. Fixed costs include insurance, depreciation, financing, taxes, and licensing.

The fixed and variable breakdown enhances the flexibility of such information because the variable costs can be applied on a per-mile basis to different annual mileages. Using the Cadillac Seville and Ford Escort GL, for example, the annual variable costs of $1,780 and $1,320 are based on 20,000 miles per year. Dividing these two figures by 20,000 shows the variable costs per mile to be 8.9 cents and 6.6 cents, respectively. To determine the cost per mile for, say, 12,000 miles per year, it would only be necessary to multiply the variable cost per mile by 12,000 and add the fixed annual cost to arrive at the total fixed and variable costs as follows:

Car Model	Mileage	Var. Cost/ Mile	Total Var.	Total Fixed	Total Var. & Fixed
Cadillac	12,000 miles × $.089 =		$1,068 +	$7,101 =	$8,169
Ford Esc.	12,000 miles × $.066 =		$ 792 +	$3,730 =	$4,522

A variation of this principle can be employed in determining the profit contribution of various products before fixed costs.

PRODUCT MIX AND PROFITABILITY

Product mix refers to the combination of products sold in one period as compared with another. Since the contribution to profit (profit before fixed costs) is likely to be different for each item, a change in quantities will affect the total profit. Exhibit 4.7 includes four products for which the unit selling prices, unit variable costs, and unit profit before fixed costs are shown. Note that the product in column 1, with a profit of 42.1% and the lowest selling price, shows the highest profit of the four products. The product in column 3 has the lowest profit before fixed costs (30.2%). The bottom two lines show two different mixes of quantities that will be used in the next exhibit to show the impact of product mix 1 and product mix 2 on their respective break-even points.

The total units shown in Exhibit 4.8 for mix 1 and mix 2 are 85,000. The 85,000 is made up of 45,000 units for type A and type B filler assembly units and 40,000 units for type A and type B heat exchangers. The units making up

EXHIBIT 4.7

PRODUCT MIX AND PROFITABILITY

	Col. 1	Col. 2	Col. 3	Col. 4
	Filler Assembly Type A	Filler Assembly Type B	Heat Exchanger Type A	Heat Exchanger Type B
Selling Price per Unit	$67.51	90.08	75.36	105.19
Less: Variable Cost per Unit	39.07	59.25	52.60	67.56
Profit before Fixed Cost	$28.44	30.83	22.76	37.63
Percent Profit	42.1%	34.2%	30.2%	35.8%
Units Sold (Mix 1)	5,000	40,000	30,000	10,000
Units Sold (Mix 2)	40,000	5,000	10,000	30,000

45,000 for the two types of filler assemblies are reversed in mix 2. The same is true of the two types of heat exchangers in which the quantities making up the 40,000 in mix 1 are reversed in mix 2. The range of units within the two mixes was based on the worst case and the best case scenarios. A summary of the results follows:

	Mix 1	Mix 2	Change
Total Sales	$7,253,400	7,060,100	Decrease
Profit after Fixed Costs	1.2%	4.2%	Increase
Break-even Point	6,997,935	6,261,016	Decrease
Sales above Break-even	255,465	799,084	Increase
Percent Profit above Break-even	35.56%	37.51%	Increase

On review of these two exhibits, the general manager's interest was drawn back to Exhibit 4.7. He felt after reviewing the profit before fixed costs that the type A heat exchanger in column 3 should show a higher percentage profit than the type B heat exchanger. He felt that the two heat exchanger types should have about the same profit relationship to each other as the two filler assembly types. Further discussion revealed that the unit variable cost was correct and that the additional profit should be derived through an increase in the selling price.

To determine what the selling price should be, the following steps were taken:

1. Determine the relationship of the profit before fixed cost between the type A and type B filler assemblies. This was done by dividing the profit before fixed cost in column 1 by the same figure in column 2 ($28.44 ÷ $30.83 = 92.2%).

EXHIBIT 4.8

TESTING PROFITABILITY AND PRICING FOR TWO PRODUCT MIXES

	Product Mix 1				Product Mix 2			
	Total Sales	Percent	Break-even Sales	Balance above Break-even	Total Sales	Percent	Break-even Sales	Balance above Break-even
Total Units	85,000				85,000			
Total Sales Dollars	$7,253,400	100.00%	6,997,935	255,465	$7,060,100	100.00%	6,261,016	799,084
Less: Variable Costs	4,819,052	66.44	4,649,428	169,624	4,411,900	62.49	3,912,509	499,391
Profit before Fixed Costs	$2,434,348	33.56%	2,348,507	85,841	$2,648,200	37.51%	2,348,507	299,693
Less: Fixed Costs	$2,348,507		2,348,507	—	$2,348,507		2,348,507	—
Pretax Profits	$ 85,841		—	85,841	$ 299,693		—	299,693
Percent Pretax Profits	1.2%		—	33.56%	4.2%		—	37.51%
Break-even Sales	$6,997,935[1]				$6,261,016[2]			

[1] Break-even sales = $2,348,507 divided by 33.56%.

[2] Break-even Sales = $2,348,507 divided by 37.51%.

2. The 92.2% was multiplied by the profit before fixed cost in column 4 with the following result: $37.63 × 92.2% = $34.69.

3. The revised profit before fixed cost of $34.69 was added to the variable cost of $52.60 to arrive at the new selling price of $87.29. The new profit as a percentage of the new selling price is $39.6% ($34.69 ÷ $87.59 = 39.6%).

A comparison of the old and new figures for the type A heat exchanger follows:

	Type A Heat Exchanger	
	Per Column 3	Per Revision
Selling Price/Unit	$75.36	87.29
Less Variable Cost/Unit	52.60	52.60
Profit before Fixed Cost	$22.76	34.69
Percent Profit	30.2%	39.6%

The revised selling price, though determined through arithmetic based on comparative analysis, was acceptable to the general manager. His feeling was that the $75.36 selling price was obviously erroneous. The revised price of $87.29 fell in line with related products whose selling prices were well established and accepted in the marketplace.

SUMMARY

This section has thus far concentrated on the common deficiencies found in the product costing procedures followed in many, if not most, companies. The major cause of these inadequacies is arbitrariness. Chapter 1 dealt with the most common errors in the application of manufacturing costs to products. Chapter 2 dealt with misapplication of SG&A costs and showed the distortions not only to intracompany pricing but to market segment pricing as well.

Because one of the main sources of manufacturing cost distortions is the use of a single plantwide costing rate when several rates should be used, chapter 3 was devoted to showing how overhead costs should be broken down by cost centers. Since the illustrative example was a machine-paced operation, the resulting overhead rates were based on machine hours rather than direct labor. This chapter also showed how the overhead costing rates for basic cost centers can be refined further by adjusting the basic rate by the differential costs.

Chapter 4 showed the importance of properly identifying fixed and variable overhead costs, as well as showing how the fixed and variable breakdown can be used for calculating the contribution to profit (profit before fixed costs). It also showed how break-even costs can be determined for two or more different mixes of products. Also included in this chapter was an illustrative example of how the fixed and variable concept can be used to test the pricing of products within a product line.

The fixed and variable concept can also be applied to intracompany pricing to provide management with useful information relating to the profit contribution of the individual plants involved in intracompany pricing. This will be covered in chapter 5.

Avoiding the Pitfalls in Intracompany Costing and Pricing

Intracompany transfer pricing is no less controversial than pricing products for sale to outside customers. Component manufacturing plants that sell to their end product counterparts are just as aggressive in seeking high prices as are outside suppliers. And, conversely, the buying plants and divisions press to obtain as favorable a price as possible.

It is not unusual for a purchasing unit to transfer its purchases to the outside when lower prices are available from suppliers outside the company. In fact, some companies have established policies permitting their units to favor outside suppliers when lower prices are available. What is frequently overlooked is that buying on the outside can be less profitable to the company even at lower prices. Such was the case with the metal products division of a well-known company. The purchasing agent of this division found that he could obtain components at a 3% lower price than the transfer price from a sister division. In making the comparison of outside and intracompany prices, an important factor was overlooked: The fixed costs of the selling division were 21% of that division's sales. Underabsorption of fixed costs for the lost sales of the selling division exceeded the 3% saving in the purchase price.

As a result of this finding, company policy was changed. Since little, if any, selling effort was required in making intracompany sales, all future intracompany pricing had to be reduced by the selling and advertising expenses, which in this case amounted to 4.4% of sales. The obvious logic behind this decision was that selling and advertising were not necessary when selling within the company. This is similar to the philosophy that the government follows in awarding defense contracts that invite all interested companies to submit bids; selling and advertising expenses are disallowed.

Intracompany prices are sometimes manipulated to make an unprofitable unit appear to be less unprofitable. This was the case in a company in which a new acquisition produced losses rather than the promised profits. To reduce the amount of reported loss, the vice-president responsible for the acquisition mandated that transfer prices for products sold to the newly acquired company would be based on standard costs with no profit markup. Since the selling plants were highly profitable, their reduction in profits was very small in relation to the more favorable impact on the new company. Nonetheless, this practice is incorrect because it obscures the true picture.

INTRACOMPANY PRICING: A REVIEW
OF THREE CASES

It should be obvious from the foregoing examples that the accounting procedures used for determining intracompany prices can result in distortions on the income statement—the degree of distortion depending on the method used. Exhibit 5.1 illustrates three income statements for a company with a number of plants. Of some nine plants, only three were involved in intracompany transfers. Plants 1 and 2 manufactured components that were sold to Plant 3, which made the end products that were sold to outside customers.

CASE 5.1:

Plant 1 had total sales of $270,000, of which roughly half were sold to plant 3. The contribution to profit, after variable costs were deducted from total sales, amounted to 35%, and the return on investment was 20%. Plant 2 had sales of $337,000, of which $270,000 were sold to outside customers and $67,000 to plant 3. The income statement of this plant shows a profit contribution of 40% of all sales and a return on investment of 20%.

The intracompany sales price charged to plant 3 by plants 1 and 2 was the same as the prices charged to outside customers. The components received by plant 3 amounted to $209,000, which was the aggregate of $135,000 from plant 1, $67,000 from plant 2, and $7,000 from outside suppliers. As such purchases are received, they are charged to the material account—as is the practice in most companies.

EXHIBIT 5.1

IMPACT OF THREE TRANSFER PRICING METHODS
ON INCOME STATEMENT RESULTS*

CASE 5.1: *Intracompany Sales Charged at Outside Selling Price and Picked up as Material*	Plant 1	Plant 2	Plant 3	Sub-total	Elim-ination	Total
Total Sales	270	337	405	1,012	202	810
Variable Cost of Sales						
Material	108	135	209	452	202	250
Direct Labor & Overhead	67	68	149	284	—	284
Total Variable Cost of Sales	175	203	358	736	202	534
Profit Contribution—$	95	134	47	276	—	276
Profit Contribution—Percent	35	40	11	27	—	34
Fixed Costs						
Manufacturing	40	54	14	108	—	108
General & Administrative Exp.	20	27	20	67	—	67
Total Fixed Costs	60	81	34	175	—	175
Pretax Profit	34	54	13	101	—	101
Investment—$	170	270	65	505	—	505
Return on Investment—Percent	20	20	20	20	—	20

CASE 5.2: *Intracompany Sales Charged at Variable Cost and Picked up as Material*	Plant 1	Plant 2	Plant 3	Sub-total		Total
Total Sales	223	311	404	938		938
Less Intracompany Sales	88	40	—	128		67
Outside Sales	135	271	404	810		810
Variable Cost of Sales						
Material	108	135	135	378		378
Direct Labor & Overhead	68	67	149	284		284
Subtotal	176	202	284	662		662
Less Intracompany Sales	87	41	—	128		128
Net Variable Cost of Sales	89	161	284	534		534
Profit Contribution—$	46	110	120	276		276
Profit Contribution—Percent	34	41	30	34		34
Fixed Costs						
Manufacturing	40	54	14	108		108
General & Administrative Exp.	20	27	20	67		67
Total Fixed Costs	60	81	34	175		175
Pretax Profit	−14	29	86	101		101
Investment—$	170	270	65	505		505
Return on Investment—Percent	−8	11	132	20		20

CASE 5.3: *Intracompany Sales Charged at Outside Selling Price but Split into Material and Fixed Cost*	Plant 1	Plant 2	Plant 3	Sub-total	Elim-ination	Total
Total Sales	270	337	405	1,012	202	810
Variable Cost of Sales						
Material	108	135	135	378	128	250
Direct Labor & Overhead	68	67	149	284	—	284
Total Variable Costs	176	202	284	662	128	534
Profit Contribution—$	94	135	121	350	74	276
Profit Contribution—Percent	35	40	30	35	36	34
Fixed Costs						
Trsfr. in: Fixed Cost & Profit	—	—	74	74	74	—
Manufacturing	40	54	14	108	—	108
General & Administrative Exp.	20	27	20	67	—	67
Total Fixed Costs	60	81	108	249	74	175
Pretax Profit	34	54	13	101	—	101
Investment—$	170	270	65	505	—	505
Return on Investment—Percent	20	20	20	20	—	20

* Figures in $000. Small errors due to rounding.

Company units that follow the practice of making purchases from outside suppliers when the outside prices are lower often overlook a key factor shown in this case. Note that the profit contribution for plant 3 is 11% of sales rather than 35% and 40%, respectively, for plants 1 and 2. The reason for the lower figure in plant 3 is that in addition to variable costs, the fixed costs and profit of the selling divisions are included in the material cost, thus reducing the profit contribution. Management, in seeing such a low profit contribution, could easily be misled and should therefore be appraised of the reason.

If plant 3 manufactured its own components instead of purchasing them internally, the profit contribution would increase for plant 3 but decrease for plants 1 and 2—other things remaining equal. The consolidated total of the three plants is correctly shown because the intracompany purchases of $135,000 from plant 1 and $67,000 from plant 2 add up to the $202,000 shown in the elimination.

CASE 5.2:

In this case, shown in the middle of the exhibit, the intracompany sales are priced only at variable costs. Since the remaining costs and profits relating to sales made to plant 3 were excluded from the selling price, the pretax profit of $34,000 for plant 1, shown in case 5.1, has dropped to a loss of $14,000. In plant 2 the profit of $54,000 has declined to $29,000—a total decline of $73,000. The pretax profit in plant 3, on the other hand, has increased from $13,000 to $86,000—an increase of $73,000. Management could be misled by these figures and make decisions detrimental to the profitability of plants 1 and 2. Note in the total column, in which all three plant figures have been consolidated, that the total profit for the three plants is $101,000—and that this figure is the same in all three cases.

CASE 5.3:

One might well ask if there is any way in which transfer pricing calculations can be improved to avoid the profit distortions shown in case 5.2. The answer is yes, as shown in "Accounting for Interplant Sales," by Raymond H. Baughman, *Management Accounting,* September, 1970. Baughman, in his article, proposes that the intracompany transfers be broken down into two figures: (1)

variable costs, and (2) fixed costs plus profit. With such a breakdown available, only the variable costs of $128,000 would be charged to the material account. The nonvariable costs, amounting to $74,000, would be included in the fixed cost section of the income statement as transfers in of fixed costs and profit. Availability of this figure would serve a useful purpose. If, for example, management felt that the $13,000 pretax profit for plant 3 was inadequate, identification of the $74,000 separately would show how much of plant 1 and 2 costs and profits are being absorbed by plant 3 and still yielding a 20% return on investment.

To accomplish this, the selling plants would have to separate the variable costs from the fixed costs plus profit. The selling plants need not be reluctant to reveal the profit portion included in the sales because the profit would be lumped together with the fixed costs.

Some would argue that since purchases of material are a variable cost of production, transfer in of fixed costs and profit should be categorized as variable to give effect to true cost behavior.

In line with this thinking, case 5.3 has been revised in Exhibit 5.2 to show the $74,000 transfer-in figure in the variable, rather than the fixed cost section of the income statement. Insofar as the purpose of identifying the fixed cost plus profit transfer separately is concerned, it does not matter in which section

EXHIBIT 5.2

IMPACT OF CASE 5.3 TRANSFER PRICING METHOD AFTER REVISION*

CASE 5.3: *Intracompany Sales Charged at Outside Selling Price but Split into Material and Fixed Cost*	*Plant 1*	*Plant 2*	*Plant 3*	*Sub-total*	*Elim-ination*	*Total*
Total Sales	270	337	405	1,012	202	810
Variable Cost of Sales						
Material	108	135	135	378	128	250
Direct Labor & Overhead	68	67	149	284	—	284
Trsfr. in: Fixed Cost & Profit	—	—	74	74	74	—
Total Variable Costs	176	202	358	736	202	534
Profit Contribution—$	94	135	47	276		276
Profit Contribution—Percent	35	40	11	27		34
Fixed Costs						
Manufacturing	40	54	14	108		108
General & Administrative Exp.	20	27	20	67		67
Total Fixed Cost	60	81	34	175		175
Pretax Profit	34	54	13	101		101
Investment—$	170	270	65	505		505
Return on Investment—Percent	20	20	20	20		20

* Figures in $000. Small errors due to rounding.

this figure appears just so long as it is set out separately rather than being lumped in as material cost.

There is a difference, however, when these figures are used for determining the break-even point of sales. Exhibit 5.3 illustrates this point. This exhibit shows the break-even calculation for plant 3 in case 5.3 both before revision and after revision. Note that the shift of $74,000 from the fixed cost category to the variable does not affect the pretax profit or the return on investment—both of which remain the same.

The break-even point of sales prior to revision shows a required sales level of $361,000 or 89% of the $405,000 sales. After revision, the break-even drops to $293,000 or 72% of the $405,000 sales. Since the pretax profit for both remain unchanged, the difference in break-even volume is attributable to the shift of the $74,000 from the fixed to the variable category.

This is depicted graphically in Exhibit 5.4 for four increments of change, of which two are contained in Exhibit 5.3. Both the sales and pretax profits

EXHIBIT 5.3

CALCULATION OF BREAK-EVEN POINT FOR PLANT 3*

	Case 5.3 prior to Revision		Case 5.3 after Revision	
	Dollars	Percent	Dollars	Percent
Sales	405	100.0%	405	100.0%
Less Variable Costs				
Material	135	33.3	135	33.3
Direct Labor & Overhead	149	36.9	149	36.9
Transfer in: Fixed Cost & Profit	—	—	74	18.3
Total Variable Costs	284	70.1	358	88.5
Profit Contribution	121	29.9	47	11.5
Fixed Costs				
Trsfr. in: Fixed Costs & Profit	74		—	
Manufacturing	14		14	
General & Administrative Exp.	20		20	
Total Fixed Costs	108		34	
Pretax Profit	13		13	
Break-even Point prior to Revision:				
108 divided by 29.9% =	361			
Percent of Total Sales	89%			
Break-even Point after Revision:				
34 divided by 11.5% =			293	
Percent of Total Sales			72%	

* Figures are in $000.

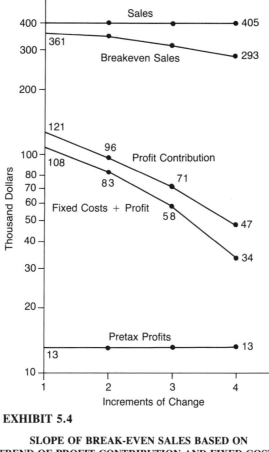

EXHIBIT 5.4

**SLOPE OF BREAK-EVEN SALES BASED ON
TREND OF PROFIT CONTRIBUTION AND FIXED COSTS**
(Figures based on plant 3 in case 5.3)

are shown as straight lines because they remain constant for the four increments. Increment 1 corresponds with plant 3 as shown in case 5.3 of Exhibit 5.1. Increment 2 is based on a reduction of $25,000 in the profit contribution as well as the fixed cost plus profit amount. As the variable costs are increased, the profit contribution and fixed cost categories decrease by an equivalent amount. This shift of more costs to the variable category causes the break-even point to edge downward.

Increment 3, like increment 2, is adjusted by another $25,000, with a further movement downward of the break-even point. The final increment reduction is $24,000, to arrive at a break-even figure of $293,000—corresponding with the figures shown in Exhibit 5.3 as case 5.3 after revision.

SUMMARY

Chapter 8 on cost-based pricing for defense work points out that government auditors are sometimes suspicious that transfer pricing within a company may result in pyramiding of profits and thus overstate the selling prices. The purpose of this chapter has been to throw more light on intracompany pricing by comparing several methods.

CHAPTER 6

Relationship of Product Costs to Prices

The objective of product cost estimating is to provide a guide for pricing and a means for monitoring the profitability of the different products in the line.

PRODUCT CHARACTERISTICS

The various expenses that make up product cost are treated differently, depending on whether the product is customized according to the customer's specifications or standardized according to the specifications established by the manufacturer. Products can thus be categorized into two general types: customized and standard.

Customized products are considered to be unique to the customer, because the customer, rather than the manufacturer, determines the design and specifications. The manufacturer sometimes recommends changes in design to improve performance of the product or to simplify production. Selling prices for customized products are essentially cost based. The cost per unit is usually large and the number of units produced relatively small.

Standard products are those products for which the manufacturer, rather than customer, establishes the design and specifications. These products are sold out of stock rather than being built to order. Because standard products are very similar to those made by competitors, selling prices are governed by the competitive forces of the marketplace. The cost per unit and selling price per unit are generally smaller than for the typical customized product.

Column A in Exhibit 6.1 shows the buildup of total product cost. Manufacturing costs are identified by the three elements of cost: material, direct labor, and overhead. Material is defined as that material which is visible in the end product, while direct labor is defined as "touch labor." This is the labor directly associated with running the machine that makes the components and performs the operations that assemble the components into a finished product.

When a product is painted or plated, the question frequently arises as to whether the paint and plating deposited on the product should be treated as material or overhead. The test is materiality and measurability. Caustics, degreasing solvents, and/or chemicals used to prepare the surface for painting or plating are generally categorized as indirect because these items are not usually substantial in cost nor are they considered to be measurable. Both paint and plating material (silver and copper, for example) are material in cost and are measurable by the surface area covered. Accordingly, they are properly treated as direct material.

Direct labor is considered direct when the machine operator or assembler of the product performs a task directly related to each unit produced. A task such as material handling is categorized as indirect labor since a large variety of materials are moved and cannot be directly associated with individual products.

In addition to the aforementioned indirect costs, factory overhead includes all indirect support costs such as foremen, group leaders, and floor men in the production cost centers. In the service cost centers (departments), it includes the general manager and staff, personnel, cost accounting, production control/ scheduling, manufacturing engineering, quality control, purchasing, and maintenance. Also included are such nonlabor costs as electricity, gas, depreciation, maintenance materials, factory supplies, and stationery as well as other office expenses and occupancy-related costs.

Column B of Exhibit 6.1 shows each of the three elements broken down into standard and variance. Although standard costs are used mostly for standardized products, some companies do use standard costs for manufacture of customized products. However, they must also book the actual costs.

This column also includes tooling, such as molds and dies. For customized products, tooling is considered to be the property of the customer and is billed with the first shipment. For standard products, tooling is frequently treated as overhead and is allocated to the product through an overhead rate. This is acceptable only if the products on which the tooling is used are fairly homogeneous. If the tooling is large in some products but small in others, then such tooling should be identified by product and charged accordingly.

Column C adds the nonmanufacturing expenses to arrive at total product

EXHIBIT 6.1

BREAKDOWN OF TOTAL PRODUCT COST

BREAKDOWN OF TOTAL PRODUCT COST

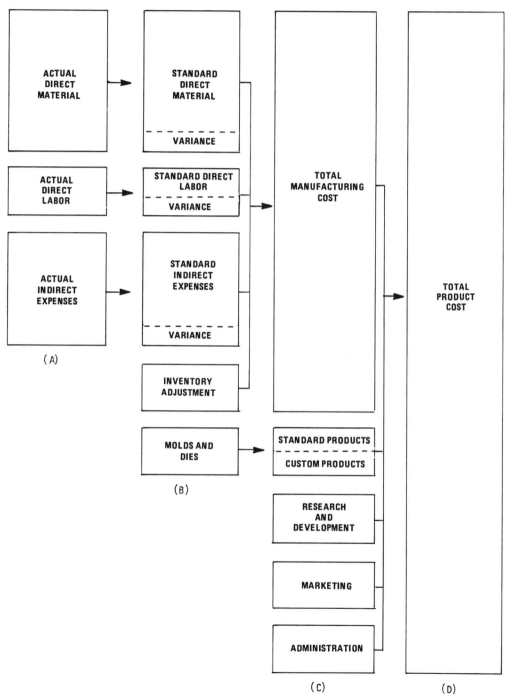

cost. (See chapter 2 for further discussion of nonmanufacturing costs.) Once the total product cost is determined, a markup is applied to arrive at the selling price. As noted earlier, the selling price for customized products is cost based, but for standardized products it is determined by the marketplace. This does not mean that the cost-based price used for customized products is blindly accepted by the customer: The quoted price and the manufacturer's performance and reputation are additional factors that are compared with other bidders before the order is placed.

PREPARATION OF PRODUCT COSTS

Product cost estimates for customized products are prepared whenever a request for quotation (RFQ) is received from a customer or prospective customer.

For standard items, product costs are established annually for all active items and any new ones included in the sales forecast. These are frozen for inventory valuation purposes. However, all companies using standard costs should also maintain an updated file of the standards for labor and material price changes, as well as changes in design and method of manufacture. Although inventories would continue to be valued at the frozen values, current costs should be available to update product costs so that new cost/selling price comparisons can be made.

Differences in Cost Classification

Product costing for customized products classifies certain expense items differently than is done for products that fall in the standardized category. For example, setup and rework are charged directly to the customer order rather than through an overhead costing rate based on machine hours, labor, or some other basis. The reason is that the setup and rework, which are small per unit of standard product, are larger for customized products. Setup and rework are also likely to vary from one customer order to another. To include these in the overhead costing rate for customized orders, as is done in costing standardized products, could result in overcosting some products and undercosting others. There are other items which, like setup and rework, are treated differently for customized products than they are for the standard items. This will be covered in chapter 7.

RFQ Processing Time Must Be Minimized

The data needed in processing RFQs can require the input of as many as six different disciplines. The disciplines involved and functions performed are as follows:

1. *Engineering:* Screens the incoming RFQs to determine from the customer drawings and product specifications if the factory has the capability to make the product. If not, the customer should be advised within a reasonable time. Included with the letter written by the marketing manager could be whatever brochures are available as to the types of products made by the company and an invitation to submit future RFQs.

2. *Manufacturing Engineering:* Identifies the equipment on which the order would be processed as well as the production time and labor requirements. Also determines what setup time is required and the cost of tooling, if applicable.

3. *Purchasing:* Provides current prices for material and purchased components.

4. *Production Control:* Reviews the production schedule to determine if the requested delivery data can be met. Here again, if the requested date cannot be met, the customer should be advised as soon as possible of the earliest date that the order can be shipped. Other bidders may be in the same position. If so, the one coming closest to meeting the required delivery data stands a better chance of being selected.

5. *Cost Accounting:* Develops material, labor, and overhead costs. Adds the SG&A costs and applies the markup to arrive at the desired selling price.

6. *Marketing:* Reviews the costs and finalizes the selling price.

The company that treats the customer as a second-class citizen by allowing the RFQ process to be delayed is risking rejection: The customer may remove the company from its list of prospective suppliers. A study made for the Elto Company (name disguised) is illustrative of loose controls in monitoring the RFQ processing procedure. The results of the findings are shown in Exhibit 6.2. The figures were based on observations made on different dates rather than following a single batch of RFQs through the entire process.

Although the total of 20 RFQs in the backlog shown in column 1 may seem small, it represents almost a third of the total number received each month. The total of 23 elapsed days shown in column 2 for processing RFQs does not bode well for a company that requires this much time. It was obvious from these figures that management was not monitoring the effectiveness of its cost estimating/pricing function. A relatively simple control would be to require that a routing form be attached to each RFQ and that each of the department heads indicate the time and date of receipt of each RFQ and initial the time and date of completion. All completed routing forms should be reviewed regularly and explanations requested in instances in which processing time in any department exceeds two days.

EXHIBIT 6.2

RFQ BACKLOG AND CUMULATIVE ELAPSED TIME

	Col. 1 RFQ Backlog	Col. 2 Number of Elapsed Days from Date of Mailing
Delivery Time from Customer	—	2
Screening Process	3	5
Manufacturing Engineering	2	8
Purchasing	5	12
Production Control/Scheduling	4	15
Cost Accounting	5	19
Marketing	1	21
Delivery Time to Customer	—	23
Total	20	23

In addition to expediting the processing operation, the various individuals should be alert to any cost reduction or other suggestions that might benefit prospective customers. The engineering department, for example, might be able to recommend a more simplified design of the product, or the manufacturing engineer may be able to recommend a sectionalized tool which, although more expensive, would actually be more economical if the customer anticipates ordering additional quantities in the future. The saving would be in maintenance costs because repairs could be limited to replacing only the damaged section rather than building a new tool. Suggestions such as these will make for a good rapport with the customer and a greater likelihood that the customer will be more favorably disposed to accepting the price even if higher than the closest bidder.

SUMMARY

The purpose of this chapter has been first to distinguish between two major categories of products—those that are customized for each customer's needs, and those that are produced to inventory for sale to more than a single customer.

The second purpose has been to point out that in pricing customized products, prices are based on cost to a much greater extent than on prices in the marketplace—as is the case with standardized products. Since prices can justifiably be based on cost, it is important that costing be based on good business sense. For this reason, each customer order is quoted individually as it is received, and is reviewed by the various disciplines involved in producing the final product. Each of the disciplines provides information relating to its own input in producing the end product. In the process of providing quotation information, timeliness is of the essence.

Because of the magnitude of customized products sold not only to commercial companies such as utilities but to the military and space agencies, this category of products warrants further discussion in the chapters that follow.

CHAPTER 7

Cost-Based Pricing: Commercial Customers

With the ever-increasing demand for high technology products used in commercial and government applications, the pricing of such highly engineered products differs from similar products required for less critical uses. Costs such as engineering, quality, rework, and others, which are substantially greater in the customized applications, must be excluded from the overhead pool and applied to individual jobs on a direct-charge basis to ensure equitable pricing.

Nuclear components, which require substantially the same cost treatment as products produced for defense and space exploration, will be used as an illustrative example of the differences in costing between standard and customized products. Early nuclear valves were built to the then existing specifications for standard commercial (industrial) valves. When nuclear valves entered the picture, the industry established standards that specified wall thicknesses and dimensional parameters as well as temperature/pressure ratings. This did not satisfy the Atomic Energy Commission (AEC), which had to cope with the public's developing fears that nuclear power plants could emit radioactivity. The AEC exerted pressure on the industry to come up with specifications that would guard against accidents that could release radioactivity.

IMPACT OF TIGHTER SPECIFICATIONS ON COSTS

The advent of these stricter requirements has had a great impact on the amount of inspection, quality assurance effort, engineering, contract administration,

EXHIBIT 7.1

INSPECTION, HOLD, VERIFICATION, AND APPROVAL POINTS
CODE CLASS I STAINLESS STEEL VALVE

	Manufacturer	Customer	Code	Total
Procedures/Drawings	100	55		155
Purchase Orders	15			15
Certifications				
Body	35	35	35	105
Bonnet	35	35	35	105
Disc	25	25	25	75
Seats	15	15		30
Bushing	10	10		20
Bolting	15	15	15	45
Other	30	30		60
	165	165	110	440
Data Book	1	1	1	3
Inspection at Vendor				
Body	8	8		16
Bonnet	8	8		16
Disc	16	16		32
Seats	16	16		32
Bolting	5	5		10
Other	2	2		4
	55	55		110
Inspection in Process				
Body	22	21	16	59
Bonnet	17	16	11	44
Disc	9	8	4	21
Seats	7	6		13
Bushing	4	3		7
Other	30	1	1	32
	89	55	32	176
Grand Total	425	331	143	899

rework, and other costs. In addition, the manufacturing cycle was greatly lengthened because of many interruptions for inspection and the need for rework to meet code and customer requirements.

Inspection. The cost of inspection for nuclear valves is more than double that required for commercial-type valves. There can be as many as 900 inspection, hold, verification, and approval points as illustrated in Exhibit 7.1. This exhibit summarizes the requirements of a large customer of one of the valve manufacturing companies.

Manufacturing Interruption. The impact of increased inspection, not only by the manufacturer's personnel but by the customer representatives and third-party inspectors, results in production delays and consequently a much longer manufacturing cycle during which costs keep increasing and investment is tied up.

Quality Assurance. In the manufacture of industrial-type valves, the quality function does not go much beyond the inspection stage. With the more demanding requirement for code adherence in making nuclear valves, the quality assurance function must relate to the total controlled manufacturing system. To do this, quality assurance must take responsibility for the following:

· audit and control of suppliers to ensure conformance to code and contract requirements;
· internal training of inspection personnel;
· audit and control of internal departments for conformance to code and contract requirements;
· control of internal quality standards;
· development and monitoring of programs for calibration of measuring equipment; and
· control of quality documentation.

In a study of the industry, the opinion expressed by several valve manufacturers is that the net effect on cost of assuring conformance can more than triple the cost of the quality function.

Engineering. Engineering must also expand its role. It must go far beyond the relatively simple requirements of commercial types the customer can order by a simple designation such as catalog number. But when nuclear valves are being ordered, the customer (usually a utility company) must provide a design specification along with the order for each different type valve. Accordingly, for each and every contract, engineering must:

· design the end product according to the design specifications that were furnished;
· certify that the design meets code and contract requirements;
· spell out specifications for purchase of material by customer order;

- make detail drawings for the shop based on customer design specifications and write instructions and test procedures; and
- coordinate customer requirements with manufacturing procedures.

According to industry engineers, engineering costs in a nuclear product can be expected to be double or triple the cost of the commercial counterpart.

Contract Administration. In any product in which manufacturing procedures are spelled out in great detail and documentation for each step is required, a close liaison must be maintained between the manufacturer and the customer. This liaison goes much further than the conventional customer service function. It must do the following:

- act as contact with the customer, providing the necessary liaison on all matters relating to the contract;
- monitor status of the job and prepare progress reports;
- review all correspondence relating to the contract;
- furnish customer with any information required;
- monitor witness inspection dates; and
- close out orders and finalize documentation.

Rework. In a commercial-type valve, rework would normally be considered as overhead and charged to the various products through an overhead costing rate. In many cases, the parts would be scrapped rather than investing additional labor and overhead in rework. In nuclear valves, rework is an unavoidable cost because even the slightest defects must be corrected. Since the degree of required rework can vary widely from one valve to another, this cost must be product specific.

Mixed Production. Companies manufacturing the commercial-type valve in the same facility that is used for making nuclear valves can expect to find costs of the commercial type increasing. This is due to the normal tendency to upgrade lower-graded products when two disparate types are being manufactured.

The foregoing are some of the factors that greatly impact the need for more definitive costs—particularly when commercial and nuclear valve types are being made in the same facility. Costs that have traditionally been classified as indirect must now be considered as direct. The traditional definition of what is direct and what is indirect must be abandoned in favor of a definition that will recognize costs that are identifiable and supportable as direct charges to each contract.

IDENTIFYING COSTS DIRECTLY WITH THE CONTRACT

It has been traditional in some valve manufacturing companies to consider as overhead such items as packing, gaskets, bolting, welding material, purchased services, incoming freight, shipping preparation, engineering/drafting, rework, and other costs. In light of the more demanding requirements in highly engineered products, these costs have increased greatly in magnitude. They can also vary widely from one contract to another. Because of these variations, inclusion of such costs in the overhead costing rate could result in allocations to contracts that are incorrect.

Supply-type Items. In most companies, items of relatively small value are expensed at time of purchase and charged to an overhead account. These costs are charged to products through an overhead costing rate. This is an acceptable expedient when items like a nut cost only 10 cents each, gasket material only a few cents a sheet, and welding material so little that it can practically be ignored. Since the aggregate cost of supply-type expenses like the foregoing can amount to as much as $1,500 for a nuclear valve, it is highly desirable that such items be treated as direct material and charged directly to the contract on which used.

Incoming Freight. In some companies, incoming freight is treated as an overhead expense. When valve manufacturers were, by and large, making castings in their own foundries, incoming freight was not as substantial an item as it is now when many companies purchase their castings from outside foundries. If these higher costs are included in overhead as in the past and allocated to the various products through an overhead rate applied on the basis of production time, the amount charged to individual valves could be greatly distorted. This distortion occurs because production time in a valve does not correctly reflect the material-related costs. Note in Exhibit 7.2 that the line representing material cost in the various sizes is quite different in slope than the line representing production time. A more accurate approach would be to identify the amount of incoming freight actually incurred by each size casting and to add this amount to the cost of the casting as material.

Rework. The requirement for nondestructive examinations refers to certain additional operations that need to be performed when defects such as sandholes are found. These are as follows:

· gouging,
· welding,

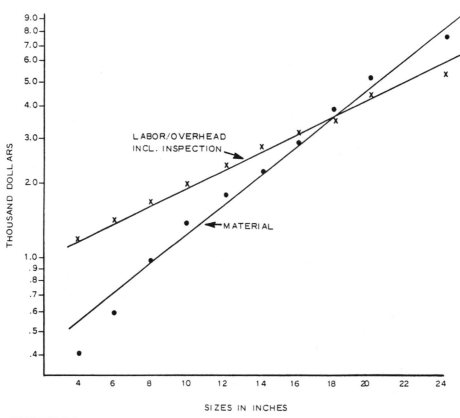

EXHIBIT 7.2

**COST COMPARISON
LABOR/OVERHEAD CONTENT VERSUS BASE MATERIAL FOR THE
600# CS PRESSURE SEAL VALVES*
COST PER UNIT**

· grinding,

· hand dressing,

· X-ray (if sand holes in the casting are still present, the cycle starts again),

· heat treating,

· remachining, and

· inspection.

   Companies that include rework as part of overhead are allocating such costs to the various valves on the basis of production time required to make the valve. Obviously, when the rework operations can be specifically identified with the valve on which they are being performed, it would be more accurate to have the individuals doing the work charge their time to the specific valve and identify the time as direct labor.

Special Tooling, Fixtures, and Patterns. The cost of these items could have a wide range. Special tooling could cost as much as $18,000, while patterns and fixtures could amount to more than $5,000—depending on the type of valve. Since these costs are product specific, the cost should, like material, be charged directly to that valve rather than spreading such costs through an overhead rate. It is conceivable that fixtures, tooling, and patterns could be used for a subsequent order. The method of amortizing such costs against orders is a separate issue—the treatment of which depends on the negotiations made with the customer.

Shipping Costs. Traditionally, some companies consider shipping to be part of the selling group of expenses, rather than identifying them as part of the manufacturing cost. Before the advent of the nuclear valve, the commercial types could be loaded on trucks with little or no protective packing so that shipping cost was merely a handling expense. This is no longer the case with the more sophisticated nuclear valves, which must be crated to protect the weld end and the operating mechanisms. The crating and wrapping of a large valve, which can weigh as much as an automobile, could amount to as much as $2,500. The operations required to prepare the valve for shipment should be identified as direct labor and charged to the specific valve.

Product Engineering. The concept of product engineering has been expanded greatly with the introduction of nuclear products. The function now includes design, writing instructions to the shop and purchasing department, preparing detail drawings, writing test procedures, and coordinating with the customer. The product engineering effort can start as much as a year before the shop begins to build the valve. Because of the foregoing factors, as well as the requirement to match costs with revenues, product engineering—as well as other related expenses—must be charged as direct costs when incurred. Application of such costs through a manufacturing overhead rate rather than a direct charge will not yield correct product costs. Take the case of a customer ordering two or more valves of the same type while another customer orders the same number of valves but each of a different type. Application of this cost through an overhead rate would penalize the first order. The product engineering charge should therefore be treated as direct rather than indirect labor.

Contract Administration. This is a liaison function in which the administrator or project manager acts as a coordinator between customer and company. He or she must review all correspondence, monitor the status of the job, advise the customer of witness inspection dates, and close out the orders and finalize the documentation. The effort required for each contract is not likely to vary with the amount of shop production time required to make the product, so this expense should not be allocated through an overhead rate but rather through a direct charge.

PRODUCT COST FEEDBACK

Many job cost systems accumulate costs by job but fail to compare these costs with the original estimate on which the selling price was based. This is an exceedingly important step which can be very helpful in achieving greater accuracy in cost estimating. The cost history record, which provides for a simple product cost feedback, is illustrated in Exhibit 7.3. This record contains two sets of figures: (a) unit costs of orders shipped, and (b) unit cost history record.

The upper portion of the exhibit is a breakdown for individual products that have been shipped during the period. Material, labor, overhead, and tooling/pattern costs, as well as nonmanufacturing costs and selling prices, are shown on a per-unit basis. Each of these is compared with the original cost estimate made at the time the selling price was determined. A comparison is also made of the total actual product cost and selling price.

The lower portion of the exhibit lists unit cost and selling price history for individual products. It recasts the actual costs for the individual products. The items shown in this portion are all 20″ 150# carbon steel gate valves. In place of the labor and overhead costs, this record shows the labor hours in the various departments (cost centers). Hours are preferable in making comparisons of jobs at different periods of time because they eliminate the inflationary effects of wage increases.

The two reports in Exhibit 7.3 can highlight where further analysis is required. Note in the upper portion of the exhibit, for example, that the 12″ 900# carbon steel valve shows quite a difference between the actual and estimated cost of the body—$3,123 versus an estimated cost of $2,138. The breakdown of the difference of $985 is shown in Exhibit 7.4. The understated cost was caused by the assumption that an elliptically shaped body would be used in making this valve. In an elliptical shape only the major dimension is 12″, while the minor dimension is somewhat less than 12″. Since a round shape was called for, 360 more pounds of material was required. In addition, certain other associated costs were understated. Obviously, the selling price was also understated, resulting in a 15% loss rather than an 18% profit.

Companies that fail to make this type of comparison are missing an

EXHIBIT 7.3

UNIT COST AND SELLING PRICE OF ORDERS SHIPPED

		Total Material Cost						Tools & Patterns	Total Labor and Overhead				Total Mfg. Cost	Non-Mfg. Cost	Total Product Cost	Selling Price	% Profit
Order #	Qty.	Body	Bonnet	Disc	Operator	Other	Total		Machining	Welding	Assy. & Test.	Total					
4" 300 S.S.																	
Actual Cost 22113	2	$ 327	268	54	966	235	1,850	24	617	318	299	1,234	3,108	410	3,518	5,044	30%
Estimate	2	620	460	35	834	213	2,162	—	721	350	371	1,442	3,604	580	4,184	5,044	17
12" 900# Ca St																	
Actual Cost 26126	1	3,123	991	165	3,904	1,341	9,524	2,140	3,174	1,597	1,578	6,349	18,013	1,040	19,053	16,602	(15)%
Estimate	1	2,138	874	126	2,004	1,027	6,169	2,515	2,056	1,019	1,037	4,112	12,796	796	13,592	16,602	18
20" 150# Ca St																	
Actual Cost 23957	2	1,288	154	229	—	376	2,047	15	682	362	320	1,364	3,426	804	4,230	5,910	28%
Estimate	5	1,015	148	297	—	260	1,720	—	607	365	342	1,314	3,034	760	3,794	5,910	36
30" 150# Ca St																	
Actual Cost 24628	2	2,943	349	441	—	688	4,421	—	1,474	716	757	2,947	7,368	1,149	8,517	20,200	58%
Estimate	2	4,984	300	501	—	861	6,646	5,028	2,215	1,097	1,119	4,431	16,105	1,296	17,401	20,200	14

PRODUCT: 20" GATE VALVE

UNIT COST AND SELLING PRICE OF ORDERS SHIPPED

		Total Material Cost						Total Hours					Total Mfg. Cost	Non-Mfg. Cost	Total Product Cost	Selling Price	% Profit
Order #	Qty.	Body	Bonnet	Disc	Operator	Other	Total	Upgrade	Machining	Welding	Assy. & Test.	Total					
21428	3	$1,285	163	246	—	346	2,040	3	57	14	21	95	3,521	1,519	5,040	5,910	15%
21585	2	1,273	162	241	—	345	2,021	4	58	12	18	92	3,502	1,307	4,809	5,910	19
23561	2	1,311	189	220	—	298	2,018	5	71	29	22	127	3,982	1,275	5,257	5,910	11
23957	5	1,288	154	229	—	376	2,047	4	63	16	21	104	3,426	804	4,230	5,910	28

EXHIBIT 7.4

COMPARISON OF ACTUAL AND ESTIMATED COSTS

	Estimated Cost	Actual Cost	Difference
Body Weight (pounds)	1,450	1,810	360
Cost of Body	$1,888	2,444	556
Heat Charts	—	15	15
Charpy Tests	—	45	45
Film	200	455	255
Rough Machining	50	164	114
Total	$2,138	3,123	985

important step in the process of management control. In the case of the 30″ 150# carbon steel valve, the opposite was true. When the estimate was prepared, it was assumed that the existing tools and patterns could no longer be used, so an additional $5,028 for new tools was included. Because of the resulting overstatement of this and the other associated costs, the total product cost was overstated. Because of the existence of a strong seller's market at the time, the customer did not dispute the price. As a result, an unusually large profit was realized—58% rather than the estimated 14%.

SUMMARY

The advantage of good feedback should be obvious: It gives high visibility to the difference between the actual product cost estimates and the original estimates on which the selling prices were based. This is particularly important for highly engineered products that change from job to job and whose determination of selling prices are more heavily influenced by cost than is the case with standardized products.

CHAPTER 8

Cost-Based Pricing: Government Contracts

The previous chapter discussed cost-based pricing as it relates to highly engineered, customized products sold to commercial (industrial) customers—utility companies, for example. As was also pointed out earlier, many expenses classified as indirect in the manufacture of standardized products revert to direct charges when highly engineered products are produced.

Because of the extended focus of the media on overpriced items purchased by the military, auditors have naturally felt pressured to dig more deeply for the answers. Prior to the outburst of criticism, the office of the Assistant Secretary of Defense had pointed out the need for more accuracy in the bills of material, production schedules, and inventory records, as well as cost transfers. This chapter will deal with bills of material as they relate to material and direct labor costs used for costing and pricing products.

DIRECT MATERIAL

The logical source of information for determining the quantitative material content of the various products is the engineering bill of materials (B/M). It shows the type and quantity needed to ensure that the product fulfills the design requirements and specifications set forth by the customer, whether it be a commercial customer or a government agency. The quantities of the various materials provide for such losses as blanking scrap in metal stamping, and turnings, for example. But they do not provide for production rejects. A reasonable allowance for such rejects must be added as a separate factor shown by point of origin.

The engineering bill of material must be converted to a manufacturing bill to show the material requirements by sequence of operations in the various production cost centers. The manufacturing bill also provides for inclusion of unit price data (pounds, inches, weight, etc.). The unit price multiplied by the quantity shows the material cost for each type of material. Availability of manufacturing bills for past periods can be helpful as checkpoints in preparing current product cost estimates.

DIRECT LABOR RATES AND PRODUCTION TIME

The same manufacturing bill broken down by operations within the production cost centers provides such information as number of employees at each operation, their labor grades, and the time required to perform each operation.

Forecasting Direct Labor and Overhead Rates

Government auditors, in reviewing procedures followed by contractors in developing overhead rates, are wary when the amount of forecasted labor is lower than past history indicates. This could occur when such items as setup and rework are classified as overhead in the forecast and direct labor when charging these costs to the various jobs. Such a case is as follows:

	Forecast	As Charged to Products
Direct Labor	$16,316	19,154
Overhead	28,208	25,370
Total	$44,524	44,524
Overhead Rate	173%	132%

If the forecasted overhead rate of 173% were to be applied to the actual direct labor charged to products, the overhead would amount to $33,136 ($19,154 × 173%), rather than $25,370, as shown in the second column. This could also occur if the forecasted labor was based on standard costs but applied to the actual labor, rather than standard. To avoid this multiplier effect of overhead buildup in product costs, the figures used in developing overhead rates must be consistent with the figures used in charging costs to the products.

Changes in Make/Buy Policy

Comparing the current forecast with historical experience can be helpful in revealing changes in make/buy policy wherein the company may revert to purchasing components on the outside rather than manufacturing them in-house—or the comparisons may suggest the reverse action. If such changes are made in any magnitude, they could affect the material/labor ratio. Increasing the volume of outside purchases would reduce direct labor and therefore the in-house volume level of production. Transfer of outside purchases to in-house production, on the other hand, would increase the volume level. Any such changes would affect the labor base for calculating overhead rates. Companies have been found to make such reversals midyear without updating the forecast from which the overhead rates were originally determined.

Scrap and Rework

In developing scrap and rework allowances for product cost estimating purposes, plantwide percentages should be avoided because the cost of some products would more than likely be overstated and others understated. Some companies do not segregate scrap and rework in the chart of accounts. In such cases the information should be maintained on a statistical basis as long as the data is complete. Whether these items are segregated in the books or maintained statistically, trends and cost relationships can be made available and should be utilized for improved product costing.

Scrap and rework are usually greater in the early stages of a contract. A leveling off can be expected as production moves out of the early stages and volume increases. The data should be studied to determine when unusually high scrap and rework costs occur and the reasons. It is at this point that management should be apprised so that corrective action can be taken as early as possible.

Setup

Some companies have been found to prorate setup time over the number of pieces in the lots being produced. Since all lots are not likely to be uniform, setup costs can be overstated and understated, depending on the lot size.

In reviewing the reasonableness of setup costs being charged to the various jobs, production schedules in the forecast period should be compared with production schedules in prior periods. This comparison should determine if spare parts are scheduled for production at the same time as the end products on which the parts are used. If the spares are not scheduled at the same time, it means that additional setup costs will be incurred.

INTRACOMPANY TRANSFERS

Some of the areas likely to be questioned by auditors have been covered in earlier chapters. Another likely candidate could be procurement from affiliates as compared with outside suppliers. This is based on the suspicion that purchasing from other units within the company may result in pyramiding of profits and thus overstating selling prices that are not only cost based but profit based as well.

Intracompany transfer pricing was discussed in chapter 5. The exhibits included in that chapter reviewed several methods that can be used in transfer pricing and their impact on profits. The case studies were presented in an income statement format together with a consolidation which eliminates intracompany transactions to avoid doubling up of sales. A review of the different methods should be helpful.

Many companies have erred because of hasty decisions made in comparing outside purchase costs with costs of products made in-house. Chapter 5 discusses this.

AVAILABLE VERSUS PRACTICAL CAPACITY

A large underabsorbed amount of overhead charged to a government contract can trigger questions from an auditor even though the underabsorption is due to the use of tight standards which do not allow for valid downtime, such as equipment maintenance and downtime required when changeovers are made from one job to another. Overhead rates should be based on practical rather than available capacity so that allowances for unavoidable downtime are provided for in the overhead costing rates. Determining practical capacity requires several steps in which the base for calculating overhead—whether direct labor or machine hours—must allow for necessary downtime. This was illustrated in chapter 3.

Exhibit 3.1 in chapter 3 showed the available capacity in the first column in which the equipment for the various production cost centers was listed by type and number. The number of shifts, shown in the next column, is based on the economics of machine utilization. If the investment in equipment is high, then three shifts may be necessary, as is the case for both compression and injection molding. The less expensive equipment may require only two shifts, while the older, less expensive machines may be run only one shift (or less).

The machine hours available per day are the extension of the number of machines by the number of shifts shown in the third column. The next factor—and an important one—is the anticipated percentage of time that the equipment can be utilized after providing for unavoidable downtime and maintenance.

The difference between available capacity and practical capacity is not small. Exhibit 3.1 showed the total available capacity in a 21-day month to be 41,832 machine hours. This compares with 28,413 machine hours after adjustment to practical capacity based on the overall 67.9% utilization of equipment. The overhead rates at practical capacity would, on the average, be about 50% higher than at available capacity. Even though higher, the rates based on practical capacity are far more likely to be accepted by government auditors than attempting to spread a large pool of presumed "idle plant cost" to the various products.

IT ISN'T ALWAYS POSSIBLE TO GO BY THE BOOK

As discussed earlier, the manufacturing bill of materials shows the material quantities and prices as well as the production time and labor grades broken down by operations in each of the production cost centers. This is the ideal, but the reality is that receipt of an invitation to bid does not always allow time to develop a computerized engineering B/M and a manufacturing bill. More often than not, it will be necessary to locate the manufacturing B/M for a similar product made in the past and to adjust the costs to fit the product for which the current bid is to be prepared. For entirely new products, it would be necessary to go through the steps outlined in chapter 6.

THE LEARNING CURVE AS A GUIDE TO COSTING AND PRICING

The Air Force, in its *Guide for Evaluation of Cost Projections,* promotes the value of the learning curve (which is actually a straight line on log log graph paper) in achieving reduced costs through the following:

· simplification of product design;
· good plant layout;
· introduction of automated equipment where feasible;
· improved material handling, such as motorized conveyors in lieu of manual carting;
· good production planning and coordination of functions;

· increased specialization wherein each operator becomes more highly skilled;

· reduced number of production rejects; and

· reduction of rework and setups.

The principle of the learning curve is that each time the total production quantity doubles, the cumulative average production hours will be a fixed percentage of the cumulative average hours of the quantity that was doubled. An 80% learning curve indicates a 20% decrease in the cumulative average hours with each doubling of quantity.

If, for example, the first 10 units were produced in an average time of 10,000 hours, the first 20 should average 8,000 hours, the first 40 should average 6,400 hours, and so on. A 90% learning curve assumes a reduction of 10% with each doubling. Although the foregoing calculations result in cumulative average costs of all items produced, this line on graph paper is paralleled by another line of the same slope showing the cost, or hours of individual units. The relationship between figures on the cumulative average cost line and on the unit cost line is unchanged. There is a decimal factor, computed on the basis of a mathematical formula which shows this relationship for any given percentage slope. For the 80% learning curve, this factor is 0.6781; for the 90% curve, it is 0.8480. For more detailed discussion of factors and other formulas relating to the learning curve, see chapter 31 of *Handbook of Business Planning and Budgeting,* edited by Thomas S. Dudick and Robert V. Gorski, Van Nostrand Reinhold, 1983.

To find the cost of a given unit at any point, it is necessary to multiply the figure on the cumulative average line by 0.6781 for an 80% learning curve and 0.8480 for a 90% curve. If the unit cost of any individual unit is known, the average cost of all units up to and including that one may be calculated by dividing this figure by the factor.

Using the Learning Curve in Price Negotiation

The learning curve is an effective tool for price negotiation. However, the production requirement must be large enough to facilitate measurement of learning efficiency that results in cost reduction. This tool has received large acceptance in the aerospace industry and also has application in the electronics industry, machine shops, and nondefense industries producing nonstandard products. It can be used in tract housing in which 100 or more houses are being built. The learning curve in this case should be broken down by craft rather than using a single overall learning curve percentage.

The expected efficiency of production varies with the nature of the operations. The greatest potential for cost reduction applies to labor-intensive operations; the least in operations performed on automated equipment. A 100% learning curve indicates no potentiality for learning—a 50% curve is unrealistic because this would indicate that the second half of a doubled quantity can be produced in zero hours.

Good records of production hours must be maintained. In addition, reductions in efficiency will take place during vacation and holiday periods.

The Mechanics of Developing a Learning Curve

Exhibit 8.1 lists four lots in column 1. Column 2 shows the production hours required to complete each of the four lots. The figures in these two columns are shown cumulatively in columns 3 and 4. Column 5 shows the cumulative average labor hours for each of the cumulative labor hour quantities for the four lots. These figures are determined by dividing the cumulative labor hours in column 4 by the cumulative production figures in column 3. The figures in column 5 are multiplied by the adjustment factor of 0.6781 to determine the labor hours per unit in column 6. A list of adjusting factors used for converting cumulative hours to hours per unit is shown in Exhibit 8.2.

The next step is to plot the figures in column 5 and column 6 on log log graph paper. This paper is sometimes referred to as double log because ratio, rather than arithmetic scales, are used for both vertical and horizontal scales.

When the plotting is completed as shown in Exhibit 8.3, both lines are extrapolated to 200 units—the quantity called for in the contract. The extended line shows the cumulative average for the 200 units to be 51 hours. The labor hours per unit line shows the labor hours per unit to be 35 hours (51 cumulative

EXHIBIT 8.1

DATA FOR 80% LEARNING CURVE

Lot Number	Col. 1 Production	Col. 2 Labor Hrs.	Col. 3 Cumulative Production	Col. 4 Cumulative Labor Hrs.	Col. 5 Cumulative Average Labor Hrs.	Col. 6 Labor Hrs. per Unit
A	10	1,352	10	1,352	135	92
B	10	819	20	2,171	109	74
C	20	1,288	40	3,459	86	58
D	40	2,061	80	5,520	69	47
	80	5,520				

EXHIBIT 8.2

FACTORS FOR ADJUSTING CUMULATIVE
HOURS TO HOURS PER UNIT

Learning Curve %	Adjusting Factors
96	.9411
94	.9108
92	.8796
90	.8480
88	.8155
86	.7824
84	.7484
82	.7137
80	.6781
78	.6415
76	.6041
74	.5655
72	.5261
70	.4854

average labor hours multiplied by the 0.6781 adjusting factor for an 80% learning curve).

SUMMARIZING THE CONTRACT DATA

Two key figures are needed to summarize the contract status: total contract hours completed to date, and total hours needed to complete the contract.

To determine the total contract hours completed to date, multiply the 200 hours by the cumulative labor hours indicated at the end of the extrapolated line. The cumulative labor hours shown for the entire 200 units are 51. The total hours for the entire contract would be 10,200 (200 units × 51 hours).

To calculate the hours needed to complete the contract, subtract the total hours at the point at which the extrapolation line begins from 10,200 hours (10,200 hours − 5,520 = 4,680 hours).

LINKING PRODUCT DEVELOPMENT WITH PRODUCTION

Defense contractors are often awarded contracts to develop a new product or a variation of an existing product. On conclusion of the development work, the contractor may be requested to submit a proposal for follow-on production. Obviously, learning curve data compiled in the development stage can be

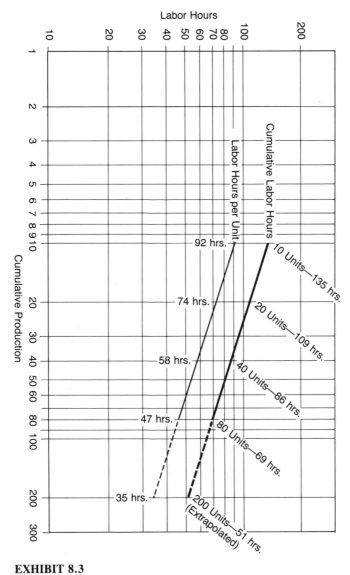

Labor Hours

EXHIBIT 8.3

valuable in estimating and pricing the production work. This was the case with a division of a large company that received a development contract which called for 48 units to be tested in the field. On conclusion of the tests, the company was invited to submit a proposal to produce 200 units. The company recognized the probability that even more follow-on work would be requested, so it bent every effort to prepare an acceptable bid proposal. The company reviewed its

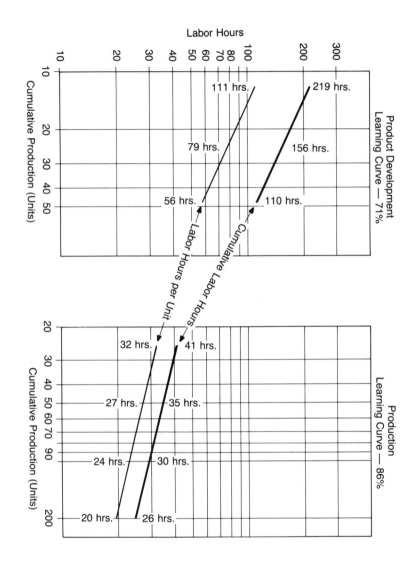

figures relating to the development contract, in which the labor hours per unit were reduced from 111 hours for the first 12 units to 56 hours per unit for the 48 units called for in the contract. In a discussion between the engineering and division managers, it was agreed that the labor hours could be reduced further with the introduction of special tooling that enabled a number of the operations to be automated. With the purchase of such tooling, there was also agreement that the 200 units could be produced for 20 hours per unit.

The learning curve for the development order was compared with the anticipated learning curve for the follow-on production order and appears in Exhibit 8.4. A copy of this was attached to the bid proposal, which also included the cost of the proposed tooling that would become the property of the government. The production order was awarded to the company, undoubtedly because of the well-documented link with the progress made in developing the first 48 units.

CHAPTER 9

Verifying Cost-Based Pricing through Estimate to Complete Analyses

The old saying, "There's many a slip between the cup and the lip," can be applied to costing and pricing highly engineered, single-customer products being manufactured in relatively small quantities.

Unlike standard multicustomer products that are in continuous production, highly engineered products can require months or years to complete. Often, in the course of manufacture, the customer may request changes that will affect the product cost and selling price. Naturally, this justifies a price add-on, which is often overlooked because of a breakdown in communications.

The use of an estimate to complete analysis on a regular basis will disclose such omissions early in the production cycle, rather than waiting until the order is closed out. If a product is being manufactured and price-tested stage by stage, a monthly Estimate to Complete analysis can be very useful to management in monitoring not only its costs, but the prices that are based on such costs. If, for example, stage 1 was undercosted and therefore underpriced, the company will be more conversant with the unforeseen problems and omissions which could spill over to succeeding stages. Such costs can then be taken into account immediately.

The Estimate to Complete analysis is important when the customer requests changes midway in the production cycle. Being cognizant of this and other problem areas, the company can take this into account when preparing the add-on price. Estimates to complete can be developed in more than a single format—depending on the product and the method of manufacture. The following case studies illustrate the formats used by three companies, each of which produces a different type product.

CASE 9.1: GOVERNMENT CUSTOMIZED EQUIPMENT

This case study is based on a company that manufactures highly sensitive electronic measuring instruments for the government. Exhibit 9.1 illustrates the format used for the Estimate to Complete analysis. The manufacturing cost elements are broken down into material, direct labor, and overhead. In addition to manufacturing cost, general and administrative costs are shown separately as G&A and added to the manufacturing costs to arrive at the total product cost. The RFQ (request for quotation) resulted in a total quoted selling price of $276,716, which, based on a total cost of $261,053, would have yielded a profit of $15,663.

The exhibit, in addition to showing the breakdown of product cost, also breaks down the elements into the following five categories: (a) incurred costs; (b) RFQ estimate; (c) billings; (d) cost of sales; and (e) cost to complete.

The total costs incurred to date are divided by the RFQ estimate to determine the percentages by element. See line F.

Year to date cost of sales is also divided by the amounts shown in the RFQ estimate for the individual cost elements. See line G.

Total billings to date are divided by the total selling price to arrive at the percentage of the selling price received to date. See line H.

Although 46% of total costs have been shipped, only 44% of the selling price could be billed against these shipments—indicating that the contract is already in a loss position. The cost to complete is $151,447 (RFQ estimate of $279,769 less cost of sales of $128,321).

CASE 9.2: COMMERCIAL CUSTOMIZED EQUIPMENT

This study is based on a company that manufactures customized industrial equipment. Since this product requires a fair amount of engineering before it can go into production, the Estimate to Complete shows the engineering as a separate category. The following categories are shown in Exhibit 9.2: (a) engineering and burden; (b) factory labor and burden; (c) factory material; (d) purchased systems and designs; and (e) variances.

As in case 9.1, the figures contained in this exhibit provide the means for monitoring the performance of the job against the latest cost estimate. They

EXHIBIT 9.1

ESTIMATE TO COMPLETE ELECTRONIC INSTRUMENTS

		Material	Direct Labor	Over-head	Total Mfg. Cost	G&A	Total Cost	Profit	Selling Price
Incurred Costs									
Through Previous Month		76,937	16,316	23,208	116,461	8,253	124,714		
Current Month		6,128	2,421	4,697	13,246	1,332	14,578		
Total	A	83,065	18,737	27,905	129,707	9,585	139,292		
RFQ Estimate									
Original Estimate		155,200	43,435	43,435	242,070	18,983	261,053	15,663	276,716
Additional to Complete		—	—	15,343	15,343	3,373	18,716	–18,716	—
Total	B	155,200	43,435	58,778	257,413	22,356	279,769	–3,053	276,716
Billings									
Through Previous Month									110,652
Current Month									11,175
Total	C								121,827
Cost of Sales									
Through Previous Month		65,765	13,478	20,370	99,613	8,253	107,866		
Current Month		11,171	2,838	5,114	19,123	1,332	20,455		
Total	D	76,936	16,316	25,484	118,736	9,585	128,321		
Cost to Complete									
Invty. End Current Month		6,128	2,421	2,421	10,970	—	10,970		
Amount Yet to Be Spent		72,135	24,698	30,873	127,706	12,771	140,477		
Total	E	78,263	27,119	33,294	138,676	12,771	151,447		
Percent of RFQ Estimate									
Total Incurred Costs (A Divided by B)	F	54%	43%	47%	50%	43%	50%		
Total Cost of Sales (D Divided by B)	G	50%	38%	43%	46%	43%	46%		
Total Billings to Date (C Divided by B)	H								44%

EXHIBIT 9.2

COST TO COMPLETE CUSTOMIZED INDUSTRIAL EQUIPMENT

	Col. 1 Sales Original	Col. 2 Mfg. Check	Col. 3 Estimate Difference	Col. 4 Projected Cost	Col. 5 Actual Cost To Date	Col. 6 Actual Cost Current	Col. 7 Estimate to Complete	Col. 8 Projected Sales Original
Engineering and Burden								
Engineering Hours	1,575	1,575	—	1,575	1,325	150	250	—
Engineering Labor	11,812	11,812	—	11,812	9,938	1,125	1,874	—
Engineering Burden	13,388	13,388	—	13,388	11,263	1,275	2,125	—
Total Engineering and Burden	25,200	25,200	—	25,200	21,201	2,400	3,999	—
Factory Labor and Burden								
Machining Hours	790	760	30	750	250	175	500	40
Machining Labor	4,187	4,028	159	3,975	1,325	928	2,650	212
Machining Burden	8,453	8,132	321	8,025	2,675	1,872	5,350	428
Assembly Hours	800	800	—	800	—	—	800	—
Assembly Labor	4,240	4,240	—	4,240	—	—	4,240	—
Assembly Burden	8,560	8,560	—	8,560	—	—	8,560	—
Total Factory Labor/Burden	25,440	24,960	480	24,800	4,000	2,800	20,800	640
Factory Material	38,040	36,590	1,450	35,375	11,789	8,252	23,586	2,665
Purchased Systems and Designs	31,320	31,320	—	31,320	7,830	—	23,490	—
SUBTOTAL	120,000	118,070	1,930	116,695	44,820	13,452	71,875	3,305
Variances								
Machining Labor	—	—	—	140	22	15	118	(140)
Machining Burden	—	—	—	270	44	31	226	(270)
Material Purchase Price	—	—	—	1,953	597	418	1,356	(1,953)
Total Variance	—	—	—	2,363	663	464	1,700	(2,363)
TOTAL COST	120,000	118,070	1,930	119,058	45,483	13,916	73,575	942
Divisor	.666	.656		.661	.661		.661	
Gross Profit Percent	33.4%	34.4%		33.9%	33.9%		33.8%	
Gross Profit Dollars	60,000	61,930		60,942	23,326		37,616	
Selling Price	180,000	180,000		180,000	68,809		111,191	
Material Variance Percent	—	—		5.5%	5.1%	5.1%	5.7%	
Machining Labor Variance Percent	—	—		3.5%	1.8%	1.6%	4.4%	

also provide the documentation for progress billings as well as any add-on pricing.

Sales Original. These are the RFQ estimates used as a guide in determining the selling price. Most companies receive a continuous flow of requests for quotation from potential customers. Often, because of leadtime limitations, insufficient time is available for detailed development of the estimates. Because of this and uncertainty of the problems that will be encountered in the development process, cost estimates are closer to being raw than finished standards. Often, development estimates are based on historical costs of similar jobs.

Manufacturing Check. When the company is awarded the order and has completed a prototype, it is in a better position to develop estimates in the production stage that come closer to standards. When this manufacturing check comes up with adjustments, the new estimates are posted in this column.

Estimate Difference. This column shows the amount of difference between the original estimates shown in column 1 and the manufacturing check column.

Projected Cost. This is the revised projection based on the results of the manufacturing check.

Current and Actual Costs to Date. Total costs of $45,483 factored by the divisor of 0.661 shows sales value of $68,809 at this stage.

Estimate to Complete. The figures in this column represent the difference between the projection shown in column 4 and actual cost to date in column 5.

Projected versus Sales Original. The figures in this column show the amount by which the various cost elements in the latest projection in column 4 deviate from the figures shown in column 1.

The exhibit shows the Estimate to Complete in terms of dollars. The dollar figures are necessary for accounting purposes. For management purposes, however, it would be helpful to summarize the data in a more concise fashion in which the status of the jobs is expressed in terms of percent completion, as follows:

	Projected Cost	*Actual Cost*	*% Complete*
Engineering and Burden	$ 25,200	21,201	84%
Total Factory Labor and Burden	24,800	4,000	16
Total Factory Material	35,375	11,789	33
Purchased Systems and Design	31,320	7,830	25
Variances	2,363	663	28
Total Cost	$119,058	45,483	38%
Divisor	.661	.661	
Sales value	$180,000	68,809	

EXHIBIT 9.3

ESTIMATE TO COMPLETE MAGNETRONS FOR RADAR APPLICATION
(Work-in-Process)

Month	Col. 1 Costs Incurred	Col. 2 Finished Units	Col. 3 Relieved from WIP	Col. 4 WIP Balance	Col. 5 Estimate to Complete	Col. 6 WIP Bal. Incl. Estimate to Comp.	Col. 7 Units to Be Completed	Col. 8 Value of Units to Be Completed	Col. 9 Current Prod'n. Variance	Col. 10 % Completed	Col. 11 Current Prod'n. Variance
Jan.	10,000	—	—	10,000	90,000	100,000	100	100,000	—	10%	—
Feb.	20,000	3	3,000 (2,427)	27,000	62,000	89,000	97	97,000	(8,000)	30%	(2,427)
Mar.	40,000	45	45,000 (4,633)	24,427	19,146	43,573	52	52,000	(8,427)	55%	(4,633)
Apr.	32,000	26	26,000 22,030	35,060	35,000	70,060	26	26,000	44,060	50%	22,030
May	38,000	26	26,000 25,030	25,030	—	25,030	—	—	25,030	100%	25,030
	140,000	100	40,000 100,000								40,000

A glance at the figures in the last column shows that the engineering effort is 84% complete. A total factory percentage completion (total cost less engineering and burden) would show a figure of 26% ($24,282 divided by $93,858), which could easily be included in the tabulation. Thus, management would know that the engineering effort is close to completion while the manufacturing effort is only about one-fourth completed.

CASE 9.3: STANDARDIZED ELECTRONIC UNITS

The product in this study consists of magnetrons used in radar applications. In the two preceding case studies, the Estimate to Complete reports reflected the work-in-process (WIP). When completed, WIP was relieved and cost of sales was charged. Since the magnetrons are made in production quantities, they move from WIP to finished goods inventory awaiting shipment. For this reason, the Cost to Complete figures discussed here reflect the cost accounting procedures followed by the company in tracing the Cost to Complete information through the work-in-process and finished goods accounts. The transactions illustrated in this study cover 100 units priced at $1,000 each.

Exhibit 9.3 summarizes the work-in-process transactions from January through May. The first month shows that $10,000 in costs were incurred and that no units were completed, leaving a work-in-process balance of $10,000. Since the total cost for 100 units is $100,000, and $10,000 has been incurred, the percentage completed in column 10 is shown as 10%, while the Estimate to Complete in column 5 is shown as $90,000. In February an additional $20,000 was incurred—making a total of $30,000 to date.

Three units have been completed in February, making the work-in-process balance $27,000. A check with the factory revealed that their estimate for completion of the remaining 97 units is $62,000 (column 5). The WIP balance of $27,000 plus the estimate to complete of $62,000 amounts to $89,000—which becomes the estimated actual cost of 97 units. Since the standard value of these 97 units is $97,000, there is a favorable variance of $8,000. Because this is the variance for the entire 100 units to be produced, it must apportioned to reflect only the number of units completed to date. Since $27,000 represents the portion completed and $89,000 is the total cost, the percentage of completion is 30.3%. Taking this percentage of $8,000, we arrive at $2,427 as the portion of the variance which is assignable to the completed work.

The next period shows that $40,000 in costs was incurred and that 45 units were completed. The WIP relief amounts to $45,000 (45 at $1,000). The new work-in-process balance becomes $24,427, which was arrived at as follows:

February WIP Balance (Col. 4)	$27,000
Plus February Variance (Col. 3)	2,427
Plus March Costs Incurred (Col. 1)	40,000
Total	$69,427
Less WIP Relief (Col. 3)	45,000
March WIP Balance (Col. 4)	$24,427

On completion of the 100 units, the actual costs incurred are shown in the column 1 total as $140,000. WIP relief in column 3 is made up of $100,000 representing relief from work-in-process at standard cost plus a net variance of $40,000.

Production transferred to finished goods is gross production, which exceeds the number of completed good units because of the inclusion of rejects and life test destruction. The rejects are shown in Exhibit 9.4 in columns 3 and 4, while units destroyed in life test are shown in columns 5 and 6. Note that these columns add up to 45 of the 145 shown in column 1.

In February five units were moved from production at the standard cost of $1,000 each (columns 1 and 2). One of the units was rejected and another was destroyed in life test. Although five units were moved out of work-in-process physically, this was reduced to three, which is the number used to relieve work-in-process. Although this illustration assumes that all rejected and life-tested units were charged back to the same month's production, this does not usually work out in actual practice. The number of units in the book inventory agrees with the physical inventory. The units in physical inventory are valued at 82% of the sales price of $1,200, or $984. Accordingly, the ending inventory was valued at a total of $2,952 (columns 12 and 13).

In the month of March, 70 more units were transferred from production at $1,000 each, bringing the book inventory up to $72,952 ($2,952 in February plus $70,000 input in March). The value of rejects was $23,000, and units destroyed in life test $2,000 (columns 4 and 6). This reduced the book inventory to $47,952, which was further reduced by shipments of $29,520 (column 8). The book value for March amounted to $18,432 (column 10). Again, the physical inventory confirmed that the number of units in the book inventory shown in column 9 was correct at 18. Using the valuation of $984 per unit resulted in the excess cost write-off shown in column 11 as $720 for the month of March. The equivalent write-off for the preceding month was $48.

Summarizing the transactions for the period indicates that gross production transferred to finished goods was 145 units, of which 39 were rejected and 6 destroyed in life testing. Actual shipments were 100 units, which were costed at $984 each for a total of $98,400 (column 8). The difference between this

EXHIBIT 9.4

ESTIMATE TO COMPLETE MAGNETRONS FOR RADAR APPLICATION
(Finished Goods)

Month	From Prod'n.		Rejects		Life Test		Shipments		Book Inventory		Excess Cost Write-off	Physical Inventory	
	Units	Value	Units	Value	Units	Value	Units	Value	Units	Value		Units	Value
	Col. 1	Col. 2	Col. 3	Col. 4	Col. 5	Col. 6	Col. 7	Col. 8	Col. 9	Col. 10	Col. 11	Col. 12	Col. 13
Feb.	5	5,000	−1	−1,000	−1	−1,000	—	—	3	3,000	−48	3	2,952
Mar.	70	70,000	−23	−23,000	−2	−2,000	−30	−29,520	18	18,432	−720	18	17,712
Apr.	40	40,000	−12	−12,000	−2	−2,000	−35	−34,440	9	9,272	−416	9	8,856
May	30	30,000	−3	−3,000	−1	−1,000	−20	−19,680	15	15,176	−416	15	14,760
Jun.							−15	−14,760					
Total	145	145,000	−39	−39,000	−6	−6,000	−100	−98,400			−1,600		

and the standard cost of $100,000 is shown in column 11 as an excess cost write-off of $1,600.

SUMMARY

While Exhibits 9.2 and 9.3 present what appears to be a clear-cut accountability for costs broken down as to amount of production variance, number of rejects, and losses in life testing, this does not automatically ensure that the figures are correct. The key is in the manner in which actual costs and Estimates to Complete are determined.

In development contracts, for example, it is impossible to audit the minds of engineers to determine what project they should be charging their time to. This does not present as much of a problem when fully engineered products are being manufactured. Human nature being what it is, there is always a temptation, when costs are running over on one job, to begin charging another job which is not in difficulty. However, determination of the Estimate to Complete should not be a one-way avenue of communication wherein the estimator merely records furnished information. The estimator should be able to ask intelligent questions about the status of the project so that Cost to Complete figures can be supported by a familiarity with the problems and a knowledge of what action is being taken to correct such problems. Failure to do so can mislead management in assessing which products are profitable and which are marginal. It can also result in erroneous pricing.

CHAPTER 10

Additional Considerations for Cost-Based Pricing

Chapters 7 and 8 emphasized the importance of charging certain types of overhead costs directly to the customer order when the product is highly engineered and customized to one customer's specifications—as opposed to a standard product which is in continuous production and sold to many customers. Direct charging of certain types of overhead costs is necessary when they are large and when the amounts incurred vary widely from product to product. Standard products are produced in large volumes on a continuous basis. For this reason, such overhead items as rework and setup, which are very small on a per-unit basis, can be treated as overhead and charged to the products through an overhead costing rate.

There can be instances in which cost-based pricing does not require direct charging of overhead items in the manner discussed in chapters 7 and 8. Printing Binding, Inc. (name disguised) is one such example. Any rework or setup (makeready), for example, can be provided for in the downtime allowance when the labor and or machine hour base for calculating the overhead costing rates is determined. Utilization allowances are made individually for cutting/folding, sewing/binding, color, and black/white presses.

Although pricing is cost based in Printing Binding, Inc. because each customer order is unique, the overhead costing process is quite similar to that used for standardized products. Chapter 3, which illustrated the development of overhead rates, focused on a company whose operations were machine paced. For that reason, the base for distributing the overhead was machine hours. The direct labor, like overhead, was also distributed on the basis of machine hours. Many companies assume that a company is either machine paced or labor paced and select one or the other. Printing Binding, Inc. has been selected as a case study because its breakdown of functions is both labor paced and machine paced. This chapter will demonstrate how costing rates can be calculated for both labor-paced and machine-paced operations within the same company.

CASE 10.1: PRINTING BINDING, INC.

The company started in the days when linotype machines were used to cast type one line at a time. This was a vast improvement over the previous method, by which typographers set movable type by hand. Both of these methods of typesetting have been almost completely replaced by newer techniques—first, photocomposition and, more recently, electronic typesetting systems. Now, word processors are used to produce electronic manuscripts copied onto floppy disks or magnetic tapes—or transmitted by telecommunications. Such media, with proper interfacing techniques and with additional type-specification instructions, are processed through electronic typesetting equipment. The end product is high-quality type (reproduction proofs) in galleys or pages. Proofreading, correction work, and paste-up complete the preparation of the finished copy. The work is then ready for the camera to make negatives which are used in exposing the offset plates. These plates are sent to companies like Printing Binding, Inc. to print and bind the book. Prior to the adoption of electronic typesetting, the company did its own typesetting. It used letterpress rather than offset printing, so plant operations were considered to be labor paced. The company was satisfied with a single, plantwide overhead rate based on direct labor. But with the installation of the more expensive offset presses in place of letterpress printing, management recognized the need for more sophisticated costing. Accordingly, the decision was made to establish four production cost centers, each with its own costing rate.

Production Cost Centers

The four cost centers are: folding, binding, color presses, and black and white presses. Folding and binding are labor paced, while both the color and black and white presses are machine paced.

Folding. Commonly at Printing Binding, Inc., the offset plates used in the printing process provide for 16 pages to be printed on both sides of 36″ × 48″ sheets. The folding process consists of folding these sheets in a predetermined pattern so the 32 pages in the folded packet are arranged in numerical sequence. A 256-page book would require eight packets (called signatures). As the folding is done, the signatures are bundled and the process continues until the edition is complete. The bundles of signatures are then ready for the binding operations.

Binding. After folding is completed, the signatures are gathered in proper sequence, bringing all the pages for each book together. Then, depending on the style of binding, the book may be either sewn or bound using adhesives. If the book is sewn, the signatures are stitched together in sequence. Each book is held together by the sewing on the back edge of the spine. Adhesive binding holds the pages together by milling off the closed back edge of the spine and then applying the adhesive. Once the semifinished book is sewn or bound by an adhesive, it may be encased in either a hard or soft cover.

The hardcover binding is more expensive and requires additional operations and materials. Cases are made of boards and covering material, and then are stamped with the title or design. Endpapers are used to connect the front and back covers to the first and last signatures of the book. In hardcover binding, the endpapers together with the book pages are trimmed on the three outside edges. This becomes the "book block"; it is finally brought together with the cover as it is "cased in."

Papercover binding is much simpler and involves a preprinted cover to be glued to the spine of the book block. Then the cover and the book receive a final trim of the three outside edges.

Color Presses. Color presses, being larger and more complex than black and white presses, require a greater amount of maintenance, depreciation, floor space, energy, and the like.

Black and White Presses. These presses were set up as a separate cost center to distinguish between the higher overhead machine hour costs of the color versus the black and white presses.

The balance of this chapter will discuss the following steps required in providing management with fully integrated costing procedures developed from a common database:

1. projected level of activity, based on both direct labor and machine hours;
2. overhead requirements;
3. allocation of overhead to production cost centers;
4. calculation of hourly costing rates;
5. product cost estimate (job cost estimate);

6. development of the flexible budget formula; and

7. break-even analysis.

PROJECTED LEVEL OF ACTIVITY

Exhibit 10.1 sets forth the level of activity at which the business is expected
to operate in the coming year. It takes into consideration that this will also be
the level at which the fixed costs of the business will be fully absorbed and
the business will yield an acceptable return on investment.

A number of companies that were queried about their practices in establishing the level of activity were found to favor forecasts of what was anticipated
in the coming year. Others based the level on what they referred to as normal—
the expectation based on past history.

These approaches are only partly correct. The important factor that must
also be taken into account is the economics of the business. Depending on the

EXHIBIT 10.1

PROJECTED LEVEL OF ACTIVITY; DIRECT LABOR AND MACHINE HOURS

	Shifts	Direct Labor Dollars	Direct Labor Hours	Machine Hours
LABOR-PACED OPERATIONS				
Cutting and Folding				
6 Operators	1	$ 86,400	11,664	
Sewing and Binding				
5 Sewing machine operators	1	67,000		
3 Binders	1	40,500		
Total Sewing and Binding		107,500	15,550	
Total Labor-paced Operations		$193,900	27,214	
MACHINE-PACED OPERATIONS				
Color presses				
4 Pressmen	2	$ 90,800		
4 Helpers	2	55,200		
Total Color Presses		$146,000		6,800
Black and White Presses				
4 Pressmen	2	89,200		
3 Helpers	2	53,600		
Total Black and White Presses		142,800		7,760
Total Machine-paced Operations		$288,800		14,560
TOTAL LABOR & MACHINE-PACED OPERATIONS		$482,700		

nature of the business, economic considerations dictate that labor-paced operations would normally be carried on a single-shift basis, while machine-paced operations would be performed on a two- or three-shift basis—depending on the amount of capital investment. In Printing Binding, Inc., the labor-paced operations are done on a single shift, with some second-shift work during peak periods. The presses are operated on a two-shift schedule, with the probability of third-shift work in peak periods.

Exhibit 10.1 identifies the labor-paced and machine-paced operations and also lists the number of employees in each production center, the job title, payroll cost, number of shifts, direct labor hours, and machine hours. Note that the labor hours and machine hours represent the available hours. These must be adjusted to provide an allowance for unavoidable downtime (this is done in Exhibit 10.4).

OVERHEAD REQUIREMENTS

The overhead requirements listed in Exhibit 10.2 consist of the indirect employees identifiable with the production and service (support) departments. The nonlabor overhead includes the fringe benefits for direct- as well as indirect-labor employees. It also includes items that do not fit in the direct material category, as well as other support costs such as occupancy-related items, depreciation, and utilities. Note that the indirect labor payroll of $182,300 plus fringe benefits of $131,590 account for about two-thirds of the overhead of $463,900. This is not unusual.

ALLOCATION OF OVERHEAD TO PRODUCTION COST CENTERS

The allocation of overhead is shown in Exhibit 10.3. The column titled ''Overhead Requirements'' includes the same information as that shown in Exhibit 10.2, but in a different format. The columns to the right show the total amounts, the method of allocation, and the amounts allocated to the four production cost centers. The rationale used in determining the most appropriate bases for distributing the individual items is discussed next.

Superintendent. The factory superintendent felt that from past experience, his time and the effort of his steno-clerk were provided on a ''readiness to serve'' basis. He therefore estimated that their payroll allocations should be made on the basis of 30% to the two labor-paced operations (split 50/50), 30% to the color presses, and 40% to the black and white presses. The latter were allocated

EXHIBIT 10.2

OVERHEAD REQUIREMENTS

	Annual Payroll	
INDIRECT LABOR—PRODUCTION DEPARTMENTS		
1 Factory Superintendent	$ 33,500	
1 Steno-clerk	15,200	
2 General Maintenance	26,700	$ 75,400
INDIRECT LABOR—SERVICE DEPARTMENTS		
Accounting		
1 Accountant	$ 21,650	
2 Cost Clerks	23,750	45,400
Production Control		
1 Production Scheduler/Estimator	$ 19,500	
3 Expediters	42,000	$ 61,500
TOTAL INDIRECT LABOR PAYROLL		$182,300
NONLABOR OVERHEAD		
Fringe Benefits	$131,590	
Ink	28,700	
Freight	950	
Rollers	10,300	
Replacement Parts	8,200	
Oil Wipers	3,300	
Electricity	22,400	
Chemicals	7,200	
Depreciation—Equipment	32,300	
Depreciation—Building	14,500	
Real Estate Taxes	17,960	
Property Taxes	4,200	$281,600
TOTAL NONLABOR OVERHEAD		
TOTAL ALL OVERHEAD REQUIREMENTS		$463,900

more than the color presses because of the number of short runs which frequently required more monitoring and additional reports.

Maintenance. The factory superintendent required all maintenance work to be recorded on job cards showing the time spent and repair parts used. On completion of such work, the time started and time finished were to be approved by the responsible individual in each of the production centers. The allocations were based on an analysis of the job cards after adjustment for certain unusual, nonrecurring costs.

Accountant. The accountant's services were also considered to be on a "readiness to serve" basis. His payroll cost was therefore allocated in the same manner as the superintendent's and the steno-clerk's.

EXHIBIT 10.3

ALLOCATION OF OVERHEAD TO PRODUCTION CENTERS

Overhead Requirements	Basis of Allocation	Amount	Labor-paced Operations		Machine-paced Operations	
			Cutting and Folding	Sewing and Binding	Color Presses	Black & White Presses
INDIRECT LABOR—PRODUCTION DEPTS.						
1 Factory Superintendent	Superintendent's Estimate	$ 33,500	5,025	5,025	10,050	13,400
1 Steno-clerk	Superintendent's Estimate	15,200	2,280	2,280	4,560	6,080
2 General Maintenance	Job Card Analysis	26,700	4,806	4,005	11,748	6,141
Total		$ 75,400	12,111	11,310	26,358	25,621
INDIRECT LABOR—SERVICE DEPTS.						
Accounting						
1 Accountant	Accountant's Estimate	$ 21,650	3,247	3,248	6,495	8,660
2 Cost Clerks	Direct and Indirect Employees	23,750	6,650	8,787	3,800	4,513
Total		$ 45,400	9,897	12,035	10,295	13,173
Production Control						
1 Production Schedule/Estimator	Number of Jobs in Process	$ 19,500	3,900	4,875	4,875	5,850
3 Expediters	Number of Jobs in Process	42,000	8,400	10,500	10,500	12,600
Total		$ 61,500	12,300	15,375	15,375	18,450
TOTAL INDIRECT LABOR PAYROLL		$182,300	34,308	38,720	52,028	57,244
NONLABOR OVERHEAD						
Fringe Benefits	Direct & Indirect Labor Payroll	$131,590	23,686	28,950	39,477	39,477
Ink	Number of Impressions	28,700	—	—	17,220	11,480
Freight	Number of Impressions	950	—	—	570	380
Rollers	Number of Impressions	10,300	—	—	6,180	4,120
Replacement parts	Job Card Analysis	8,200	1,230	656	3,608	2,706
Oil Wipers	Number of Impressions	3,300	—	—	1,980	1,320
Electricity	Connected Load × Hours of Usage	22,400	3,584	2,688	10,080	6,048
Chemicals	Production Control's Estimate	7,200	—	—	4,104	3,096
Depreciation—Equipment	Fixed Asset Ledger	32,300	5,491	5,168	12,274	9,367
Depreciation—Building	Floor Space Occupied	14,500	2,610	2,175	6,380	3,335
Real Estate Taxes	Floor Space Occupied	17,960	3,233	2,694	7,902	4,131
Property Taxes	Floor Space Occupied	4,200	756	630	1,848	966
TOTAL NONLABOR OVERHEAD		$281,600	40,590	42,961	111,623	86,426
TOTAL OVERHEAD REQUIREMENTS		$463,900	74,898	81,681	163,651	143,670

Cost Clerks. Since these clerks made up the payrolls, maintained the quarterly records, and performed duties normally performed by a personnel department, their time was distributed on the basis of the number of direct and indirect employees.

Scheduler, Estimator, and Expediters. The effort of this group is determined by the number of jobs in process. This was used as the basis for allocation.

Ink, Freight, Rollers, and Oil Wipers. These items are all influenced by the number of impressions made by the various printing presses. The color presses were alloted 50% more of the cost allocation for these items, since there were more rollers because of the additional colors and more impressions.

Electricity. The determination of this allocation was based on the connected load in each of the four production centers multiplied by the hours of operation. While electricity was also used in the office area, no attempt was made to charge the office and then reallocate this cost (and others) to the production centers. Such recirculation of costs was not considered substantial enough to be worth the effort.

Chemicals. Chemical usage, which was localized to the presses, was estimated by the scheduler/estimator.

Equipment Depreciation. This cost was taken from the asset ledger.

Occupancy-type Costs. This included building depreciation and real estate and property taxes, as well as janitorial service. The allocation was based on the floor space occupied by the four production cost centers.

CALCULATION OF HOURLY COSTING RATES

The cost elements used in making the calculations of hourly costing rates, shown in Exhibit 10.4, are taken directly from the figures in the previous three exhibits. The section headed ''Activity Base'' in this exhibit shows the available direct labor hours and the available machine (press) hours as shown in Exhibit 10.1. This exhibit adjusts the available hours by the utilization factor to provide for the unavoidable downtime. In the case of direct labor hours, the utilization factor for both folding and binding is 85%. For machine hours, this percentage is 70% for color presses and 80% for the black and white. The section headed ''Total Overhead and Direct Labor'' shows the total overhead and the total labor dollars for the four centers. The section headed ''Hourly Costing Rates'' shows the costing rates broken down by the overhead and the labor. How these rates are used in product cost estimates is illustrated in the next exhibit.

EXHIBIT 10.4

CALCULATION OF HOURLY COSTING RATES

		Labor Paced		Machine Paced	
	Amount	Cutting and Folding	Sewing and Binding	Color Presses	Black and White Presses
Activity Base					
Direct Labor Hours Available	27,214	11,664	15,550	—	—
Direct Labor Hours Utilized—85%	22,548	9,331	13,217	—	—
Machine Hours Available	14,560	—	—	6,800	7,760
Machine Hours Utilized—Color, 70%; B/W, 80%	10,968	—	—	4,760	6,208
Total Overhead and Direct Labor					
Total Overhead	$463,900	74,898	81,681	163,651	143,670
Total Direct Labor	482,700	86,400	107,500	146,000	142,800
Total Overhead and Direct Labor	$946,600	161,298	189,181	309,651	286,470
Hourly Costing Rates					
Overhead Cost per Hour		$ 8.03	6.18	34.38	23.14
Direct Labor Cost per Hour		9.26	8.13	30.67	23.00
Total Costing Rate		$17.29	14.31	65.05	46.14

PRODUCT COST ESTIMATING

The product cost estimate (job cost estimate) shown in Exhibit 10.5 was prepared for a job that was printed in the black and white press section. The materials are made up of the cost of paper plus a 10% spoilage allowance and bindery materials. These add up to $637.81. The spoilage allowance varies depending on the nature of the work to be done.

EXHIBIT 10.5

JOB COST ESTIMATE

MATERIALS			
Paper—36″ × 48″ Sheets		$ 332.63	
10% Spoilage		33.26	
Bindery Materials		271.92	$ 637.81
DIRECT LABOR AND OVERHEAD			
Cutting and Folding—	14.0 Hrs. @ $17.29	242.06	
Sewing and Binding			
Gathering	1.7 Hrs.		
Sewing	4.9 Hrs.		
Trimming	1.0 Hrs.		
Case-in	5.4 Hrs.		
Total	13.0 Hrs. @ $14.31	186.03	
Black and White Press 27.0 Hrs. @ 46.14		1,245.78	1,673.87
TOTAL JOB COST			2,311.68
Markup—35% on Cost (26% on Sales Price)			809.09
SELLING PRICE			$3,120.77

Although the labor and overhead costs were calculated individually, the total of the two was used in each case. The $17.29 rate for the folding operation, for example, is made up of $8.03 for direct labor cost and $9.26 for the overhead. The total cost of the material, direct labor, and overhead amounts to $2,311.68.

In pricing, this company uses a markup of 35% applied to the total product cost. This becomes the selling price of the product. The 35% provides not only for the profit but the selling and administrative costs, which are not considered part of the overhead.

As in the case of material spoilage allowances, which are determined by the difficulty of the job, there are instances in which a larger crew may be required. In such cases the costing rate is adjusted to provide for the additional cost.

DEVELOPING THE FLEXIBLE BUDGET FORMULA

The flexible budget formula is a recasting of the same figures that were used to calculate the production center costing rates. The difference is that the overhead costs are now identified as to which are considered to be fixed, and those that vary with changes in the level of activity. This determination is based on the level of activity that was used in calculating the production center costing rates.

The guide to use in deciding how much of each overhead item is fixed and how much is variable is as follows: If the activity level drops 20% on a sustained basis, those overhead items that can be reduced by the same percentage are considered to be in the variable category. For example, the steno-clerk working for the factory superintendent at an annual salary of $15,200 was categorized by him as being 50% fixed and 50% variable. In terms of dollars, this would mean $7,600 fixed and $7,600 variable. If the level of activity dropped by 20%, the variable allowance would be 80% of $7,600 or $6,080—a reduction of $1,520. The total budget allowance would be $7,600 fixed and $6,080 variable—a total allowance of $13,680. In explaining this, the super-intendent hastened to add that he would not expect to cut the steno-clerk's salary. The reduction would take place in accounting, and the steno-clerk would work part time on the payroll. In the event that activity increased by, say, 20%, he would not immediately hire an additional employee. Instead, he would use overtime as a means of fulfilling the need for more help.

Usually, in calculating the variable allowances, labor hours rather than dollars are used as the base for labor-paced operations, and machine hours are used for the machine-paced operations. In Exhibit 10.6, for example, rollers are used exclusively in the machine-paced operations. Therefore, the $10,300 variable cost for rollers is divided by 10,968 machine hours (after adjustment for utilization shown in Exhibit 10.4) to arrive at a variable allowance of $.94 per machine hour. If the total machine hours of 10,968 were reduced by 20% to 8,774 hours, the allowance for rollers would be $.94 × 8,774, or $8,248. It would be more accurate to make individual allowances for the two types of presses, but since the activity levels fluctuated about the same, the superintendent preferred to keep it simple.

Some of the overhead items—freight and electricity, for example—are used in the labor-paced operations, but their variability is not applied to the labor hour activity in cutting/folding or sewing/binding. This, too, would be more accurate if individual production center operations were recognized. But since the labor hour activity in both production centers is gaited by the machine

EXHIBIT 10.6

DEVELOPMENT OF THE FLEXIBLE BUDGET FORMULA

		Annual Overhead Cost		Variable	
	Total	Fixed	Variable	Rate per Sales $	Rate per Machine Hour
INDIRECT LABOR—PRODUCTION DEPARTMENTS					
1 Factory Superintendent	$ 33,500	33,500	—	—	—
1 Steno-clerk	15,200	7,600	7,600	.0032	—
2 General Maintenance	26,700	17,900	8,800	.0037	—
Total	$ 75,400	59,000	16,400	.0069	—
INDIRECT LABOR—SERVICE DEPARTMENTS					
Accounting					
1 Accountant	$ 21,650	21,650	—	—	—
2 Cost Clerks	23,750	15,850	7,900	.0033	—
Total	$ 45,400	37,500	7,900	.0033	—
Production Control					
1 Scheduler/Estimator	$ 19,500	19,500	—	—	—
3 Expediters	42,000	28,000	14,000	.0058	—
Total	$ 61,500	47,500	14,000	.0058	—
TOTAL INDIRECT LABOR	$182,300	144,000	38,300	.0160	—
NONLABOR OVERHEAD					
Payroll Fringes	$131,590	28,950	102,640	.0428	—
Ink	28,700	—	28,700	—	2.62
Freight	950	—	950	—	.09
Rollers	10,300	—	10,300	—	.94
Replacement Parts	8,200	—	8,200	—	.75
Oil Wipers	3,300	—	3,300	—	.30
Electricity	22,400	—	22,400	—	2.04
Chemicals	7,200	—	7,200	—	.66
Depreciation—Equipment	32,300	32,300	—	—	—
Depreciation—Building	14,500	14,500	—	—	—
Real Estate Taxes	17,960	17,960	—	—	—
Property Taxes	4,200	4,200	—	—	—
TOTAL NONLABOR OVERHEAD	$281,600	97,910	183,690	.0428	7.40
TOTAL ALL OVERHEAD	$463,900	241,910	221,900	.0588	7.40

hour activity of the presses, the machine hours were used for these expenses rather than splitting them by labor hours and by machine hours.

Sales Are Not Normally Used as a Base

Normally, the bases for the flexible budget would be the same as those used for calculating the costing rates. In this case, management preferred to relate the indirect labor control to sales because each month's sales volume was known sooner than the labor hours and machine hours. Accordingly, the indirect labor plus payroll fringe benefits show the variable allowances as so many cents per sales dollar.

Going back to the illustration of the steno-clerk, the variable allowance is shown as $.0032 per sales dollar. If sales dropped 20% to $1,920,000, the variable budget allowance for this item would be $.0032 × $1,920,000, or $6,080. Since fixed costs are also part of the flexible budget formula, the fixed cost of $7,600 would be added to the variable cost of $6,080 to arrive at a total allowance of $13,680, which is the same figure arrived at earlier using a different approach.

The example shown here was calculated on an annual basis. For use on a monthly basis, the fixed costs would be one-twelfth of the amount shown in the exhibit, but the variable rate would remain unchanged.

THE BREAK-EVEN ANALYSIS

Exhibit 10.7 illustrates how the break-even point was calculated. The sales volume of $2,400,000, which was the basis for determining the activity level for the exhibits used in this chapter, is also the starting point in making the break-even calculation.

Variable Costs. The direct labor of $482,700 required to generate this sales level was taken from Exhibit 10.1. The total variable overhead cost of $221,990 was shown in Exhibit 10.6. The material cost $750,000 is the amount of paper and bindery material used to achieve a sales level of $2,400,000. Commissions paid to salespeople are 10% of the dollar volume of sales and therefore amount to $240,000. All variable costs add up to $1,694,690, or 70.61% of sales. Subtracting this from the total sales of $2,400,000 yields a profit contribution of $705,310, or 29.39% of sales.

Fixed Costs. The manufacturing fixed costs of $241,910 were also taken from Exhibit 10.6. To this was added $180,000 to cover general and administrative expenses (G&A). These include the owner of the business and a small staff.

EXHIBIT 10.7

BREAK-EVEN ANALYSIS

	Projected Volume	Percent	Break-even Volume	Volume Above Break-even
SALES	$2,400,000	100.00	1,435,556	964,444
Variable Costs				
Material	$750,000			
Direct Labor	482,700			
Variable Overhead	221,990			
Sales Commissions	240,000			
	1,694,690	70.61	1,013,646	681,044
CONTRIBUTION TO PROFIT	705,310	29.39	421,910	283,400
Fixed Costs				
Manufacturing Fixed Cost	241,910			
General & Administrative	180,000			
	421,910		421,910	—
PRETAX PROFIT	$ 283,400		0	283,400
Pretax Profit Percent	11.81%			29.39%

$$\text{BREAK-EVEN CALCULATION} = \frac{\text{Fixed Costs}}{\text{Contribution to Profit Percent}} = \frac{\$421,910}{29.39\%} = \$1,435,556$$

These two fixed costs, totaling $421,910, when subtracted from the profit contribution of $705,310 leave a pretax profit of $283,400, or 11.81% of sales.

Break-even Volume. This computation requires only two figures: (1) total fixed costs; and (2) contribution to profit as a percentage of sales. To arrive at the break-even volume, the fixed costs are divided by the percent contribution to profit. This is shown in the lower part of the break-even calculation in Exhibit 10.7.

Since *break-even* means no profit and no loss, a profit can only be made on the sales above the break-even level. This is illustrated in the last two columns of Exhibit 10.7.

In the column headed "Break-even Volume," the break-even sales of $1,435,556 are multiplied by the variable percentage of 70.61%—showing that the variable costs at the break-even point amount to $1,013,646. When this figure is subtracted from break-even sales, the contribution to profit equals the fixed costs—leaving no profit.

The "Volume above Break-even" column amounts to $964,444. This is obviously the portion of the sales from which the profit is derived. To verify this, the $964,444 was multiplied by the variable percentage of 70.61% to determine the amount of variable cost, which is shown to be $681,044. Inasmuch as the fixed costs have already been accounted for in break-even sales, the contribution to profit in this column is actually the pretax profit shown in the first column. The pretax profit, then, is not 11.81% of total sales; it is 29.39% of the sales above break-even. Stated another way, since the break-even sales represent 60% of total sales (break-even sales of $1,435,556 divided by total sales of $2,400,000), the year's profit is made in the final 40% of the year.

SUMMARY

In cost-based pricing, as well as pricing of standard products, it is important that product cost estimates be realistic. A fully integrated cost system which utilizes a common database is the first step in assuring consistency in costing as well as realism. The seven exhibits discussed in this chapter show how the same database can be used to develop costing rates for assignment of overhead to products, identify fixed and variable costs for use in forecasting, and develop make/buy studies, break-even analyses, and marginal pricing. Both break-even analysis for testing prices for a new product and marginal pricing will be discussed in chapter 19.

CHAPTER 11

Structuring Product Costs for Computerization

The stage-by-stage breakdown of total product cost, as presented graphically in Exhibit 6.1 in chapter 6, applies to standardized as well as customized products. Product cost differences between the two are principally in the categorization of certain expenses and variations in cost flow in the manufacturing process.

VARIATIONS IN COST FLOW

A custom product unlike a standard product is an entity unto itself—production flow and costing being patterned toward making a customer-specific product. When completed, it is shipped to the customer directly out of work-in-process rather than out of a finished goods warehouse as is the case with standard products. In a number of companies, customized products are made from standard components that are interchangeable. Thus, the production flow for the components can be quite similar to the flow in making standard products for stock, while the assembly of the finished unit would be treated as a customized product.

A standard product is usually built to stock and sold out of finished goods. The production flow can be pictured as a steady stream of material, labor, and overhead flowing into work-in-process through the various operations within the production cost centers. From work-in-process, the flow is through finished goods warehouses from which shipments are made.

Exhibit 11.1 shows the cost flow for customized products on the left side and the flow for standardized products on the right side. Note that the work-in-process inventory for customized products is broken down by job—each job representing a customer's order. In the case of standardized products, work-in-process is broken down by the production cost centers. The production cost center breakdown varies from company to company, so the names of the centers are not shown in the exhibit.

Defining the Three Cost Elements in Standard Products

Manufacturing costs are broadly identified by material, direct labor, and overhead costs. Material can be defined as that material which is visible in the finished product, while direct labor can be defined as "touch labor"—that labor directly associated with making the product.

Material Cost. When a product is painted or plated, the question frequently arises as to whether the paint and plating deposited on the product should be treated as material or overhead. The test is materiality and measurability.

Caustics, degreasing solvents, and/or chemicals used to prepare the surface for painting or plating are generally treated as overhead (indirect) because these items are not substantial in cost, nor is it considered practical to measure the usage per unit of product. Both paint and plating, such as copper and silver, are material in cost and are measurable by the amount of surface area to be covered. Accordingly, they are properly treated as direct material.

Direct Labor. This element of cost is considered direct when the machine operator or assembler of the product performs a task directly related to each unit produced. A task such as material handling is classified as indirect labor since the material handler moves a large variety of items.

Factory Overhead. In addition to the aforementioned indirect costs, factory overhead includes all indirect support costs such as foremen and group leaders in the production centers; it also includes the general manager and staff, personnel department, cost accounting, production control/scheduling, manufacturing engineering, quality control, purchasing, and maintenance. Also included are such nonlabor costs as electricity, depreciation, repair materials, supplies, gases, and occupancy-related costs.

COMPUTERIZING THE MANUFACTURING PROCESS SHEET

Reference is made in chapter 18 to the importance of using a common database for all costing. The data, which originates in the engineering bill of material,

TWO BASIC COST FLOWS

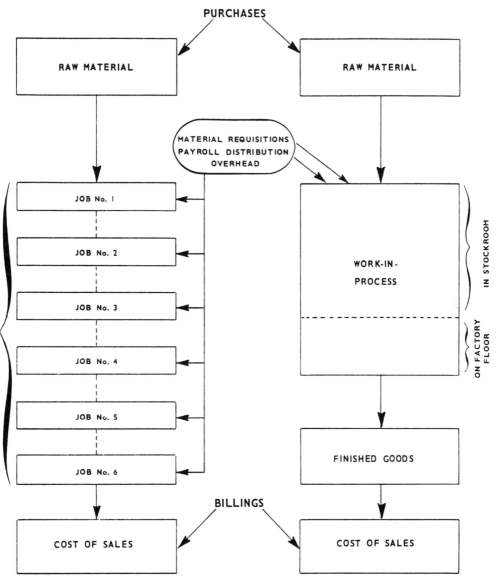

EXHIBIT 11.1

TWO BASIC COST FLOWS

EXHIBIT 11.2

MANUFACTURING PROCESS SHEET BRASS STEM—LEVEL 04

MANUFACTURING PROCESS SHEET

ISSUE DATE	ISSUE #	REVISED:				SHOP ORDER #
DRAWING #		LAST C.A.				DATE ISSUED

P.C. 01	BASIC 02608	SUFFIX 1	MACH. CODE 0008	REFERENCE	
PART NAME STEM					
MTL. CODE 20-2800	KIND BRASS		SIZE .280 DIAMETER		QTY. TO MAKE
SHAPE COIL	SPEC. 26-4	TEMPER	HARDNESS		RAW MTL. REQMT.
UNIT LBS.	PER/M GROSS 37.8	PER/M NET 17.0			REQD COMPLETION DATE

ROUTING

MACHINING, COATING, INSPECTION, COMPONENTS STOCKROOM   LEVEL (04)

OPN. #	OPERATION DESCRIPTION	EQUIPMENT	DEPT.	SET-UP HRS.	LAB. GRD.	PROD. HRS./M	LAB. GRD.	NO. MACH.	NO. MEN	COST CENTER
010	CUT-OFF & HEAD	HEADER	MACHG	3.0	10	.15	5	2	1	0447
020	ROLL THREAD	ROLLING MACHINE	MACHG	2.0	10	.50	5	2	1	0450
030	HEADING	HEADER	MACHG	12.0	13	.81	12			0761
050	DEGREASE	DEGREASER	COATG			.07	4			0568
	INSPECT		QC							

128

provides the product cost information on manufacturing process sheets similar to Exhibit 11.2. The material specifications are shown in the upper part of the form along with the identification of the part, part number, routing, and level of production. The lower part of the form shows the operations within the cost centers in which this part is processed, the equipment used, production hours, labor grade of the operators, the number of machines, and size of the crew. The manufacturing process sheets for the various manufacturing levels are next structured to obtain the total product cost.

COMPUTERIZED PRODUCT COSTS

The structuring process (sometimes referred to as treeing up) for the three elements of cost is shown in Exhibit 11.3. The arithmetic relating to the material costs is shown in Exhibit 11.4. Note first that the overhead costs, broken down by the variable and fixed segments, are listed by operation and cost center on the cost routing sheet in the upper part of the exhibit (columns 8 and 9), as are the material costs in columns 10 through 14. The calculation of brass used in level 4 for making the stem (machine code 0008) is shown in the middle section of the exhibit. The starting quantity of brass is shown in column 11, while column 12 shows the net amount of brass after deducting the standard allowance for turnings. The stem is drilled to provide space for the valve, which is inserted in a later operation. Note that the turnings account for 55% of the starting brass quantity.

$$\frac{(37.8 \text{ lb.} - 17.0 \text{ lb.})}{37.8 \text{ lb.}} = \frac{20.8 \text{ lb.}}{37.8 \text{ lb.}} = 55\%$$

Column 13 shows the standard recovery cost for the sale of scrap, which will reduce the cost of brass charged to the stems from which the scrap was obtained. The cost of sales figures at the lower third of the exhibit show the reconciliation of the brass cost for 2,255 units with the data contained in the cost routing sheet for product 01-02608-5036.

Exhibit 11.5 shows the same cost routing sheet as the one in Exhibit 11.4, inasmuch as this is still the same product. The middle third of this exhibit shows the development of the total labor cost of making the stem. The cost centers and operation numbers are listed along with the labor costs incurred in each. As in the preceding exhibit, the cost of sales figures in the lower third of this exhibit show the reconciliation of the $14.76 labor cost with the figures derived from the cost routing sheet.

EXHIBIT 11.3

PRODUCT STRUCTURE

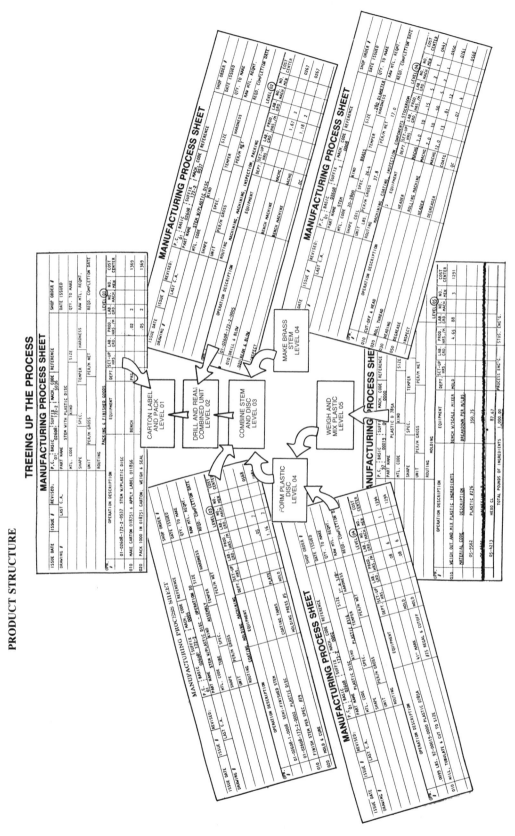

TREEING UP THE PROCESS

COST ROUTING SHEET
PRODUCT 01-02608-5036

	1	2	3	4	5	6	7	8	9	10	11	12	13	14	15
PRODUCT ID	OPR NO.	BM LEVL	QUANTITY	START OPN.	COST CNTR.	STND HRS/M	LABOR RATE	VARBLE OVHEAD	FIXED OVHEAD	R/M CODE	R/M GROSS	R/M NET	SCRAP RECOVY	STANDARD R/M COST	U M
01—02608—5036	010	01	1.00000	010	1369	.02	2.497	1.749	3.407	018751				128.6900	2
01—02608—5036	010	01	1.00000	010						011856				8.0500	2
01—02608—5036	020	01	1.00000	020	1369	.05	2.497	1.749	3.407						
. 01—02608—0537	010	02	1.00000	010	0267	1.67	2.473	2.093	3.678						
. 01—02608—0537	020	02	1.00000	010	0267	1.18	2.473	2.093	3.678						
.. 01—02608—0005	010	03	1.00000	010	0568	.05	2.752	6.022	4.282						
.. 01—02608—0005	020	03	1.00000	010	0981	1.16	2.790	1.942	3.237						
... 01—02608—0008	010	04	1.00000	010	0447	.15	1.335	4.182	7.121	202800	37.80	17.0	313.75	638.17	2
... 01—02608—0008	020	04	1.00000	010	0450	.50	1.335	4.182	7.122						
... 01—02608—0008	030	04	1.00000	010	0761	.81	3.396	3.326	4.933						
... 01—02608—0008	050	04	1.00000	010	0568	.07	2.752	6.022	4.282						
... 01—02608—0002	010	04	1.00000	010	1294	.08	2.773	2.978	4.413						
.... 97—00019—0000	010	05	.00990	010	1291	4.65	2.773	2.978	4.413	059562	350.75000	350.75000		250.0000	2
.... 97—00019—0000	010	05	.00990	010						055491	17.54000	17.54000		88.0000	2
.... 97—00019—0000	010	05	.00990	010						051202	3.86000	3.86000		530.0000	2
.... 97—00019—0000	010	05	.00990	010						058110	4.56000	4.56000		530.0000	2
.... 97—00019—0000	010	05	.00990	010						057326	7.02000	7.02000		34.5000	2
.... 97—00019—0000	010	05	.00990	010						054202	35.08000	35.08000		260.0000	2
.... 97—00019—0000	010	05	.00990	010						057320	87.69000	87.69000		114.2100	2
.... 97—00019—0000	010	05	.00990	010						055407	86.64000	86.64000		160.0000	2
.... 97—00019—0000	010	05	.00990	010						057315	3.51000	3.51000		225.0000	2
.... 97—00019—0000	010	05	.00990	010						059536	70.15000	70.15000		102.5000	2
.... 97—00019—0000	010	05	.00990	010						059537	224.48000	224.48000		60.0000	2
.... 97—00019—0000	010	05	.00990	010						051214	21.05000	21.05000		11.7500	2
.... 97—00019—0000	010	05	.00990	010						054213	87.67000	87.67000		72.5000	2

COSTING THE BRASS
(COSTS ARE PER/M)

1. MULTIPLY GROSS WEIGHT (COL. 11) × STANDARD COST (COL. 14)

   37.8 Lbs. X 638.17/M = $24.13/M

2. SUBTRACT NET WEIGHT (COL. 12) FROM GROSS WEIGHT (COL. 11)

   37.8 Lbs. MINUS 17.0 Lbs. = 20.8 Lbs.

3. MULTIPLY DIFFERENCE BY SCRAP RECOVERY COST (COL. 13)

   20.8 Lbs. X 313.75/M = $6.53/M

4. FROM LINE 1 SUBTRACT LINE 3

   $24.13 MINUS $6.53 = $17.60/M

2,255 UNITS @ $17.60 = $39.68

COST OF SALES

PRODUCT ID	OPR NO.	QUANTITY	BRASS	NON-BRASS MATERIAL	LABOR	VARIABLE OVERHEAD	CUMULATIVE OPERATING COST	FIXED OVERHEAD	TOTAL COST
01 00131 AP1	0004 000 R	315,000	4,191.36	17.71	310.16	731.31	5,250.54	837.66	6,088
01 00131 A1782	0013 000 R	57,500	773.78	240.59	481.82	524.23	2,020.42	756.87	2,777
01 00131 17829	0017 000 R	243,800	3,167.79	899.12	2,187.49	2,315.74	8,570.14	3,324.75	11,894
01 01651 UAH1	0086 000 R	277,500	3,605.67	15.45	287.09	676.08	4,584.29	760.57	5,344
01 02351 7913	5250 000 R	1,200	15.59	11.59	17.31	14.93	59.42	20.94	80
01 02870 7913	5179 000 R	757	12.58	5.29	31.35	20.25	69.47	27.18	96
01 02608	5036 000 R	2,255	39.68	3.77	33.28	33.49	110.22	54.50	164
01 03407 0178	5032 000 R	8,550	137.70	29.88	148.94	186.67	503.19	241.74	744
PRODUCT TOTALS	R	952,062	12,535.70	1,472.22	3,904.79	4,940.38	22,852.74	6,655.99	29,508
PERCENT OF TOTAL COST			42.49	4.99	13.23	16.75	77.46	22.54	100.00

LEGEND: R = Rod

EXHIBIT 11.4

DEVELOPING THE PRODUCT COST—MATERIAL
COST ROUTING SHEET
PRODUCT 01-02608-5036

COST ROUTING SHEET
PRODUCT 01-02608-5036

	1	2	3	4	5	6	7	8	9	10	11	12	13	14	15
PRODUCT ID	OPR NO.	BM LEVL	QUANTITY	START OPN.	COST CNTR.	STND HRS/M	LABOR RATE	VARBLE OVHEAD	FIXED OVHEAD	R/M CODE	R/M GROSS	R/M NET	SCRAP RECOVY	STANDARD R/M COST	U M
01—02608—5036	010	01	1.00000	010	1369	.02	2.497	1.749	3.4ʊ7	018751				128.6900	2
01—02608—5036	010	01	1.00000	010						011856				8.0500	2
01—02608—5036	020	01	1.00000	020	1369	.05	2.497	1.749	3.407						
. 01—02608—0537	010	02	1.00000	010	0267	1.67	2.473	2.093	3.678						
. 01—02608—0537	020	02	1.00000	010	0267	1.18	2.473	2.093	3.678						
.. 01—02608—0005	010	03	1.00000	010	0568	.05	2.752	6.022	4.282						
.. 01—02608—0005	020	03	1.00000	010	0981	1.16	2.790	1.942	3.237						
... 01—02608—0008	010	04	1.00000	010	0447	.15	1.335	4.182	7.121	202800	37.800	17.000	313.75000	638.1700	2
... 01—02608—0008	020	04	1.00000	010	0450	.50	1.335	4.182	7.122						
... 01—02608—0008	030	04	1.00000	010	0761	.81	3.396	3.326	4.933						
... 01—02608—0008	050	04	1.00000	010	0568	.07	2.752	6.022	4.282						
... 01—02608—0002	010	04	1.00000	010	1294	.08	2.773	2.978	4.413						
.... 97—00019—0000	010	05	.00990	010	1291	4.65	2.773	2.978	4.413	059562	350.75000	350.75000		250.0000	2
.... 97—00019—0000	010	05	.00990	010						055401	17.54000	17.54000		88.0000	2
.... 97—00019—0000	010	05	.00990	010						051202	3.86000	3.86000		530.0000	2
.... 97—00019—0000	010	05	.00990	010						058110	4.56000	4.56000		530.0000	2
.... 97—00019—0000	010	05	.00990	010						057326	7.02000	7.02000		34.5000	2
.... 97—00019—0000	010	05	.00990	010						054202	35.08000	35.08000		260.0000	2
.... 97—00019—0000	010	05	.00990	010						057320	87.69000	87.69000		114.2100	2
.... 97—00019—0000	010	05	.00990	010						055407	86.64000	86.64000		160.0000	2
.... 97—00019—0000	010	05	.00990	010						057415	3.51000	3.51000		225.0000	2
.... 97—00019—0000	010	05	.00990	010											
.... 97—00019—0000	010	05	.00990	010											
.... 97—00019—0000	010	05	.00990	010											
.... 97—00019—0000	010	05	.00990	010											

COSTING THE LABOR
(COSTS ARE PER/M)

COST CENTER	OPN.	STANDARD HOURS/M	LABOR RATE(1)	LABOR COST
1369	010	.02	$2.497	$.05
1369	020	.05	2.497	.12
0267	010	1.67	2.473	4.13
0267	020	1.18	2.473	2.92
0568	010	.05	2.752	.14
0981	020	1.16	2.790	3.24
0447	010	.15	1.335	.20
0450	020	.50	1.335	.67
0761	030	.81	3.396	2.75
0568	050	.07	2.752	.19
1294	010	.08	2.773	.22
1291	010	4.65(2)	2.773	.13
				$14.76

(1) Based on hourly rate divided by number of machines operated.
(2) Factored by .0099 to reflect standard cost per/M units.

2,255 Units @ $14.76 = $33.28

COST OF SALES

PRODUCT ID	OPR NO.	QUANTITY	BRASS	NON-BRASS MATERIAL	LABOR	VARIABLE OVERHEAD	CUMULATIVE OPERATING COST	FIXED OVERHEAD	TOTAL COST
01 00131 AP1	0004 000 R	315,000	4,191.36	17.71	310.16	731.31	5,250.54	837.66	6,088
01 00131 A1782	0013 000 R	57,500	773.78	240.59	481.82	524.23	2,020.42	756.87	2,777
01 00131 17829	0017 000 R	243,800	3,167.79	899.12	2,187.49	2,315.74	8,570.14	3,324.75	11,894
01 01651 UAH1	0086 000 R	277,500	3,605.67	15.45	287.09	676.08	4,584.29	760.57	5,344
01 02351 7913	5250 000 R	1,200	15.59	11.59	17.31	14.93	59.42	20.94	80
01 02870 7913	5179 000 R	757	12.58	5.29	31.35	20.25	69.47	27.18	96
01 02608	5036 000 R	2,255	39.68	3.77	33.28	33.49	110.22	54.50	164
01 03407 0178	5032 000 R	8,550	137.70	29.88	148.94	186.67	503.19	241.74	744
PRODUCT TOTALS	R	952,062	12,535.35	1,472.22	3,904.79	4,940.38	22,852.74	6,655.99	29,508
PERCENT OF TOTAL COST			42.49	4.99	13.23	16.75	77.46	22.54	100.00

LEGEND: R = Rod

EXHIBIT 11.5

DEVELOPING THE PRODUCT COST—LABOR
COST ROUTING SHEET
PRODUCT 01-02608-5036

The overhead figures are obtained from another file in which the individual costing rates are contained. The base for applying these rates is direct labor for the labor-paced operations and machine hours for machine-paced operations.

Exhibit 11.6 summarizes the treed-up costs from the processing of rubber in level 05 up to the finished stem in Level 01. Note in Level 4 "Make Brass Stem" that the brass cost of $17.60 corresponds with the cost worked out in Exhibit 11.4, and the labor cost of $14.76 corresponds with the labor shown in Exhibit 11.5 for all five levels.

PUTTING THE THREE COST ELEMENTS TOGETHER

Although the three cost elements are separate and distinct, they do not always flow through the costing process as individual costs. Many companies treat the material, direct labor, and overhead of a finished component or subassembly as material cost in the next production cost center. That cost center, in turn, adds its own material, direct labor, and overhead and transfers the aggregate of the three to the following cost center as material. This is illustrated in Exhibit 11.7. Note that the material, labor, and overhead costs of the wash-and-coat-bulbs operation in the manufacture of cathode-ray tubes in the amount of $8,106.04 is treated as material cost in the next operation.

Other companies prefer to retain purity of all three cost elements throughout the manufacturing process, as illustrated in Exhibit 11.8. This method has an advantage in that product costs are more meaningful if each of the three cost elements can be identified at each stage of manufacture. This also simplifies the revision process when standards are updated.

The author's preference is to retain purity of the individual material, direct labor, and overhead cost elements throughout the manufacturing process. The advantage of purity over the cumulative method is that the database can then be used for additional applications that are highly useful in cost reductions, make/buy studies, break-even analyses, and marginal pricing.

Quality Control and Cost Reduction

The glass bulbs used in the manufacture of cathode-ray tubes are the single most costly items of material. Additionally, bulbs are quite fragile and therefore subject to damage such as breakage, chipping, and scratching of the face plate in all stages of production. Note in Exhibit 11.7 that the bulb costs in the wash-and-coat-bulbs operation are shown as $6,770.83.

In Exhibit 11.8 each material is reported separately rather than being combined with labor and overhead and then transferred as material. The pro-

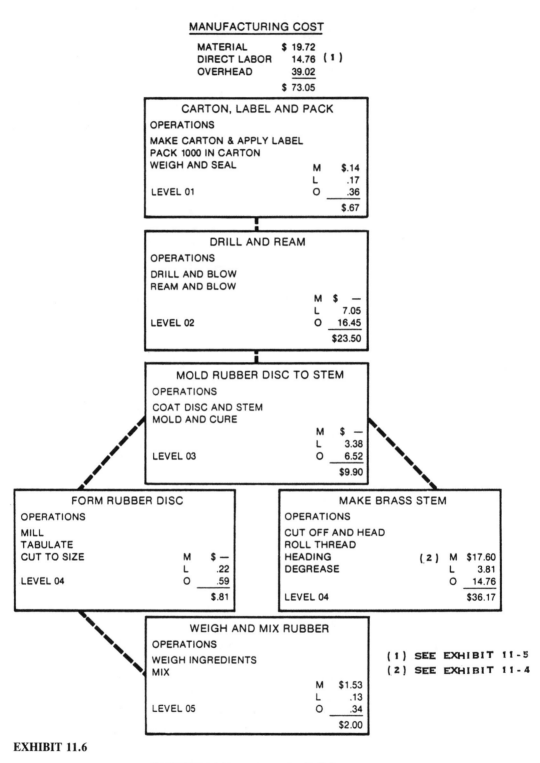

MANUFACTURING COST

MATERIAL	$ 19.72	
DIRECT LABOR	14.76	(1)
OVERHEAD	39.02	
	$ 73.05	

CARTON, LABEL AND PACK

OPERATIONS

MAKE CARTON & APPLY LABEL
PACK 1000 IN CARTON
WEIGH AND SEAL

	M	$.14
	L	.17
LEVEL 01	O	.36
		$.67

DRILL AND REAM

OPERATIONS

DRILL AND BLOW
REAM AND BLOW

	M	$ —
	L	7.05
LEVEL 02	O	16.45
		$23.50

MOLD RUBBER DISC TO STEM

OPERATIONS

COAT DISC AND STEM
MOLD AND CURE

	M	$ —
	L	3.38
LEVEL 03	O	6.52
		$9.90

FORM RUBBER DISC

OPERATIONS

MILL
TABULATE
CUT TO SIZE

	M	$ —
	L	.22
LEVEL 04	O	.59
		$.81

MAKE BRASS STEM

OPERATIONS

CUT OFF AND HEAD
ROLL THREAD
HEADING (2)
DEGREASE

	M	$17.60
	L	3.81
	O	14.76
LEVEL 04		$36.17

WEIGH AND MIX RUBBER

OPERATIONS

WEIGH INGREDIENTS
MIX

	M	$1.53
	L	.13
LEVEL 05	O	.34
		$2.00

(1) SEE EXHIBIT 11-5
(2) SEE EXHIBIT 11-4

EXHIBIT 11.6

PRODUCT COST BY MANUFACTURING LEVEL

EXHIBIT 11.7

MANUFACTURING COST OF CATHODE-RAY TUBES TRANSFERRING THE THREE ELEMENTS TO THE NEXT DEPARTMENT AS MATERIAL

	Wash and Coat Bulbs			Assemble, Exhaust, Seal, & Base			Test and Pack			Finish and Repack		
	Theo. Cost/M	% Eff.	Std. Cost/M	Theo. Cost/M	% Eff.	Std. Cost/M	Theo. Cost/M	% Eff.	Std. Cost/M	Theo. Cost/M	% Eff.	Std. Cost/M
Material												
Bulbs	$6,500.00	96	$6,770.83									
Phospor #43	137.75	60	229.58									
Phospor #75	99.13	60	165.22									
Kasil	12.48	60	20.80									
Acetic Acid	3.28	60	5.47									
Graphite Coating	3.50	90	3.89									
Total	$6,756.14		7,195.79									
Washed & Coated Bulbs				8,106.04	94	8,623.45						
Electron Guns				1,022.56	92	1,111.48						
Basing Material				27.54	90	30.60						
Total				9,156.14		9,765.53						
Based CRTs							11,347.72	74.5	15,231.84			
Salvage Credits									(1,711.35)			
Packing Material							247.25	95.0	260.26			
Miscellaneous Material							53.57	85.6	62.58			
Total							11,648.54		13,843.33			
Finished & Repacked CRTs										15,873.40	100	15,873.40
Direct Labor												
Wash and Coat Bulbs	109.90	46	238.91									
Assemble & Seal in				44.69	60	74.49						
Exhaust				75.72	60	126.20						
Base				56.50	70	80.71						
Total				176.91		281.40						
Test and Pack							57.37	57.2	100.30			
Finish and Repack										11.91	79.6	14.96
Overhead												
Wash and Coat Bulbs			671.34									
Assemble & Seal In						213.79						
Exhaust						957.86						
Base						129.14						
Total						1,300.79						
Test and Pack									1,929.77			
Finish and Repack												53.11
Total Std. Manufacturing Cost			$8,106.04			11,347.72			15,873.40			15,941.47

EXHIBIT 11.8

MANUFACTURING COST OF CATHODE-RAY TUBES MAINTAINING PURITY OF THE THREE COST ELEMENTS IN ALL FOUR DEPARTMENTS

	Wash and Coat Bulbs			Assemble, Exhaust, Seal, & Base			Test and Pack			Finish and Repack		
	Theo. Cost/M	% Eff.	Std. Cost/M	Theo. Cost/M	% Eff.	Std. Cost/M	Theo. Cost/M	% Eff.	Std. Cost/M	Theo. Cost/M	% Eff.	Std. Cost/M
Material												
Bulbs	$6,500.00	96	6,770.83	6,770.83	94	7,203.01	7,203.01	74.5	9,668.47	9,668.47	100	9,668.47
Phosphor #43	137.75	60	229.58	229.58	94	244.23	244.23	74.5	327.83	327.83	100	327.83
Phosphor #75	99.13	60	165.22	165.22	94	175.77	175.77	74.5	235.93	235.93	100	235.93
Kasil	12.48	60	20.80	20.80	94	22.13	22.13	74.5	29.70	29.70	100	29.70
Acetic Acid	3.28	60	5.47	5.47	94	5.82	5.82	74.5	7.81	7.81	100	7.81
Graphite Coating	3.50	90	3.89	3.89	94	4.14	4.14	74.5	5.56	5.56	100	5.56
Electron Guns				1,022.56	92	1,111.48	1,111.48	74.5	1,491.92	1,491.92	100	1,491.92
Basing Material				27.54	90	30.60	30.60	74.5	41.07	41.07	100	41.07
Salvage Credits									(1,711.35)	(1,711.35)	100	(1,711.35)
Packing Material							247.25	95.0	260.26	260.26	100	260.26
Miscellaneous Material							53.57	85.6	62.59	62.59	100	62.59
Total Material	$6,756.14		7,195.79	8,245.89		8,797.18	9,098.00		10,419.79	10,419.79		10,419.78
Direct Labor												
Wash and Coat Bulbs	$ 109.90	46	238.91	238.91	94	254.16	254.16	74.5	341.15	341.15	100	341.15
Assemble & Seal In				44.69	60	74.49	74.49	74.5	99.99	99.99	100	99.99
Exhaust				75.72	60	126.20	126.20	74.5	169.40	169.40	100	169.40
Base				56.50	70	80.71	80.71	74.5	108.33	108.33	100	108.33
Test and Pack							57.37	57.2	100.30	100.30	100	100.30
Finish and Repack										11.91	79.6	14.96
Total Direct Labor	$ 109.90		238.91	415.82		535.56	592.93		819.17	831.08		834.13
Overhead												
Wash and Coat Bulbs	671.34		671.34	671.34	94	714.19	714.19	74.5	958.64	958.64	100	958.64
Assemble & Seal In						213.79	213.79	74.5	286.97	286.97	100	286.97
Exhaust						957.86	957.86	74.5	1,285.72	1,285.72	100	1,285.72
Base						129.14	129.14	74.5	173.34	173.34	100	173.34
Test and Pack									1,929.77	1,929.77	100	1,929.77
Finish and Repack												53.11
Total Overhead	671.34		671.34	671.34		2,014.98	2,014.98		4,634.44	4,634.44		4,687.55
Total Std. Manufacturing Cost			$8,106.04			11,347.72			15,873.40			15,941.47

gression of glass bulbs beyond the wash-and-coat operation results in some rejects, which are included in the following glass bulb costs:

Total Glass Bulb Costs in Each Cost Center	
Wash and Coat Bulbs	$6,770.83
Assemble, Seal, and Base	7,203.01
Test and Repack	9,668.47

Note that the total bulb material cost is $9,668.47—$2,897.64 more than the $6,770.83 shown in Exhibit 11.7 for the wash-and-coat cost center. The $2,897.64 of additional material cost is partly offset by salvage credits of $1,711.35 shown in the test-and-pack operation. There were direct labor and overhead costs associated with the bulb losses in operations subsequent to the initial wash-and-coat cost center as well as in the initial center. These amounted to $341.15 for direct labor and $958.64 for overhead—more than offsetting the salvage credits. These costs are buried in the figures shown in Exhibit 11.7. Exhibit 11.8 spells out the full amount of material, direct labor, and overhead as individual items through the entire manufacturing operation. The breakdown of the three elements of cost by the cumulative method is quite different from the method in which costs are pure, as follows:

Cumulative		Pure Method
99.6%	Material	65.5%
.1	Direct Labor	5.2
.3	Overhead	29.3
100.0%	Total	100.0%

In addition to maintaining purity of the three manufacturing cost elements, it is necessary to provide a breakdown of overhead into its fixed and variable segments. This will facilitate the use of other product costing and pricing applications mentioned earlier. These are: (a) cost reduction analyses; (b) make/buy studies; (c) break-even analyses; and (d) marginal costing and pricing.

The breakdown of overhead into its fixed and variable segments was covered in chapter 4. Exhibit 4.8 utilized the fixed and variable breakdown to demonstrate the calculation of profit contribution after variable costs and the pretax break-even point of sales for two different product mixes. Note in this exhibit that the mix with the lower sales volume capitalizes on higher prices to yield a larger profit contribution and higher pretax profit as well as a lower break-even point.

Chapter 12 goes a step further in analyzing eight products and identifying those whose profitability can be improved by simplifying the product design to reduce material costs, automating to reduce labor costs, and adding special features to support premium pricing.

Profit Planning, Profits, and Pricing: A Case Study

Far too often, discussions with executives of troubled businesses reveal vagueness as to management plans for the coming year. The sales department of such a company will more than likely express its opinion that sales expectations for the coming year will change by x percent without an in-depth analysis as to underlying problems in the market. Manufacturing executives, in turn, will point out that their production plans hinge entirely on sales orders—therefore, they must remain "loose" in their plans. In short, efficient manufacturing is not compatible with hit-or-miss planning.

CASE 12.1: STEREO, INC.

Stereo, Inc. (name disguised) has an excellent marketing organization that takes its work seriously. Its sales forecasts are rarely off by more than 5%. This company was therefore selected for this case study.

Although the goals in a profit plan may not always materialize, the procedures required in the development of a plan provide a simulation wherein the various probabilities and alternatives will be evaluated in advance. Then, when things do go wrong, management will already have had its "fire drills" and will be far better equipped to cope with the unforeseen.

HOW STEREO, INC. DEVELOPED ITS PROFIT PLAN

This company manufactures a line of products that has become increasingly popular with the "boom-box" generation. Its sales had been running at about $8,000,000 per year. While its own pretax profit on sales has been averaging 8%, a competitor's annual report showed pretax profits of slightly over 10%. The management of Stereo, Inc. felt that its plans should be predicated on realization of profits that are at least as good as their competitor.

In an effort to improve the coming year's results, the market potential and company's profit goals were carefully evaluated. A study of the balance sheet showed the stockholder equity to be $3,375,000. Industry statistics indicated that competitors turned their equity two-and-a-half times a year in terms of sales. This meant that Stereo, Inc., to match the industry turnover of investment, must achieve a sales volume of $8,437,500 annually ($3,375,000 multiplied by two-and-a-half turns). The company, in matching the industry turns of equity, will realize a 25% return on equity. This would be equivalent to a 35% gross profit. The 35% gross profit became the goal for the coming year. The company was careful to spell out that attainment of this goal was predicated on two factors: (1) sales volume of $8,437,500; and (2) gross profit of $2,950,000, which would result in a gross profit of 35%.

In assessing its ability to attain the required sales volume, the sales department analyzed its territories and customers to ascertain realistically how the added volume would be obtained in the coming year. Although an in-depth market analysis assured that a sales level of $8,300,000 was attainable, the company felt it could not achieve the $8,437,500 unless it added a new product.

The most likely candidate was a low-priced stereo set whose factory selling price would have to be $60. This item had just come into the market and appeared to have a good potential because of its compact size. Although there was a good chance that the company could sell the required number, it recognized that market tests had not yet been completed (the item was just off the drawing board with some prototypes being field tested). Since only $129,700 in sales was needed to attain the desired volume of $8,437,500, the company decided to take a calculated risk that field test results would be sufficiently well received to permit this volume of sales to be made by the end of the coming year. Going ahead with this assumption, the company next turned its attention to the manufacturing budget.

Developing the Manufacturing Budget

The first step was the determination of the level of production. Beginning inventories as well as the desired level of ending inventories are factors that must be taken into account.

In projecting the anticipated volume of production, the company was not concerned with beginning inventories because it followed the practice of disposing of prior years' models through discount outlets in noncompetitive selling territories. The production volume for budget purposes was substantially the same as the sales forecast. For a summary of sales by product see Exhibit 12.1.

EXHIBIT 12.1

SALES FORECAST BY PRODUCT*

Product	Number of Units	Factory Selling Price	Total Sales
P-6	287	1.030	$ 295,600
J-2	7,000	197	1,379,700
202	20,300	122	2,484,500
610	3,350	150	498,600
F-0	11,000	150	1,649,100
707	3,150	275	867,400
810	1,900	596	1,132,900
D-1	2,160	60	129,700
Total	49,147		$8,437,500

* Small errors due to rounding.

These projected sales were given to the manufacturing manager with an indication that the goal for his operation was to come up with a budget that would produce a 35% gross profit. He, in turn, had his scheduling department determine the manufacturing needs by months. In instances in which several products used a common part, arrangements were made to produce them in a single, rather than multiple, runs. Direct labor and overhead needs were also evaluated on the basis of monthly requirements to fulfill the sales projection.

Production Cost Analysis Report

On completion, the budget projection was summarized on a production cost analysis report similar to the format used for monthly reporting of manufacturing costs against an allowance based on the month's production volume. This annualized report is shown in Exhibit 12.2. The major cost elements are shown in the first column in dollars. The second column shows the same breakdown with each of the cost elements expressed as a percentage of the sales value of production. Since the total cost of production is 67.8% of the total sales value of production, the gross profit percentage is 32.2%.

The percentage breakdown of the major cost factors can be helpful in ascertaining changes in the "mix" of production. If, for example, material as

EXHIBIT 12.2

PRODUCTION COST ANALYSIS REPORT

	Production Budget	
	Dollars	Percent
Sales Value of Production	$8,437,500	100.0
Material	3,663,040	43.4
Direct Labor	724,623	8.6
Total Material & Direct Labor	4,387,663	52.0
Indirect Labor		
Production Departments	128,560	1.5
Service Departments	398,057	4.7
Labor Fringes	284,327	3.4
Nonlabor Expenses	522,200	6.2
Total Overhead	1,333,144	15.8
Total Cost of Production	$5,720,807	67.8

a percentage of sales is significantly different from the year-to-date percentage, it shows a change in the makeup of production going through the plant. Such changes would affect the conversion cost (direct labor plus overhead). Theoretically, larger profits are made in converting than in handling material. Changes affecting conversion cost could therefore have an impact on profits. The production cost analysis report is, in effect, a dollarized breakdown of the production schedule.

The monthly version of the cost analysis report also summarizes in greater detail the material, direct labor, and indirect labor costs incurred in the various production and service departments.

The material breakdown, for example, shows the dollar value of steel, fabricated parts used, and purchased components. A continuous monitoring of the volume of purchased components will provide a clue as to whether the company should prepare a make/buy analysis as to the feasibility of expanding its own press section and reducing purchases on the outside. This would reduce the material content of the products and would increase the conversion costs, thus providing a greater potential for increasing profits—assuming that the press shop is meeting its anticipated productivity goals.

Direct labor, as well as indirect labor production, is broken down by department. Frequently, a rising trend in the assembly section can provide signals that a backlog of fabricated parts and subassemblies is being used up through conversion to finished units. On the other hand, if the volume of assembly effort is on the decline, this could mean that a glut of fabricated parts might develop if production schedules are not adjusted.

In addition, the monthly production cost analysis report shows the indirect labor in the service support departments as well as the labor-connected expenses. The breakdown by department provides a means for evaluating a possible rising trend in overhead costs. Since the monthly report would include year-to-date figures, comparisons of the current month's figures with the cumulative total (as well as the budgeted allowances) would be possible.

Gross Profit by Product Line

The total manufacturing cost in Exhibit 12.2 is $5,720,807, and reflects a gross profit of 32.2% of the sales value. The next step is to break down the 32.2% by product lines. This is done in Exhibit 12.3. The sales value of production for the eight products is shown across the top of the exhibit. The dollars, units, and sales price per unit were taken from the sales forecast in Exhibit 12.1.

The material is broken down by type of material and by the individual products. The direct labor is broken down by production cost center and also by the individual products. The same applies to total overhead, which is applied through a combination of labor-based and machine-hour based overhead costing rates.

This type of breakdown of the production budget is helpful to nonfinancial operating managers in reconciling forecasted (budgeted) costs with the manufacturing costs of the individual products and the profitability of the individual products. When the factory management can see the impact of the costs it generates on the profitability of the individual products it makes, the figures take on a new meaning.

Material costs in this exhibit were obtained by extending the quantities of the various products by the required amount of material shown in the bills of material. To these requirements, allowances were added to provide for a reasonable amount of scrap and production rejects.

The direct labor allowances are based on time studies made by the industrial (manufacturing) engineers. Here, too, normal allowances for unavoidable delays and other downtime were included to ensure that labor costs would be reasonably attainable.

Overhead was assigned to the products in the following two ways:

1. Machine hour rates were applied to hours of machine time of the various presses. The direct labor cost was included as part of the machine hour costing rate.

EXHIBIT 12.3

FULL COSTING BREAKDOWN OF PRODUCT LINE*

	P-6	J-2	202	610	F-0	707	810	D-1	Total
Sales Value	295,600	1,379,700	2,484,500	498,600	1,649,100	867,400	1,132,900	129,700	8,437,500
Units	287	7,000	20,300	3,350	11,000	3,150	1,900	2,160	
Unit Price (Rounded)	1,030	197	122	150	150	275	596	60	
Material									
Steel	2,818	96,746	84,751	2,169	53,210	21,323	103,806	16,446	381,269
Fabricated Parts	74,344	27,694	135,063	104,925	—	283,203	80,435	14,005	719,669
Purchased Components	49,938	382,342	872,126	148,897	769,580	152,969	229,440	10,810	2,562,102
Total Material	127,100	452,782	1,091,940	255,991	822,790	457,495	413,681	41,261	3,663,040
Direct Labor									
Semiautomatic Presses	1,306	43,781	31,252	8,767	23,106	22,852	136,103	15,984	283,151
Automatic Presses	10,833	67,607	67,591	640	41,789	14,541	10,804	1,841	215,646
Assembly	6,759	28,788	60,929	16,574	31,422	33,112	41,799	6,443	225,826
Total Direct Labor	18,898	140,176	159,772	25,981	96,317	70,505	188,706	24,268	724,623
Total Overhead	31,208	260,440	308,313	46,963	182,857	128,386	328,738	46,239	1,333,144
Total Manufacturing Cost	177,206	853,398	1,560,025	328,915	1,101,964	656,386	931,125	111,768	5,720,807
Gross Profit Percent	40.1	38.1	37.2	34.1	33.2	24.3	17.7	13.8	32.2

* Small errors due to rounding.

2. In the assembly section, overhead was added to the product cost through a rate applied to allowable labor hours for assembling the products. Differences between the allowed costs and the actuals were accounted for as variances.

After the material, direct labor, and overhead requirements for each of the products were determined, the total manufacturing cost of each product was subtracted from the projected sales to arrive at the gross profit by individual product. This profit was then divided by sales to arrive at the gross profit percentages. These percentages are as follows in order of profitability from the highest to the lowest.

Product	Gross Profit
P-6	40.1%
J-2	38.1
202	37.2
610	34.1
F-0	33.2
707	24.3
810	17.7
D-1	13.8
Average	32.2%

Since the gross profit percentages of products 707, 810, and D-1 are well below the overall average of 32.2%, management realized immediately that if the sales mix should change so that sales of these three items increased and sales of the more profitable items dropped, the 32.2% average would drop even lower. On making this observation, management immediately targeted the last three items for study. Knowing that prices could not arbitrarily be changed, the study effort was directed first to cost reduction possibilities—to be followed with decisions as to changing the selling prices. Inasmuch as the gross profit reflects full costing, the decision was made to break down manufacturing costs into their fixed and variable segments to determine the profit contribution of each of the eight products; a better evaluation of the selling prices could then be made.

The Profit Contribution Approach

Since the profit contribution approach is based on the separation of fixed and variable costs, the first step was to determine which of the manufacturing costs varied with changes in volume of production and which would remain relatively fixed within the normal operating range. Material and direct labor were considered to be completely variable. Such overhead costs as expendable tools, lubricants, factory supplies, and material handlers were considered to be variable. Depreciation, occupancy-related costs, and supervision were treated as fixed costs. The actual determination was made by department heads responsible for the costs. The breakdown of the total manufacturing cost of $5,720,807 into its fixed and variable segments is as follows:

BREAKDOWN OF MANUFACTURING COST

	Variable	Fixed	Total
Material	$3,663,040		3,663,040
Direct Labor	724,623		724,623
Indirect Labor			
Production Depts.		128,560	128,560
Service Depts.		398,057	398,057
Labor Fringes	100,000	184,327	284,327
Nonlabor Costs	160,548	361,652	522,200
Total	$4,648,211	$1,072,596	$5,720,807

The next step was to make the variable and fixed distribution to the various products. In Exhibit 12.4, the projected sales volume was considered as 100%. For analytical purposes, the variable costs were broken down by material, direct labor, and variable overhead. This would be helpful in determining if any of the products contained an unusually high amount of one or more of the cost elements. If, for example, labor content is large, it may be possible to automate the fabrication operations. Although fixed costs would increase, the direct labor reductions should more than offset the increase in fixed costs. If material cost content is high, it may be possible to redesign the product and/or use substitute material. Stereo, Inc., being a relatively new company, was aware that it needed improvements.

The column "Total Variable Costs" shows the percentage of variable costs to total sales for each product. The difference between these percentages and 100% shows the profit contribution of the individual products.

For purposes of showing the whole picture so that profit contribution can be reconciled with the gross profit percentages, the fixed manufacturing cost figures have also been included. The gross profit figures are shown in the last column. For convenience in making the comparisons between profit contribution and gross profit, both have been listed in Exhibit 12.5.

While the major differences in profitability of products are obvious, the two figures are not expressed in the same common denominator—as evidenced

EXHIBIT 12.4

ELEMENTS OF PRODUCT COST AS A PERCENTAGE OF SALES*

Product	Sales $	Sales %	Material $	Material %	Direct Labor $	Direct Labor %	Variable Overhead $	Variable Overhead %	Total Variable Costs $	Total Variable Costs %	Profit Contribution %	Fixed Overhead $	Fixed Overhead %	Total Mfg. Cost $	Total Mfg. Cost %	Gross Profit %
P-6	296	100	127	42.9	19	6.4	7	2.3	153	51.7	48.3	24	8.2	177	59.9	40.1
J-2	1,380	100	453	32.8	104	10.2	50	3.7	643	46.7	53.3	210	15.2	853	61.9	38.1
202	2,485	100	1,092	44.1	160	6.4	58	2.3	1,309	52.7	47.3	251	10.1	1,560	62.8	37.2
610	499	100	256	51.3	26	5.2	9	1.9	291	58.4	41.6	38	7.5	329	65.9	34.1
F-0	1,649	100	823	49.9	96	5.8	35	2.1	954	57.8	42.2	148	9.1	1,102	66.8	33.2
707	867	100	457	52.7	71	8.1	26	2.9	554	63.8	36.2	103	11.9	656	75.7	24.3
810	1,133	100	414	36.5	189	16.7	68	6.1	670	59.3	40.7	261	22.9	931	82.3	17.7
D-1	130	100	41	31.8	24	18.7	9	6.7	74	57.2	42.8	38	28.9	112	86.2	13.8
TOTAL	8,439	100	3,663	43.4	725	8.6	262	3.1	4,648	55.1	44.9	1,073	12.7	5,720	67.8	32.2

* Small errors due to rounding. $000 omitted.

147

EXHIBIT 12.5

COMPARISON OF PROFIT CONTRIBUTION AND GROSS PROFIT PERCENTAGES

	Before Adjustment			*After Adjustment*	
Product	*Profit Contrib- ution*	*Gross Profit*	*Product*	*Profit Contrib- ution*	*Gross Profit*
P-6	48.3%	40.1%	P-6	108%	125%
J-2	53.3%	38.1%	J-2	119%	118%
202	47.3%	37.2%	202	105%	116%
610	41.6%	34.1%	610	93%	106%
F-0	42.2%	33.2%	F-0	94%	103%
707	36.2%	24.3%	707	81%	75%
810	40.7%	17.7%	810	90%	55%
D-1	42.8%	13.8%	D-1	95%	43%
Average	44.9%	32.2%	Average	100%	100%

by the averages, which are 44.9% for profit contribution and 32.2% for the gross profit. To convert the figures to a comparable basis, the marginal contribution percentages for the various products were divided by 44.9%. The gross profit percentages were likewise divided by 32.2%. Thus, both columns were expressed in terms of an average based on 100%.

With the profitability of the eight products expressed in terms of a common denominator represented by 100%, it was possible to compare the profit contribution percentages directly with the gross profit percentages.

In reviewing the gross profit column, management showed concern with the poor showing of the 810 and the D-1 products because the profitability was about half that of the average—55% for product 810 and 43% for product D-1. However, the profit contribution percentages showed a profitability of 90% and 95%, respectively, which comes closer to the average.

In fact, the spread of percentages was much narrower for the marginal contribution column than for gross profit. Under the former the spread ranged from 81% to 119%, while for gross profits the range was 43% to 125%. In the first case, the spread was 38 points from the lowest to the highest, while in the second it was 82 points.

It was also noted under the marginal contribution approach that three of the eight products showed higher than average profitability, while five showed lower than average. In the gross profit column the reverse was true—five products were more profitable than average and three were less profitable.

These differences between the two methods of measuring profitability were obviously due to the effect of the fixed cost content in the various products.

Some of the fixed costs were of a general purpose nature, such as the personnel, cost accounting, and general manager functions. However, there were enough other fixed costs that were directly associated with a cost center to warrant further investigation into profitability based on the inclusion of fixed costs specifically applicable to certain products. Since the low profitability of products 707, 810, and D-1 was quite evident, the study was concentrated more heavily on these three initially.

Study of the Manufacturing Process

A review conducted with the industrial engineer disclosed that these three products required a number of parts that were fabricated on the slower semi-automatic presses. These particular presses were large and even more expensive than some of the fully automatic types because of the need for frequent maintenance. Also, because they were slow, large storage areas were needed to accumulate the fabricated parts until an optimum size batch could be readied to send out for plating. Since the presses were not automatic, they required full-time operators—causing labor costs to be high as well.

If the introduction of product D-1 is successful and a sales volume of $750,000 to $1,000,000 develops, the company could justify the purchase of additional high-speed automatic presses that would reduce labor costs. Fixed costs per unit would also decline because of the larger volume of component parts that would be produced in-house. In addition, several thousand square feet of factory space would be released for storage of finished goods with a saving in rental of outside facilities.

While the main focus was on products 810 and D-1 initially, product 707, the third product of below-average profitability, also used parts made on the slower presses, but not to as great an extent. The company was concerned because a significant competitor was selling the 707 equivalent for a price that was 8% lower.

Since the material and direct labor costs together amounted to 61% of the selling price, the engineering group was instructed to make a cost reduction study. The competitor's product was purchased and completely disassembled. The cost of each part was calculated, as was the estimated direct labor cost. Estimates were also made of the overhead costs. The competitor's design was simpler and the circuitry less complicated. On completion of the study, it was determined that adoption of the simpler design would reduce the percentage of material and labor costs to 54% of the sales value compared with 61%. The gross profit would then increase from 24.3% to an estimated 30% for this product.

These calculations are summarized in Exhibit 12.6. The cost breakdown is shown before and after the design change. Comparisons are based on the same sales value. With these changes the company could now meet the competitive price of $254. The profit at manufacturing level was then projected to 30.2% from 24.3%.

EXHIBIT 12.6

REDUCING THE COST OF PRODUCT 707 TO MEET THE COMPETITIVE PRICE*

| | Old Design | | New Design | |
	$	%	$	%
Total Sales	$ 867	100.0	867	100.0
Factory Price/Unit	275		254	
Total Units	3,150		3,413	
Less Variable Costs				
Material	$ 457	52.7	407	46.9
Direct Labor	71	8.1	62	7.2
Mfg. Overhead	26	2.9	27	3.1
Total Variable Costs	554	63.7	496	57.2
Profit Contribution	313	36.3	371	42.8
Mfg. Fixed Costs	103		109	
Total Mfg. Cost	656		605	
Mfg. Gross Profit	$ 211		262	
Mfg. Gross Profit %	24.3%		30.2%	

* $000 omitted.

Changes in the circuitry of product 707 resulted in improvements that could be made in several other products. The engineering study also resulted in some premium features that could be incorporated in existing products to support a price increase. The premium features effectively added three additional products to the line because of these new features.

The company had to wait several months to determine the acceptance of product D-1 in the marketplace before embarking on the purchase of automatic presses to reduce the high labor content of products D-1 and 810. Product D-1 was successfully launched and demand accelerated sufficiently to warrant purchase of the automatic presses.

Management's goal of increasing the average gross profit from 32.2% to 35% of sales did not materialize until the final quarter of the year for which the profit plan was prepared. This is to be expected, inasmuch as the attainment of this goal called for an extensive engineering study and market testing a new product.

AN ADDENDUM TO THIS CASE STUDY

This type of integrated analysis in which profit planning, profit yield, and pricing are linked can be highly productive. As an addendum to this case study, management became interested in an approach in determining the impact on profits when (a) volume drops; (b) the inflation rate rises; and (c) competition reduces prices.

Exhibit 12.7 shows the impact of a 10% drop in sales volume (column B); a rise in the inflation rate to 10% (column C); and a 10% price reduction because of competitive pressures (column D). Dollar figures are shown in the top half of the exhibit and percentages in the lower half.

Sales Volume Drops 10%. Since sales have been reduced to 90% of the base period sales shown in column A, variable costs also drop to 90% of the base

EXHIBIT 12.7

IMPACT OF VARIOUS MARKET AND ECONOMIC CHANGES

	Base Period (A)	Volume 10% Loss (B)	Inflation up 10% (C)	10% Price Reduction (D)
		Figures in Dollars		
Sales	$8,438	7,594	7,594	6,835
Less Variable Costs				
Material	3,663	3,297	3,627	3,627
Direct Labor	725	653	718	718
Variable Overhead	262	236	260	260
Total Variable Cost	4,650	4,186	4,605	4,605
Profit Contribution	3,788	3,409	2,989	2,230
Mfg. Fixed Costs	1,073	1,073	1,180	1,180
Total Mfg. Cost	5,723	5,259	5,785	5,785
Mfg. Gross profit	$2,715	2,335	1,809	1,050
		Percentage Breakdown		
Sales	100.0%	100.0%	100.0%	100.0%
Less Variable Costs				
Material	43.4	43.4	47.8	53.1
Direct Labor	8.6	8.6	9.4	10.5
Variable Overhead	3.1	3.1	3.4	3.8
Total Variable Cost	55.1	55.1	60.6	67.4
Profit Contribution	44.9	44.9	39.4	32.6
Mfg. Fixed Costs	12.7	14.2	15.6	17.2
Total Mfg. Cost	67.8	69.3	76.2	84.6
Mfg. Gross Profit	32.2	30.7	23.8	15.4

period variable costs. The percentage relationship of variable costs to sales remains at 55.1%, as shown in the base period. Similarly, the profit contribution percentage remains the same in column B as in the base period. Fixed costs, unlike the variable costs, remain unchanged. The manufacturing gross profit therefore drops from 32.2% to 30.7% of sales.

Inflation Rises to 10%. Costs follow increases in the inflation rate more closely than prices do. Column C therefore shows an increase in variable costs to 60.6% of sales, and the profit contribution percentage drops to 39.4%. Since fixed costs, consisting mostly of indirect labor, will also increase, the manufacturing gross profit drops to 23.8% of sales.

Competition Forces a 10% Price Reduction. Column D shows the impact of a 10% price decrease with costs remaining unchanged. Variable costs, as a percentage of the reduced sales, now become 67.4% of the reduced sales, while profit contribution has decreased to 32.6% of sales. Because of the reduction in sales dollars, the manufacturing gross profits have dropped to 15.4% of sales.

As a practical matter, when inflation is on the rise, the inventory consists of preinflation level costs that could reduce the amount of increase in variable costs temporarily. This could also be true of fixed costs when indirect labor cost increases because of salary increases.

CHAPTER 13

Markup Factors in Pricing

The most commonly used markup factor is the application of a single percentage to the total manufacturing cost. In many cases, this percentage factor also includes an allowance for SG&A. If one were to inquire as to what portion of the markup covers SG&A, the probability is that the line of demarcation is unknown. In many instances one will find that the factor had been established sometime in the past and that it is arbitrarily adjusted from time to time.

SG&A costs are too large to be lumped together with the provision for profits. Several annual reports at the time of this writing showed that Pfizer's SG&A expenses amounted to 82% of manufacturing cost (cost of sales), while Warner Lambert's SG&A amounted to 115%. For Xerox, the SG&A expenses were 61% of products and services sold; the equivalent percentage for IBM amounted to 67%.

Except in unusual cases, the markup factor for pricing should be reserved exclusively for the profit. SG&A costs should be calculated and shown separately by market segments such as original equipment manufacturers, distributors, and retailing chains. (See chapter 2 for a more detailed discussion of market segment pricing.)

Four types of markups in use are summarized in this chapter. Illustrative examples of each are provided in exhibits.

Manufacture of Sculptures: The markup for this product is applied to prime cost (material + labor). No markup is applied to overhead.

Special Transformers: The amount of markup varies with the size of the order. The markup applied to material is different than the markup applied to labor. No markup is applied to overhead.

Traditional Markup: A single markup is applied to total manufacturing cost. This was found to be the most common method for applying the markup.

Return on Investment (ROI): Two markup factors are used. The first is applied to material consumption and provides for a return on investment in inventory. The second is applied to conversion costs and provides for a return on investment on fixed assets.

MARKUP APPLIED TO PRIME COST

The first case study is based on Artco, a company that makes decorative sculptures. The second deals with a division of ElectroMag which makes transformers that are sold to a sister division. The purchasing division discontinued purchasing large quantities and stocking them. The reason given was the frequency of changes because of high-technology advances in the end product that it sells. In view of this, the end product division requested that future deliveries of transformers be made according to just-in-time delivery schedules twice each month. Since this would mean numerous short runs and higher costs, the transformer division was faced with the question of how to price the shorter runs and more frequent shipments.

CASE 13.1: ARTCO

Although the marketplace normally determines prices, there are cases in which judgment must play a large part in determining what the price will be. This was the case with Artco, a company that makes decorative sculptures of various types. Creativity is an important ingredient in determining which types will sell and which will not. For this reason a single, across-the-board percentage based on manufacturing cost would not suffice. Artco recognized this and classified the products by categories based on the anticipated markup that might be realized. Each of the categories assumed a different markup multiple that was applied to the prime cost (material + direct labor) of each of the products.

Exhibit 13.1 lists 24 of the current line of sculptures broken down into four separate multiple factor categories. Note in the first group that the markup multiple is 2 or 200%. This means that the material plus direct labor is doubled

EXHIBIT 13.1

MANUFACTURE OF SCULPTURES

Product ID	Material	Direct Labor	Total Prime	Markup Factor	Selling Price
C	10.10	30.60	40.70	2	81.40
D	3.90	21.55	25.45	2	50.90
F	2.85	21.40	24.25	2	48.50
G	3.40	39.90	43.30	2	86.60
H	3.95	21.45	25.40	2	50.80
I	26.80	56.80	83.60	2	167.20
J	7.80	40.05	47.85	2	95.70
Q	24.35	40.25	64.60	2	129.20
T	8.05	30.60	38.65	2	77.30
W	25.80	10.30	36.10	2	72.20
A	20.40	51.75	72.15	3	216.45
O	14.80	48.40	63.20	3	189.60
B	7.55	10.15	17.70	4	70.80
E	8.15	12.80	20.95	4	83.80
M	2.45	9.80	12.25	4	49.00
U	11.75	19.35	31.10	4	124.40
V	23.10	26.75	49.85	4	199.40
K	2.80	10.70	13.50	5	67.50
L	17.10	40.15	57.25	5	286.25
N	2.05	21.60	23.65	5	118.25
P	4.25	9.75	14.00	5	70.00
R	6.95	20.95	27.90	5	139.50
S	21.05	8.25	29.30	5	146.50
X	7.15	25.15	32.30	5	161.50

to arrive at the selling price. The multiple provides for recovery of overhead as well as profit. The manufacturing process is highly labor intensive, and overhead is a relatively small cost in relation to material and labor. Management therefore preferred not to go through the mechanics of including the overhead costs in the base to which the multiples are applied.

The assignment of markup multiples is a matter of judgment based on estimates as to how the various sculptures would appeal to the purchaser. There are cases in which a multiple can be set too high and is later moved to a lower multiple. This was the case with product I and product Q, both of which started at a higher multiple which was later reduced to a lower level. There were also instances in which a low-cost item assigned a low multiple was later moved to a higher level. This was the case with product P. Multiples are not limited to the four shown in the exhibit. Limited editions, in which the production volume is intentionally kept low, warranted multiples as high as 6 or 7. Multiples are also fine tuned to, say, $2\frac{1}{2}$, $3\frac{1}{2}$, $4\frac{1}{2}$, etc.

MARKUP BASED ON SIZE OF ORDER

CASE 13.2: ELECTROMAG

The transformer division of ElectroMag (name disguised) was instructed by the purchasing division to make future shipments on a just-in-time delivery basis. This did not sit too well with the general manager of the transformer division. He objected to what he termed a piecemeal and uneconomical approach in producing and shipping his product. He cited figures shown in Exhibit 13.2.

EXHIBIT 13.2

**EXTRACT OF JIT (JUST IN TIME)
DELIVERY SCHEDULE**

Spec. #3304-192: 10 on 10/7; 9 on 10/23; 5 on 11/7
Spec. #3305-194: 37 on 10/14; 9 on 10/23; 5 on 11/7
Spec. #3308-195: 39 on 10/11; 9 on 10/23; 5 on 11/7
Spec. #3550-198; 39 on 10/11; 9 on 10/23; 5 on 11/7
Spec. #3630-199; 10 on 10/7; 9 on 10/23; 5 on 11/7
Spec. #3679-199; 10 on 10/7; 2 on 10/11; 6 on 11/7

The transformer division general manager argued that from an overall company basis it may appear to be inconseqential whether this burden should be placed on the buying or selling division. Such is not actually the case because the saving in clerical effort in the buying division is accomplished at the expense of shorter runs with greater material usage, lower labor efficiency, and added clerical cost in the selling division.

After several meetings between representatives of the two divisions, the general manager of the transformer division agreed to the adoption of just-in-time delivery provided that the pricing would be adjusted to compensate his division for increased material losses and the lower labor efficiency because of the reduced number of units in the smaller orders. Since transformers represented a relatively small cost in the end product, the purchasing division agreed to the use of markup factors based on the size of the order.

The revised pricing schedule is shown in Exhibit 13.3. Separate factors

EXHIBIT 13.3

ALLOWANCES FOR MATERIAL AND LABOR DIFFERENTIAL

Quantities	Material Differential	Labor Differential
1	100%	200%
2	50	160
3	20	120
4	10	100
5 to 9	8	60
10 to 24	6	40
25 to 49	4	30
50 to 99	2	15

were established for material differentials and for labor differentials. These differentials ranged from 2% to 100% for material and from 15% to 200% for labor. The order sizes to which the markup factors applied are for quantities of 1, 2, 3, 4, 5 to 9, 10 to 24, 25 to 49, and 50 to 99.

SINGLE MARKUP PERCENTAGE BASED ON MANUFACTURING COST

There are instances in which a single markup percentage based on total manufacturing cost is acceptable.

CASE 13.3: METAL PRODUCTS, INC.

Formed Metal Products, Inc. is an example. This company stamps out metal parts made of steel. The parts are all made of the same material, and the ratio of material to labor and overhead content is fairly consistent. The single markup percentage is considered by management to be a reasonably reliable trend indicator. (See Exhibit 13.4.)

This exhibit uses three different vertical scales and a horizontal time scale broken down by months of the year. The bottom portion of the exhibit is a combination of a bar and line chart. The bars show the production costs in each of the months, while the line shows the sales value per thousand parts produced. The bars include a breakdown of material, direct labor, and overhead cost. The overhead is further split into its fixed and variable segments.

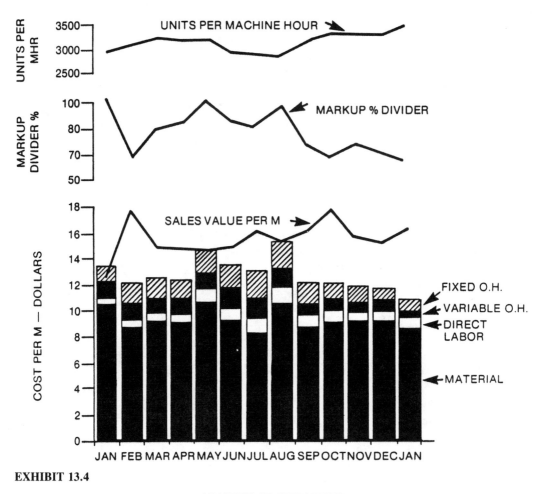

EXHIBIT 13.4

ANALYSIS OF OPERATIONS
USING THE TRADITIONAL MARKUP FACTOR

The line in the middle graph shows each month's production costs as a percentage of sales value. Management's goal is to keep costs from rising above 70% of the sales value. This graph enables management to tell at a glance whether the goal is being achieved, while the bottom graph shows the relationship between the manufacturing cost elements, total production cost as reflected by the height of the bars, and sales value.

The uppermost graph shows the average production rate per machine hour in each month. This rate of production is key to the other relationships shown in the exhibit. Experience has shown that when the production rate per machine hour is above 3,000 per machine hour, costs per 1,000 parts remain low and the production cost as a percentage of sales value (middle chart) can be expected to be 70% of sales value, or lower.

Using the month of February for illustrative purposes, note that the total production cost is $12.35 per 1,000 and that approximately 3,100 units were produced per machine hour. The sales value based on these figures is as follows:

$$\frac{\text{production cost of } \$12.35}{\text{markup divider of } 69.5\%} = \text{sales value of } \$17.177$$

Cases 13.1 and 13.2 show that a single one-size-fits-all markup cannot be applied universally. The Artco company recognized that buyers of sculptures were interested in products that reflected creativity in design. For this reason, judgment had to be excercised in selecting the proper markup multiple.

The markup problem in the transformer division of ElectroMag was different. Here, the transformer division could no longer produce to stock because of the rapidity of technological changes in the end product and the requirement by its sister division to make shipments on a just-in-time basis. As a result, the markup factors were developed by order size.

The Formed Metal Products company can use the traditional single markup factor applied to total manufacturing cost because the metal parts are homogeneous. The fourth type of markup which is not used to any great extent warrants serious consideration.

MARKUP FOR RETURN ON INVESTMENT PRICING

Factory investment controllable by the factory is made up principally of inventory and fixed assets such as plant, property and equipment-net of accumulated depreciation. Since items like accounts receivable are excluded, one will sometimes find that the factory investment can approximate the shareholder equity.

Material content of a product is the vehicle on which the markup for inventory investment is based. A material-based markup factor must therefore be developed. Conversion cost (direct labor + overhead) is the markup vehicle for recovering the investment in plant, property, and equipment inasmuch as the manufacturing operation cannot convert material into finished products without the facilities. A conversion-cost markup factor must therefore also be developed.

Exhibit 13.5 contains two graphs. The lower graph shows the actual sales and profit figures over a five-year period broken down by quarters. The upper

EXHIBIT 13.5

**SALES, PROFIT, AND INVESTMENT TURNOVER
BY QUARTERS**

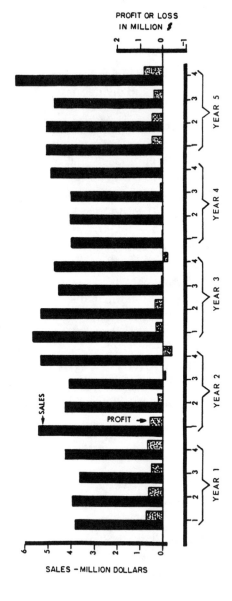

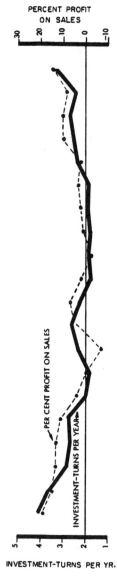

PERCENT PROFIT
ON SALES

PROFIT OR LOSS
IN MILLION $

INVESTMENT-TURNS PER YR.

SALES – MILLION DOLLARS

PER CENT PROFIT ON SALES

INVESTMENT-TURNS PER YEAR

SALES

PROFIT

YEAR 1   YEAR 2   YEAR 3   YEAR 4   YEAR 5

line graph shows the percent profit on sales for each quarter and investment turns per year for each of the quarters. Note that a loss or near-loss situation exists when the investment turns are below twice a year. This is true from the third quarter in year 3 through the third quarter in year 4. Year 1 is based on a different product mix than the rest of the years. It shows greater profitability and a higher number of investment turns because the amount of investment was lower than in succeeding years, in which the acquisition of another less profitable company resulted in a higher investment and generally lower investment turns.

In year 5, sales for the four quarters added up to $21.3 dollars and profits were $2.2 million, averaging 10.3% of sales for the year. This percentage is shown in the upper graph with fluctuations over the four quarters. The average turns of investment for the year averaged 2.7 times. The arithmetic relating to the foregoing is shown in Exhibit 13.6.

EXHIBIT 13.6

Calculations for Year 5		
Total Sales	$21.3 Million	
Total Profit	2.2 Million	
Percent Profit	10.3%	(ROS)

Turns per Year:

Sales divided by investment $= \dfrac{\$21.3 \text{ million}}{\$ 7.9 \text{ million}} = 2.7\times$

Return on Investment:

Percent profit $\times$ 2.7 turns $= 27.8\%$ (ROI)

IMPACT OF ECONOMIC VOLATILITY ON PRICES AND PROFITS

Downward pressure on prices and profitability is frequently attributed to actions by competitors. Periods of economic volatility are quickly forgotten once the waters again become smooth. The 1970s were a period of stress to many companies. Many have forgotten the impact of double-digit inflation, a period during which costs rose faster than prices; an oil embargo which resulted in fuel shortages; government price controls; a severe recession in 1973–1975; intensification of foreign competition; and the onset of another downturn in the economy in 1979 and 1980.

Profit planning procedures, as they relate to product cost estimating and pricing, must take into account the impact of changes in the economy. Readers can profit from an overview of events that transpired during the 1970s and their impact on costs, prices, and profits.

CASE 13.3: A STUDY OF SIX COMPANIES IN THREE INDUSTRIES

A sharp recession in 1973–1975 had a different impact on the companies that were studied. Note in Exhibits 13.7 and 13.8 that profitability of the two chemical companies and two steel companies peaked at the midpoint of the recession. The earnings of these companies were also fairly high in 1979 when the economy began to falter once again. On the other hand, the two tire and rubber companies shown in Exhibit 13.9 were in a downtrend both in 1974 and 1979. Although Firestone earnings improved in 1979, after a bad 1978 the improvement in 1979 was shortlived because of the mandated recall of several million Steelbelted Radial 500 tires. These are a few examples of the impact of economic forces that can affect cost, prices, and profitability. Exhibits 13.7a, 13.8a, and 13.9a contain excerpts for each of the 10 years taken from the annual reports of the six companies. This year-by-year diary of events reviews operations for each of the years.

CALCULATING THE RETURN ON INVESTMENT MARKUP

The text related to Exhibit 13.6 states that material and conversion costs are the two vehicles for applying markup factors which result in prices that provide a profit allowance based on the amount of factory investment. The following steps are shown in Exhibit 13.10:

Column 1: Using the annual financial plan as the source, the total manufacturing cost is broken down to show the material and conversion costs separately. The gross profit of $5,432,915 (also taken from the annual financial plan) divided by the total manufacturing cost of $11,442,235 shows the gross profit to be 47.5% of total manufacturing cost.

Column 2: Factory investment is broken down to show the portion of the investment that is related to material. This includes not only the material in raw material stores but the material portion in work-in-process and in finished goods. This amounts to $1,321,500. The remainder of $6,020,300 is related to conversion cost. It becomes obvious from these figures that the dollar investment for inventory in this company is substantially less than it is for the conversion cost related to converting material to finished goods.

$$\text{TURNS PER YEAR} = \frac{\text{SALES}}{\text{SHAREHOLDER EQUITY}}$$

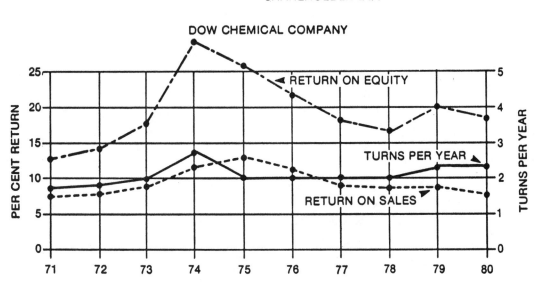

DOW CHEMICAL COMPANY

ALLIED CORPORATION

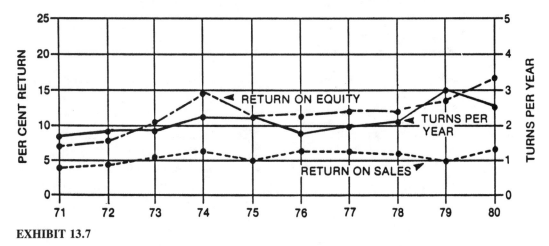

EXHIBIT 13.7

IMPACT OF ECONOMIC VOLATILITY ON EARNINGS

EXHIBIT 13.7a

EXCERPTS FROM ANNUAL REPORTS

Dow Chemical Company		Allied Corporation
Good product mix and higher prices. However, Federal controls more lax on wages than on prices.	**1971**	Some products being phased out to improve mix. Products with good profit potential being expanded.
Two lengthy strikes.	**1972**	Strong competition kept prices from rising to the amount permitted by Price Commission.
Material cost increases unprecedented. Price increase of 50% needed. Prices are substantially lower than this.	**1973**	Made vigorous gains despite soaring inflation, stultifying effect of wage and price controls and economic uncertainty.
In spite of these negatives company turned in remarkably sound performance.	**1974**	When the recession made itself felt later in the year, automotive product sales weakened.
Company able to maintain global selling prices and even make some gains sorely needed to recover increased raw material and fuel costs.	**1975**	Demand for most products reduced because of recession.
Sales higher but profits lower due to low prices. Recovery from 1975 recession slow.	**1976**	Sales of some high volume products were down but higher prices partly offset decline.
Sales grew about 10% but profits decreased by 9%. Prices did not cover the new cost increases.	**1977**	Weaknesses in economy hurt performance of some products but rapidly rising earnings in oil and gas operations made up the difference.
Government environmental regulations are fastest growing cost.	**1978**	Earnings of chemicals suffered because of industry overcapacity which kept prices down.

EXHIBIT 13.7a (cont'd)

EXCERPTS FROM ANNUAL REPORTS

Dow Chemical Company		Allied Corporation
Company benefitted from robust demand and improving prices.	**1979**	Company acquired an electrical and industrial product manufacturer to balance cyclical nature of chemical operations.
Year of record sales and earnings. Company became world's most profitable chemical company despite global economic conditions that included a major recession.	**1980**	In spite of recession, company had exceptionally good year that achieved highest earnings in its history. Divestiture program was major factor because it eliminated most of the coal, coke and gas pipeline losses.

(This identifies a major weakness in using a single markup factor based on total manufacturing cost.) The gross profit markup, which was 47.5% of total manufacturing cost, becomes 74.0% of total investment.

Column 3: The 74.0% return on investment is an intermediate step in arriving at separate markup factors for material and conversion costs.

Column 4: As was illustrated in Exhibit 13.6 and the related text, investment turns adjust for the difference between return on sales and return on investment. For this reason, it is necessary to determine separate investment turns for investment related to material and to conversion cost. The turns are calculated by dividing the material cost in column 1 by the related investment shown in column 2. Note that the turns are based on manufacturing cost rather than sales. The resulting investment turns are 3.64 times for material and 1.10 times for conversion cost.

Column 5: The next step in determining the individual markup percentages is to divide the overall gross profit markup of 74.0% in column 3 by the 3.64 turns for material and 1.10 turns for conversion cost. The markup percentages become 20.3% and 67.2%, respectively.

Column 6: This column shows the markup dollars as they relate to material and to conversion costs. The material cost shown in column 1 is multiplied by 20.3% and the conversion cost by 67.2%. These two figures add up to the gross profit of $5,432,915 shown originally in column 1.

$$\text{TURNS PER YEAR} = \frac{\text{SALES}}{\text{SHAREHOLDER EQUITY}}$$

REPUBLIC STEEL CORPORATION

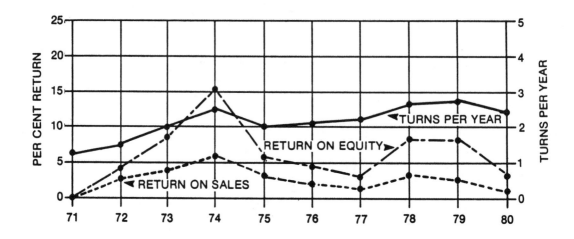

BETHLEHEM STEEL CORPORATION

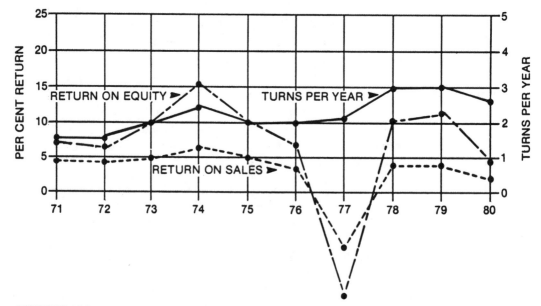

EXHIBIT 13.8

IMPACT OF ECONOMIC VOLATILITY ON EARNINGS

EXHIBIT 13.8a

EXCERPTS FROM ANNUAL REPORTS

Republic Steel		Bethlehem Steel
High inflation; record imports of foreign steel; unbalanced product mix, and price weakness.	**1971**	Losses incurred in shipbuilding and efforts to enter shelter market. (modular housing)
Improved product mix and higher profits. Problem areas include higher inflation, higher imports and price controls that limit price increases to less than 2%.	**1972**	High losses in shipbuilding operations. Long-term contracts did not anticipate inflationary pressures. Modular housing factory closed down.
Strong steel demand. Profits down because of rigid price controls. Foreign steel being sold at higher prices than domestic producers are allowed.	**1973**	Profit margins disappointingly low because of Federal price controls. Imported steel commands premium prices far above domestic prices.
Net income improved for the third consecutive year with 1974 setting an all time record. Inflationary presses severe on capital intensive industries and purchasing power of the dollar.	**1974**	Strong demand for steel. However, shipments adversely affected by shortage of coking coal caused by strike of coal miners. Price controls loosened, permitting price increases.
Upswing in demand interrupted by severest recession since the 1930s. Shipments lower because customers are liquidating inventories.	**1975**	The recession has affected the company more than anticipated. Shipments lower because customers are liquidating inventories. Recent price increases do not cover increasing costs.
Recovery from severe recession resulted in higher demand. This increase was mostly in the less profitable consumer goods industry.	**1976**	Steel demand from capital goods sector not as great as anticipated. Price increases not sufficient to offset increasing costs.

EXHIBIT 13.8a (cont'd)

EXCERPTS FROM ANNUAL REPORTS

Republic Steel   Bethlehem Steel

1977

Shipments down because of the flood of foreign produced steel. Flat rolled steel under price pressure. Most encouraging development is recognition by Washington of steel industry problems.

Dramatic downturn in profitability attributable to long recession, unfavorable market product mix, foreign steel imports, and market as well as government resistance to price increases.

1978

Earnings were the second best in the company's history. Would have been higher if it were not for record steel imports.

The company enjoyed a substantial turnaround which result in a 10.3% return on equity.

1979

Favorable first nine months interrupted by sharp decline in automotive business. Impact of heavy inflation aggravated by inequity of wage-price controls.

Shipments and profits down sharply in fourth quarter due to general economic slowdown and continuing inflationary pressure.

1980

A good fourth quarter was capped as one of the most convulsive years in steel's history. The year reflected the onset of a general economic recession, and particularly the trials and tribulations of the auto industry. Steel demand plunged 40% in two months.

Because of the recession, very low shipment and production levels combined with higher costs and inadequate price relief reduced net income by 56% and 46% from 1979 and 1978, respectively. In September, the government reinstated an improved Trigger Price machanism.

Applying the Factors to Products

Exhibit 13.11 shows the difference in gross profit when the single markup factor is applied to total manufacturing cost as compared with the two markup factors applied individually to material and to conversion cost.

$$\text{TURNS PER YEAR} = \frac{\text{SALES}}{\text{SHAREHOLDER EQUITY}}$$

GOODYEAR TIRE & RUBBER COMPANY

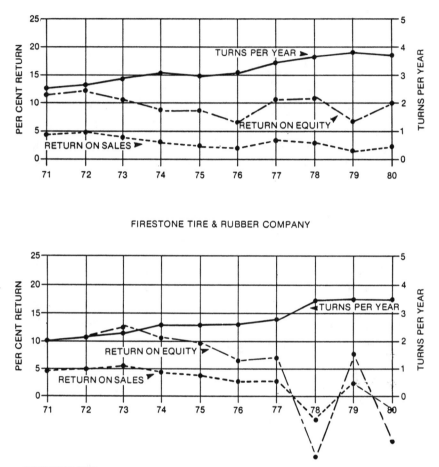

FIRESTONE TIRE & RUBBER COMPANY

EXHIBIT 13.9

IMPACT OF ECONOMIC VOLATILITY ON EARNINGS

The upper half of the exhibit shows two products to which the single markup factor of 47.5% is applied to total manufacturing cost. The resulting gross profit is 32.2% of sales for both products.

But when the individual markup factors are applied to material and to conversion cost, the gross profit becomes 21.8% of sales for product A-6731 and 31.4% for product A-6849. The reason for the lower gross profit for the

EXHIBIT 13.9a

EXCERPTS FROM ANNUAL REPORTS

Goodyear Tire & Rubber Company		Firestone Tire & Rubber Company
Company attained record levels of sales and net income despite downward economy, strikes, and increased foreign competition.	**1971**	Record sales and improved earnings resulted principally from stronger replacement market sales and higher automotive production.
Sales and net income again attained record levels.	**1972**	High sales and earnings reflect record production in auto industry and general business recovery.
Strikes in seven plants resulted in loss of 2,000,000 manhours, and lower earnings. Other adverse factors were escalating material and labor costs, and raw material shortages.	**1973**	Year of significant growth. Net earnings at record levels despite prolonged strike, rising material and payroll costs. Small price increase allowed in October did not cover increased costs.
Company is the first in the industry to exceed $5 billion sales level in spite of recession and inflation.	**1974**	Sales of $3.674 billion set a new record. In the face of energy shortages, slowdown in auto industry and intense tire competition, the company felt it maintained a good level of profits.
Sales and net income reached another record level. Company is benefitting from growing trend in the new radial tires. Recovery from recession should begin no later than mid-1976.	**1975**	Poor economic conditions, inflation and a depressed auto industry exerted downward pressure on sales and profits. Industry shipments to vehicle manufacturers down 16%.
Company established a new record in sales while net income declined. A 130 day strike resulted in a third quarter	**1976**	Company had a strong year going when a 131 day strike occurred mid-year. In view of upturn in the economy

EXHIBIT 13.9a (cont'd)

EXCERPTS FROM ANNUAL REPORTS

Goodyear Tire & Rubber Company		Firestone Tire & Rubber Company
loss. High inflation and reduced foreign earnings.		and upsurge in auto sales, it is expected that tire shipments will be high.
Fourth quarter net income fell 19% because of weaker prices, lower factory production and increased foreign translation losses.	**1977**	Softer prices, higher factory costs and wage increases triggered by inflation severely eroded second earnings.
In spite of dramatic fluctuations in the value of the dollar abroad, substantial progress was made in offsetting effects of currency translation. Competition in pricing has been intense.	**1978**	Sales reached record highs but earnings were substantially depressed, resulting in a net loss. Negotiations with the National Highway Traffic Safety Administration to recall Steel Belted Radial 500 tires concluded.
Sales set another record, but net income adversely affected by heavy charges for improving manufacturing facilities, discontinuance of some product lines and expensive labor settlement.	**1979**	Net income was $112.9 million compared with 1978 loss of $148.3 million. Car sales and driving by motorists because of energy shortages well below normal.
The recession dampened markets in many segments of the business. Auto industry orders are down.	**1980**	The company incurred a $106 million dollar loss from product recalls and phaseout of some businesses in U.S. and abroad.

first product becomes obvious when a comparison is made between the material and the conversion cost content of the two products. In product A-6731, material makes up 75% of the total manufacturing cost, while in product A-6849 the material content drops to 44% of total manufacturing cost.

EXHIBIT 13.10

CALCULATION OF RETURN ON INVESTMENT MARKUP FACTORS*

	Col. 1 Manufacturing Cost	Col. 2 Factory Investment	Col. 3 Gross Profit Markup % Based on Investment	Col. 4 (Col. 1 Divided by Col. 2) Investment Turns	Col. 5 (Col. 3 Divided by Col. 4) Gross Profit Markup % Converted to % of Mfg. Costs	Col. 6 (Col. 1 Times Col. 5) Markup % Applied to Mfg. Costs
Material	$ 4,816,080	1,321,500	74.0%	3.64 ×	20.3%	977,910
Conversion Cost	6,626,155	6,020,300	74.0%	1.10 ×	67.2%	4,455,005
Total	11,442,235	7,341,800	74.0%	1.56 ×	47.5%	5,432,915
	5,432,915	5,432,915				

Gross Profit = 47.5% of Mfg. Cost
Gross Profit = 74.0% of Investment

* Differences due to rounding.

172

EXHIBIT 13.11

GROSS PROFIT MARKUP BASED ON SINGLE FACTOR:
47.5% OF MANUFACTURING COST

Manufacturing Cost	Product A-6731	Product A-6849
Material	$ 822,790	413,681
Conversion Cost	279,174	517,444
Total Manufacturing Cost (TMC)	1,101,964	931,125
Gross Profit = 47.5% of TMC	523,433	442,284
Total Sales	$1,625,397	1,373,409
Gross Profit as a % of Total Sales	32.2%	32.2%

GROSS PROFIT MARKUP BASED ON TWO FACTORS:
20.3% OF MATERIAL; 67.2% OF CONVERSION COST

Manufacturing Cost	Product A-6731	Product A-6849
Material	$ 822,790	413,681
Conversion Cost	279,174	517,444
Total Manufacturing Cost (TMC)	1,101,964	931,125
Gross Profit:		
20.3% of Material	167,008	83,977
67.2% of Conversion Cost	187,605	347,722
Total Gross Profit (Markup)	354,613	431,699
Total Sales	$1,625,397	1,373,409
Gross Profit as a % of Total Sales	21.8%	31.4%

Since the investment in material can be quite different than the investment in facilities and related support costs, each should have its own markup factor.

The next chapter will discuss the forces of inflation that affected product costing and pricing for a period of six decades. This extended period was used because it illustrates the historical extremes that can be experienced when the price index can move from a low of about 40% to a high of over 350%. Since our economy is presently burdened by the greatest debt in history, it would be well not to ignore the past.

CHAPTER 14

Dealing with Inflation in Product Costing and Pricing

Inflation is a byproduct of the modern-day economy in which many government and private activities are financed by credit. Defense spending and construction are examples. When a nation's savings are not sufficiently large to finance such projects, the money supply is frequently increased with inflation as the byproduct.

A 60-YEAR REVIEW OF THE CONSUMER PRICE INDEX (CPI)

The inflation rate discussed here is the Consumer Price Index. Exhibit 14.1 shows the CPI by years for each of six decades. The plotting has been done on semilog paper to reflect percentage, rather than absolute changes. Thus, the slopes of the various lines can be compared directly—the steeper the slope, the greater the percentage change.

This exhibit shows how inflation has been rising in the United States for six decades. Note that in this 60-year period there were only three times in which the forces of deflation halted or slowed the upward trend of consumer prices.

> *1931–1940:* This decade shows two periods in which deflationary forces took over. One of these occurred in the first three years. This period was the aftermath of the Great Depression. The last three years were

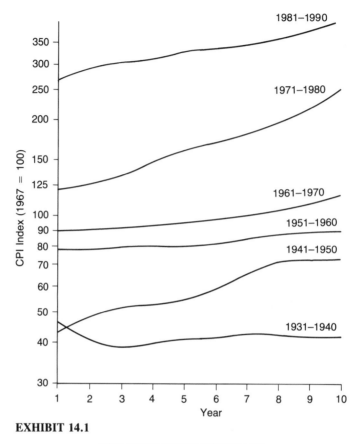

EXHIBIT 14.1

INFLATION TREND BY DECADE

the result of the Secondary Depression, which began in 1937 and lasted until the end of the decade.

1941–1950: The high rise of the price index from 1941 to 1948 was the outgrowth of World War II. Since wars are financed by credit to cover the massive outlays for armaments, production was heavily concentrated on defense needs rather than consumer goods. The pent-up demand for consumer items following cessation of hostilities caused the price index to peak in 1948. When demand was largely satisfied, the upward climb was temporarily stabilized in the last three years.

1951–1960 and 1961–1970: These two decades show a slower rate of increase, but the trend continued upward. In 1969 and 1970, the slope of the upward trend became steeper.

1971–1980: Chapter 13 referred to the volatility of this decade and its impact on product costing and pricing. The 1970s had two recessions, the first of which was the severest since the 1930s. Unlike the Great Depression and the Secondary Depression, there was no noticeable slowing of the inflation rate. President Johnson's "guns and butter" philosophy contributed greatly to the upward rise in prices. The 1973 oil embargo—accompanied by substantial oil price increases—added momentum to the already rapid acceleration of prices, which had risen from 44.1% in 1941 to 246.8% in 1980.

The following section illustrates the impact of inflation on a well-known consumer product—the postage stamp. It traces the price from 1932 when the first-class postage stamp was only 3 cents, to 1988 when the price reached 25 cents. This section also shows how the actual prices compare with the adjusted prices that are based on the April 3, 1988 CPI.

IMPACT OF INFLATION ON THE POSTAGE STAMP

Inflation is one facet of the economy that touches everyone. The greater the amount of "fiat" money in circulation, the higher the rate of inflation. The greater the rate of inflation, the greater the frequency and magnitude of price increases.

CASE 14.1: POSTAGE STAMP PRICE INCREASES

This can be demonstrated by the price increases in first-class postage from July 6, 1932 to April 3, 1988. The first increase from 3 cents to 4 cents took approximately 26 years. The next four increases were made during the 1970s, which was a decade of high volatility. This is the first time that more than two increases were made within a decade. The next four increases were made in the decade of the 1980s—the second time that four increases were made within the same decade. Actually, the move from 15 to 20 cents was all part of the same rate case. The Postal Rate Commission (PRC) would only grant a 3 cent increase, which was put into effect in March 1981. At the same time, the governors of the Postal Service asked the commission to reconsider the case for the full 5 cents. They did not make the review but held with their original recommendation of 18 cents—at which point the governors modified the PRC decision (which they can do under the law) and put in effect a 20-cent rate in November 1981. The increase from 20 cents to 22 cents took about four years, while the next increase to 25 cents took about three years.

Exhibit 14.2 compares the actual prices with the prices after adjustment for inflation.

EXHIBIT 14.2

IMPACT OF INFLATION ON POSTAGE

	Col. 1 First-Class Postage	Col. 2 CPI	Col. 3 Adjusting Factor	Col. 4 Price Adjusted to 4/3/88 CPI
Jul. 6, 1932	$.03	40.8	8.635	$.26
Aug. 1, 1958	.04	86.8	4.059	.16
Jan. 7, 1963	.05	91.1	3.867	.19
Jan. 7, 1968	.06	102.0	3.454	.21
May 16, 1971	.08	120.8	2.916	.23
Mar. 2, 1974	.10	143.1	2.462	.25
Dec. 31, 1975	.13	166.3	2.118	.28
May 29, 1978	.15	193.3	1.823	.27
Mar. 22, 1981	.18	265.2	1.328	.24
Nov. 1, 1981	.20	280.4	1.256	.25
Feb. 17, 1985	.22	312.7	1.127	.25
Apr. 3, 1988	.25	352.3	1.000	.25

The exhibit adjusts the first-class postage stamp prices for each of the years from 1932 through April 3, 1988 to the inflation level on the date of the latest increase. This was done in the following steps:

1. The Consumer Price Index was determined for each of the dates on which a price increase went into effect (column 2).

2. This figure for each date was divided into the CPI on the date of the latest increase to arrive at the adjusting factor (column 3).

3. The adjustment factor for each of the dates was multiplied by the price shown in column 1. This adjusts the actual price on each of the dates to the April 3, 1988 CPI (column 4).

These steps are illustrated as follows for the adjustment of the July, 1932 price of 3 cents to the price after adjustment to the April, 1988 CPI:

$$\frac{\text{Apr. 3, 1988 CPI}}{\text{Jul. 6, 1932 CPI}} = \frac{352.3}{40.8} = 8.635 \text{ adjusting factor}$$

The 1932 price of 3 cents multiplied by the adjusting factor of 8.635 equals 25.9 cents (rounded to 26 cents).

This type of analysis, which can be applied to manufactured products as well as postal rates, makes it possible to monitor the extent to which product prices include recovery of higher costs due to the inflationary pressures. When the adjusted prices in column 4 are lower than the actual prices shown in column 1, this is not always an indication that pricing is incorrect; it could mean that greater efficiency has been achieved through better production flow or automation. Differences between the actual and adjusted prices as they relate to manufacturing operations will be discussed next.

PRICING OPTIONS IN COPING WITH INFLATION

Competition and inflation are part and parcel of today's economy; both will be around for a while—a long while. Until the 1960s, the United States was "king of the hill." Competition was domestic rather than worldwide. Since the 1960s, competition has greatly intensified. Adam Smith, in his book, *The Roaring 80's,* cites Ezra Vogel, who points out that Japan is now the leading automobile manufacturer. He also states that of the world's 22 largest and most modern steel plants, 14 are in Japan and none are in the United States.

Countries like Korea and Taiwan are quickly evolving into competitors whose costs and prices are lower than not only those of the U.S. but Japan as well. As was pointed out in chapter 13, management must deal with competition as well as inflation when pricing decisions are made.

What are the pricing options in inflation? In responding to this question, the raw options are: (1) absorb the cost increases and maintain a constant dollar profit, or (2) pass the cost increases along and maintain a constant profit percentage.

Absorbing the Cost Increases

Exhibit 14.3 illustrates the first option in which the dollar profit is maintained as a constant. In this exhibit (and the one that follows), a 20% inflation rate for material is assumed and a 10% rate for all other manufacturing costs except depreciation, which is treated as a fixed cost. However, an adjustment is made to the total manufacturing cost in each quarter to provide for replacement expenses for property, plant, and equipment.

The $5,432,000 gross profit shown in the base period of this exhibit is kept constant for all four quarters. However, this option results in a drop in the percentage of gross profit on sales in the base period from 32.2% to 21.6% in the fourth quarter. The 47.5% gross profit based on manufacturing cost drops to 27.6% in the fourth quarter. Any company that hesitates to raise prices until

EXHIBIT 14.3

IMPACT ON PROFITS WHEN COST INCREASES ARE NOT PASSED THROUGH*

			Dollar Profits Remain Constant			
	Inflation Rate	*Base Period*	*1st Qtr.*	*2nd Qtr.*	*3rd Qtr.*	*4th Qtr.*
Sales		$16,874	18,499	20,385	22,573	25,119
Material	20%	4,816	5,779	6,935	8,322	9,986
Direct Labor	10%	2,333	2,566	2,823	3,105	3,416
Variable Overhead	10%	2,862	3,148	3,463	3,809	4,190
Property, Plant, & Equipment	Fixed	1,431	1,431	1,431	1,431	1,431
Total Manufacturing Cost		$11,442	12,924	14,652	16,667	19,023
Addt'l. Replacement Cost of Property, Plant, & Equipment		—	143	301	474	664
Adjusted Manufacturing Cost		$11,442	13,067	14,953	17,141	19,687
Gross Profit—Dollars		$ 5,432	5,432	5,432	5,432	5,432
Gross Profit—% of Sales		32.2	29.4	26.6	24.1	21.6
Gross Profit—% of Mfg. Cost		47.5	41.6	36.3	31.7	27.6

* $000 omitted. Small differences due to rounding.

it determines what the competitors will do must evaluate this option in terms of what the impact on profits will be.

Passing along the Cost Increase

Exhibit 14.4 shows the impact of the second option, in which sales prices are increased so the gross profit in the percentages in the base period can be maintained.

Very few companies monitor inflation as they should. The purchasing manager is usually the first to complain of large material price increases. The sales department is more likely to "hang loose" for a while because selling becomes a bit more difficult when an increase in prices is announced. The salespeople prefer to have competitors take the first step to minimize "shopping around" by the customer to see what other supplier has not raised prices as yet.

Which Option is Correct?

The answer to this raises several questions:

1. What is the relative material and labor cost content in the products? If the material cost content is low in relation to labor, it may be more appropriate to delay price increases until the upcoming labor negotiations provide some indication as to the amount of the settlement with the union.

EXHIBIT 14.4

IMPACT ON PROFITS WHEN COST INCREASES ARE PASSED THROUGH*

	Inflation Rate	Base Period	1st Qtr.	2nd Qtr.	3rd Qtr.	4th Qtr.
		Profit Percentages Remain Constant				
Sales		$16,874	19,273	22,055	25,285	29,037
Material	20%	4,816	5,779	6,935	8,322	9,986
Direct Labor	10%	2,333	2,566	2,823	3,105	3,416
Variable Overhead	10%	2,862	3,148	3,463	3,809	4,190
Property, Plant, & Equipment	Fixed	1,431	1,431	1,431	1,431	1,431
Total Manufacturing Cost		$11,442	12,924	14,652	16,667	19,023
Add'l. Replacement Cost of Property, Plant, & Equipment		—	143	301	474	664
Adjusted Manufacturing Cost		$11,442	13,067	14,953	17,141	19,687
Gross Profit—Dollars		$ 5,432	6,206	7,102	8,144	9,350
Gross Profit—% of Sales		32.2	32.2	32.2	32.2	32.2
Gross Profit—% of Mfg. Cost		47.5	47.5	47.5	47.5	47.5

* $000 omitted. Small differences due to rounding.

2. If the material cost increase is large but expiration of the current union contract is some months off, it might be wiser to institute a price increase to cover the higher material cost.

3. Some companies in a highly competitive market may raise the question as to whether they can maintain the present price level by reducing costs with substitution of cheaper material, simplifying the design of the product, or automating. Whether these alternatives are viable depends on the amount of time required for implementation. Cost reduction considerations often come up at times like this but may require too much time to justify delaying the price increase.

4. Another approach taken by some companies is to include a statement in all quotation requests that a surcharge may be levied in the event of a large increase in the CPI. The psychology here is to lay the groundwork for a price increase without announcing an immediate price change.

WHY SOME PRODUCTS ARE LESS VULNERABLE TO INFLATION

Some products have gone through heavy periods of inflation unscathed. This is particularly true of products in which innovative changes were made. Television receiver prices, for example, hovered close to the 100% CPI level throughout the decade of the 1970s, while total U.S. goods and services rose from about 120% in 1971 to almost 250% in 1980. This is shown graphically in Exhibit 14.5.

The innovative changes made in television receivers can be illustrated by comparing the 1946 RCA 10″ 630TS table model set with its present-day equivalent, which is one-third the price of the 1946 version. The following improvements contributed not only to greatly reduced prices but to better-performing products that required very little servicing.

The 1946 set required about 30 vacuum receiving tubes, while the present-day version is solid state. The earlier set required 342 watts as compared with 33. The weight of the earlier set was 85 pounds compared with 11 pounds.

As competition heated up, the number of receiving tubes was reduced because of the introduction of tubes containing twin elements rather than only a single element. This reduced not only the number of tubes but the sockets, wiring, and related labor costs. This improvement took place first in the audio section, then in the video section, and later in the rectifier.

Transistors and solid state devices permitted further elimination of receiving tubes and provided additional cost reductions as each of the changes was implemented in the various functional areas. The solid state chassis sounded the death knell of the remaining receiving tubes. This meant cooler as well as more efficient operation and improved product reliability.

The insertion of components, inspections, and alignment tests led to further dramatic reductions in the number of production hours. The downward trend

EXHIBIT 14.5

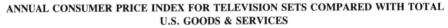

ANNUAL CONSUMER PRICE INDEX FOR TELEVISION SETS COMPARED WITH TOTAL
U.S. GOODS & SERVICES

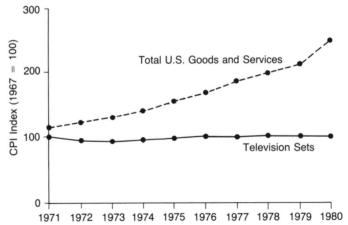

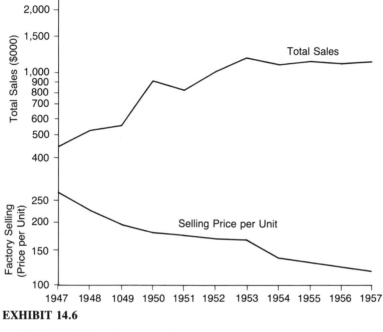

EXHIBIT 14.6

TOTAL FACTORY SALES BY SEVEN TELEVISION MANUFACTURERS

of prices is shown in Exhibit 14.6. Note that as total sales by seven television receiver manufacturers rose, the selling price per unit moved downward. Obviously, some of the cost reduction was due to higher production volume. However, the innovative changes undoubtedly contributed more to cost reduction than the increased volume. It is worthy of note that in the late 1940s and early 1950s, most receivers contained the smaller 10-inch and 12-inch picture tubes, while later in the 1950s the size of the picture tubes doubled. Also, wider deflection of the image on the screen allowed the neck of the tube to be shortened and the cabinet to be reduced in depth—resulting in additional savings.

SUMMARY

In evaluating the impact of inflation on product costing and pricing as shown in Exhibits 14.3 and 14.4, it would be simplistic to assume that one could merely apply the individual inflation rates to material and to the other manufacturing costs and then make a choice as to which of the two exhibits apply. One must first study the questions asked in the section titled, "Which Option is Correct?"

The second step is to analyze the material content to determine if more than a single rate for material is needed. Some companies use a basic commodity, copper or steel, for example, and other materials that may not be subject to the same inflation rate. This might very well suggest the use of two inflation rates for material.

The next consideration is to what degree nonmaterial costs have been affected by inflation. It may be necessary to await the next union contract negotiation date to obtain the answer. At this point, the decision must be made as to whether a price increase should be made for the material along with an estimate of terms that will be negotiated.

It is also possible that a cost reduction program could be implemented within a short time so that any price increase that is put into effect would be smaller, and thus leave the company in a more favorable position than its competitors.

The foregoing summation represents the short-term outlook. There is also a long-term overview that must be taken into account. It is a well-documented fact of life that our country has reverted from a creditor to a debtor nation during the 1980s and has entered the 1990s under an economic cloud. Although problems of the 1970s and earlier decades of this century are now history, we must not forget that history often repeats itself.

CHAPTER 15

Real-World Problems in Product Cost Estimating and Pricing

This chapter discusses problems experienced by estimators whose responsibility is to establish product cost estimates as a basis for price determination. The examples are actual. In some instances, key management personnel were interviewed to obtain their insight. The highlights of some of the interviews have been included.

INADEQUATE INFORMATION FROM THE CUSTOMER

In the survey conducted in preparation for writing this book, numerous cost estimates were reviewed and information was solicited as to difficulties experienced in developing meaningful product cost estimates. The former general manager of a subcontracting company made the following comments:

"I was quite surprised at some of the sloppy specifications we received from some of the customers. One of the customers I have in mind was a division of a *Fortune* 500 company. In some cases, my engineers had to redraw prints to make them usable by our production department. One of the most unbelievable errors was dimensional. At first, we made the changes but when we found that this was a continuing occurrence, we added an additional charge when we submitted our invoice. Our portion of the cost that went into their end product was relatively small, so we never had trouble collecting for the extra work."

When this question was asked in other companies, one general manager acknowledged that he had the same problem with one of his customers who always wanted his order "yesterday or sooner." His approach was to call the customer and explain the problem before making changes. The time required to make the changes was billed at overtime rates, which the customer accepted.

RISKS IN QUOTING ON A "SIMILAR TO" BASIS

In the course of the survey, two instances were found in which some product cost estimates were admittedly prepared by comparing the order with a similar job in the past. In both cases, the previous job on which costs were based had been manufactured about a year earlier. Within that period, the inflation rate had risen two percentage points. Because of time constraints, the estimator had forgotten to adjust the price. To make matters worse, one of the products proved to be "different than" rather than "similar to."

The survey revealed that some companies preferred not to increase prices immediately. The reason stated by one of the sales managers was: "We prefer to let the competitor take the heat for raising prices. After we learn that the prices have been increased, we increase ours." The finding, after making other reviews, was that some companies allow their prices to remain unchanged for some time, possibly to gain a larger share of the market. As was mentioned in chapter 14, some companies were found to advise their customers that a surcharge would be added to quoted prices in the event that the CPI should show a large increase. This was found to be an acceptable way to "ease into" a price increase.

IMPORTANCE OF FEEDBACK ON COST-ESTIMATING ACCURACY

Surprisingly few companies make comparisons of product cost estimates with the actual costs on completion of the job. When this was discussed with the plant manager of one of the companies, he advised that his industrial engineers establish standards for every new job and that these standards become the performance measurements. This response begged the question. Obviously, standards should be established to ensure that costs are controlled. However, comparing the actual costs with the original estimates on which prices were based highlights errors which, if not given visibility, could go on in perpetuity.

Suggested formats for feedback comparisons are shown in Exhibits 7.4 and 7.5 in chapter 7. The first of these two exhibits goes a step beyond comparing costs—it also compares the estimated profit with the profit actually realized.

The second exhibit is used by a company in which material content is very high. Because errors in estimating the material cost can contribute to a large out-of-pocket loss, the second exhibit format should also be employed.

THE COST SYSTEM MUST FIT THE NEED

As was pointed out in the early chapters of this book, a surprising number of companies have inadequate cost systems that do not provide correct information needed to prepare meaningful price quotations. Numerous articles and books emphasize the importance of recognizing differences in overhead costing rates, but many companies continue to use a single plantwide overhead rate even though there are wide overhead cost differences in the various production cost centers. (See *Cost Controls for Industry*, Thomas S. Dudick, Prentice Hall, 1962.)

In discussing this problem, a well-informed industrial engineer had this to say:

> "Last year we converted a six-girl manual assembly line to an automated operation by introducing an automatic assembly machine which required only one operator. Would you believe that the cost department continued to use that single plantwide overhead rate? I spoke to the cost manager and explained that the new automatic assembly machine cost $65,000 but instead of localizing that cost to the one operation, his accounting figures were spreading the machine cost over all the other operations which were manually performed. He didn't know what I was driving at at first, but then it dawned on him. He promised to correct this but couldn't do it until next year when the new standards were developed. Fortunately, he was replaced by someone who had a more strongly charged battery."

Although this company had been backward in the method of applying overhead to the various products, it was making use of direct costing (variable costing) in valuing inventory. At year end, when inventories had to be valued at full cost, the total fixed cost was spread over all items on the basis of the total variable overhead cost in the inventory. This assumed that the fixed cost content in all products was directly related to the amount of variable overhead. Variable overhead, like other manufacturing costs, can vary widely from one production cost center to another. Illustrative of this are three companies whose variable overhead rates are shown in Exhibit 15.1. The size of these companies ranges from a small component manufacturer with annual sales of $18 million to an appliance manufacturer with sales approximating $150 million.

EXHIBIT 15.1*

COMPANY 1
VARIABLE OVERHEAD RATES OF
A SMALL COMPONENTS MANU-
FACTURER

Parts Stamping	41%
Coil Winding	46
Furnace Processing	66
Assembly	39
Test	42
Plant Average	42%

COMPANY 2
VARIABLE OVERHEAD RATES OF
AN APPLIANCE MANUFACTURER

Metal Press Shop	213%
Machine Shop	110
Screw Machines	143
Plating	135
Assembly	67
Inspection	54
Plant Average	105%

COMPANY 3
VARIABLE OVERHEAD RATES OF
A RADIO MANUFACTURER

Sheet Metal Shop	78%
Machine Shop	71
Plating-Painting	107
Assembly	64
Inspection	53
Plant Average	65%

* The cost center names are those actually used by the three companies. *Metal Press Shop* in company 2 is the same as *Sheet Metal Shop* in company 3. *Test* in company 1 is similar to *Inspection* in companies 2 and 3.

Company 1 falls under the classification of light manufacturing. Its variable overhead rates do not fluctuate very widely from one cost center to another; the range is 39% to 66%. In this company, as in many others, all products do not use the manufacturing facilities in the same proportion. Furnace processing, which has the highest rate of the group, is bypassed entirely by some of the products. Use of the average plantwide rate of 42% would understate the products that do require the use of the furnace and would overstate the variable overhead costs of other products.

Company 2, likewise, shows differences from cost center to cost center, but the variations are greater—ranging from a variable rate of 54% to 213%. Here again, the time spent in each cost center by the various products varies depending on the amount of press shop work, amount of plating-painting required, machine shop, screw machine, and assembly work. Use of the average plantwide rate of 105% would penalize some of the products and understate the cost of others.

Company 3, smaller than company 2, shows a smaller range of variable rates than company 2. In spite of the narrower range, the highest rate is double the amount of the smallest rate (107% versus 53%). In its radio line, some of the radios use a metal cabinet, which requires more time in the sheet metal shop and painting than a radio using a plastic cabinet, which is purchased as material. Since sheet metal and plating-painting are the two highest rates in this company, use of the average rate of 65% would penalize the radios using the purchased plastic cabinets and would undercost the ones using metal.

The foregoing examples highlight the importance of taking into account the differences in the manufacturing operations.

USING THE PROFIT CONTRIBUTION PERCENT FOR MARGINAL PRICING

Because the profit contribution percent method makes it possible to analyze quickly profitability of additional sales volume without the distorting effect of arbitrarily allocating fixed costs, some companies reason as follows:

> "We now recoup all our fixed costs in the sales which we're currently booking. If I know what my variable costs are, I can set prices about 20% higher than the variable cost and come up with a lot of profitable plus business without expanding our facilities one iota. We make a well-advertised brand name product, which we can sell in bulk to a private brand distributor."

In an interview with the operations manager of another company, the conversation on the subject of marginal pricing took his turn:

> "We studied the possibilities of taking on a new product line on several occasions. Knowing the profit contribution, we determine what our additional income will be because of the added volume. We then match this

with the additional outlay of capital and other fixed-type costs needed to support the enlarged operation. If the additional outlay doesn't eat up too much of the profit contribution, we expand.''

While use of the profit contribution method is a valuable tool in determining how much prices can be reduced to obtain new business, this tool must be used with discretion. During a period of declining sales, it would be altogether too tempting to book business at reduced prices under the assumption that current business is absorbing its full complement of fixed costs. But what will happen if the ''plus'' business predominates? Normal cost controls do not set up red flags to highlight this except when profits begin to erode. Further, competitors are not likely to sit still—they too will reduce prices, possibly even further. While proponents of the profit contribution method of determining prices are quick to point out the price-cutting advantages, they are not sufficiently vocal on the dangers of unconsciously overdoing a good thing.

AMORTIZATION OF TOOLING COSTS

NatCo, Inc. (name disguised) provided for tool amortization in product cost estimates by applying an overall percentage of manufacturing cost. Tests indicated that this method was reasonable except for one product whose tooling costs were unusually high—$7.50 per unit. The percentage method assessed a charge of only $2.42 per unit, leaving a shortfall of $5.08. When this was discussed with the controller, he at first objected to making a change because it would take too much time to calculate the tooling cost for some 1,500 different items. It was explained to him that only the items requiring high tooling costs would be costed on an actual rather than a percentage basis, and pointed out further that the industrial engineer, under whose jurisdiction the tool shop falls, is in a good position to identify which tools are the most expensive. The industrial engineer agreed that he would notify the cost department of any products being quoted as to whether the tooling cost per unit would be exceptionally high.

PROVIDING FOR PRODUCTION REJECT COSTS

Chapter 1 discussed a production reject report that can be helpful in determining the rate to be used in product cost estimating. Exhibit 1.6, which is prepared weekly and is the subject of weekly meetings, shows the reject percentages for the eight products that account for 75% of the production volume. This report is used for purposes of control. Obviously, a weekly report with its week-to-week fluctuations would not be adequate for use in product cost estimating.

The production reject percentage must show more than a single week's experience—it must reflect the trend on a cumulative basis. The cost estimator must therefore accumulate the total units produced and total units rejected to arrive at a cumulative rejection percentage.

Availability of this kind of history will be more useful to the cost estimator than individual weekly figures. From such information the estimator can categorize various products by their degree of manufacturing difficulty. This should, of course, be reviewed with either the quality manager or manufacturing engineer—or both. Once the manufacturing difficulty ratings have been established by product category, all incoming requests for quotation can be identified by the category in which they fall. This should provide a more meaningful production reject rate because it can be more closely related to similar products made in the past.

ESTIMATING COSTS FOR SYSTEMS INSTALLATION

A study of two companies that manufacture equipment and make on-site installations showed that each used a different method for pricing the installation' costs. The first company, in preparing the quotations, priced the equipment separately from the installation costs.

The sales price of the second company did not distinguish between equipment and installation. The rationale followed by the second company was that it was in the business to sell systems—which included both equipment and the on-site installation of such equipment.

Semantics aside, this company's failure to distinguish between the sales price of the equipment and the sales price of the installation work precluded determination of the profit breakdown between the two functions. Since over 1,000 employees were involved in the installation work at various sites, the obvious recommendation made to the management was that for internal control purposes, the sales price and costs should be segregated even though a single price is quoted to the customer. The recommendation was implemented. After a six-month period it was found that the installation work was much less profitable than expected; equipment sales were partly subsidizing the installation work.

BASIC PRODUCT PLUS PRICE ADDERS

In pricing requests for quotation, Machine Tools, Inc. (name disguised) starts with the price of a basic machine. It then uses price adders for the various options called for in the order. Customers can choose from some 120 different options which include such features as special frames, bolster modifications, special slide features, high-speed extras, electrical modifications, and variations in lubrication systems.

The company averages as many as 10,000 requests for quotation in a year, of which approximately 10% result in firm orders. Because the typical press contains well over 2,000 parts, time limitations for quoting do not allow for step-by-step buildup of costs from purchased material to the finished product. Pricing is therefore not based on detailed costs to which markup factors are added. Instead, a price list is used for standard presses to determine the price of the basic press. The basic price is then adjusted to include the various options, which are also priced from a precalculated schedule of prices for the various options. The use of precalculated price lists from which the total price is determined is an obvious timesaver which has merit.

Unfortunately, there is a tendency in some companies to make adjustments to the adders on an arbitrary basis merely by applying an across-the-board percentage factor. Several reviews have disclosed that the percentage factors, for the most part, provided for inflation rate increases but overlooked engineering and other changes that warranted consideration in revising the pricing adders. Such was the case with a company making an entirely different product. A similar review of that company found that over a three-year period, improved bronze bearings had been added as well as a more expensive actuator, for which no adjustment was made in the prices. Failure to make periodic cost/selling price comparisons for the various adders can result in undetected losses that can go on for months at a time before they come to light.

FINE-TUNING MARKUP FACTORS

Exhibit 13.10 in chapter 13 illustrated a single markup factor for material in the interest of simplicity. There are times when more than a single markup factor should be used. Hartco Corp. (name disguised) makes numerous fabricated parts made of brass. About one-third of these are sold as fabricated parts on the outside, while the remaining two-thirds are assembled with nonbrass material to produce a finished product.

The same material markup factor was being used for both the brass fabricated parts sold outside and the finished products containing both the fabricated parts and nonbrass material. In such cases, a test should be made to determine if there is a different turnover rate for the brass used in fabricated parts and the nonbrass material used to complete the end product. If there is a large difference, then separate markup factors should be applied to the individual materials.

The same applies to the conversion costs. A review disclosed in this case that the fabrication operation required expensive equipment and high maintenance and energy costs, while the assembly operation was labor intensive, requiring a smaller investment. In view of this, the conversion costs associated with making the fabricated parts should have a different markup factor than the conversion costs related to assembly of the end product.

In developing the additional markup factors, the same format shown in Exhibit 13.10 can be used.

PROFITABILITY ANALYSIS IN PRODUCT COST ESTIMATING

Cost estimators should go beyond determining only the estimated product cost—they should include a suggested price as well as a profit calculation. The profit should be expressed not only as a return on sales, but return on investment.

Profit on sales does not reflect the return on investment. This is an important consideration, particularly when a manufacturer makes purchases for resale from a manufacturing subcontractor as well as selling products of the company's own manufacture. The investment associated with products purchased for resale is much smaller than for those products that are made by the company. The resale products do not require raw material, work-in-process, or manufacturing equipment. For this reason, the same percentage of profit on both types of sales would not mean that both products are equally profitable. This can be illustrated by the following figures for a company that makes its own pullover shirts and also makes purchases of some of the odd sizes from a subcontractor.

PULLOVER SHIRTS

	Unit Price or Cost	Made in-House	Purchased for Resale
Regular Sales	$4.75	$475,000	—
Subcontracted Sales	4.75	—	$190,000
Total		475,000	190,000
Manufacturing Cost	3.51	351,000	—
Purchased Cost	3.85	—	154,000
Gross Profit—Mfd.	1.24	124,000	—
Gross Profit—Purch'd.	.90	—	36,000
SG&A		71,000	23,900
Pretax Profit		53,000	12,100
% Return on Sales		11.1	6.4
% Return on Investment		22.2	28.8

The return on sales shows that profit on the company's own products was almost double that of the products purchased for resale—11.1% versus 6.4%. Note, however, that the 6.4% return on sales for the purchases for resale reflects the profit after a charge of $23,900 for selling, general, and administrative expenses. It is doubtful that sales of purchased items incur as much selling and administrative effort as is required for the manufactured items.

The comparison, from a return on investment concept, shows somewhat different results. During the past two years, total inventories plus net fixed assets turned over twice per year in terms of sales. (Inventory and net fixed assets were approximately equal to stockholder equity.) If we multiply the 11.1% return on sales by two turns,the resulting return on investment amounts to 22.2%.

In the case of items which are manufactured on the outside, we must exclude raw materials, work-in-process, and net fixed assets because none of these were required for the products purchased for resale. The finished goods inventory for the resale items is quite small, with annual turns of four and a half times. Converting the return on sales of 6.4% to a return on investment, the percentage becomes 28.8% compared with the 22.2% for the in-house items.

Use of subcontractors allowed this company to be more selective in the products it manufactures, thus taking advantage of longer runs, more stabilized operations, and greater efficiency. The economic advantages are somewhat intangible and therefore not readily measurable in terms of return on sales or return on investment. However, the experience of this company conclusively demonstrates that any evaluation of profitability in a company that makes purchases for resale as well as selling products of its own manufacture must evaluate profitability in terms of return on investment.

WHEN ACTUAL PRODUCT COSTS ARE WELL ABOVE THE ESTIMATE

Many new products have a tendency to run over the product cost estimate when initially run. In some cases, however, the cost can be far in excess of reason. This was the case at Plastimold, a company that made molded plastic products. Some were sold as finished products after completion of the molding operation. Others required further work such as hot stamping of letters or numerals, or insertion of spring clips or contacts. After adding several new products whose product cost estimates indicated good profitability, the company's first quarter financial statement showed a $15,000 loss on sales of $453,000. The only clue to the source of the losses available in the accounting reports was that mold costs were higher in the current year and that rework costs were excessive. This explanation fell far short of bringing to light the full picture.

In addition to the molding plant, the company also had a "feeder" plant. The molding plant's production often required some assembly work. The assembly operations—which were labor intensive—were performed at the "feeder" plant because labor costs were much lower. In the period in which the profit eroded, the same procedures were being followed, but the mix of products had changed somewhat. A large part of the new production was molding of lucite clock lenses at the molding plant and forwarding them to the feeder plant for hot stamping the numerals. Because lucite scratches easily, it was necessary to wrap each molded lens in soft tissue paper and cell-pack to avoid friction in transportation. At the feeder plant the lenses were unpacked, hot stamped, repacked, and shipped to the customer.

The lenses were molded in a two-cavity mold. Because it is impossible to make two molds exactly the same, there was a slight difference in the curvature in the two cavities in which the lenses are formed. As a result, when the numerals were stamped at the feeder plant, the printing was light on some of the lenses where the curvature was different. The reason for this was not immediately known, but after a period of investigation the difference in mold curvature in the two cavities was determined to be the cause. This had resulted in thousands of costly rejects, which had to be sorted by mold of origin and then cleaned and restamped. All this handling resulted in a substantial number that had to be thrown away.

In view of the foregoing, it was obvious why profits had eroded. As a result of this finding, the hot stamping operation was moved back to the molding plant, even though the labor rates were higher. Now, as the lenses came off the press, they were routed directly to two hot stamping machines—each adjusted to the individual curvature of the two mold cavities. On completion of the hot stamping operation, the product was packaged for the first and only time and shipped to the customer. Rejections and rework dropped substantially, and the profit picture improved markedly. As a result of this experience, a closer look was taken at some of the other operations being transferred to the feeder plant to determine whether the lower labor rate was advantageous in all cases.

IMPACT OF IMPROPERLY MAINTAINED EQUIPMENT

The preceding example illustrates a case in which a new product cost was properly estimated but manufacturing procedures were weak on two counts— first, that the hot stamping operation did not take into account the differences in mold curvature, and second, that too much handling resulted in damage to

EXHIBIT 15.2

DESCRIPTION OF DEFECTS IN 19 of 36 MACHINES

Engine Lathes

Tag 3813:	Ways are worn to the point that machine can only be used for roughing— estimated 40% loss in capacity.
Tag 3810:	Machine is old and worn out. Cannot hold .003″ used only for roughing. Estimated 40% loss in capacity.
Tag 3811:	Machine worn to point that it will turn taper of .010″ in 12″. Company will not repair unless shipped to their plant so they can completely redo bed, gibs, carriage, etc. Can only be used for roughing in current condition.
Tag 3808:	Machine needs new bronze nut in carriage. Hydraulic system needs work— otherwise OK.
Tag 3816:	Machine is old and slow with one speed of 10″ per hour. Actually obsolete—60% capacity loss estimated.
Tag 3802:	Machine worn out. Can only do rough turning. Estimated 50% loss of capacity.
Tag 3806:	Dial slips on X slide; tail stock center .003″ out—used for rough turning only; 45% capacity loss estimated.

Grinders

Tag 4003:	Old and worn; hydraulic feed grabs; dimensions will not repeat; spindle has run out.
Tag 4004:	Machine worn out. Needs factory rebuilding; 65% loss in capacity.
Tag 4006:	Same as 4004. Needs factory rebuilding. Estimated 65% loss in capacity.
Tag 4008:	Needs footing; $\frac{1}{4}$″ out of level; can only grind in one direction; 40% loss in capacity.
Tag 4002:	Needs separate foundation—out of level; 40% loss in capacity.
Tag 4106:	Speed change lever wired up to hold speed up in high—otherwise drops out of gear. Power feed does not work; 50% loss in capacity.
Tag 4104:	Ways worn, machine old and sloppy. Coolant not working. Estimated 50% loss in capacity.
Tag 4101:	Machine worn out; noise limits operation. Possible that OSHA would shut down because of noise level. Estimated 50% loss in capacity.
Tag 4108:	Machine loses RPM on cuts, clutch slips, rapid transverse table down does not shut off. Estimated 30% loss in capacity.
Tag 4102:	Used only for nozzle blades. Worn out and not usable for any other type work.

Radial Drills

Tag 3104:	Feeds erratic on all other than .004 and .007. Feeds grab and jump.
Tag 3120:	Machine worn. Bearing bad; spindle runs out; estimated 25% loss in capacity.

the lucite finish. The example that follows is an actual case (as the previous one was) in which equipment had not been properly maintained for years.

As a result, the product cost estimate, which was based on existing conditions, led to estimated costs that were too high. This has been found to be the case in far too many companies in which equipment maintenance is continually put off. Exhibit 15.2 illustrates the kinds of deficiencies that existed in 19 out of a total of 36 machines.

This is an example of when a product cost estimate based on such conditions does not provide a satisfactory base to which markup factors can be applied to arrive at selling prices. There are many such companies and divisions thereof whose operations are not competitive, but not necessarily because of inefficiency.

The equipment may be well maintained and the operations efficiently performed, but a competitor with a larger share of the market may have highly automated equipment and longer runs and therefore lower production costs. The noncompetitive, though efficient, company sometimes overcomes this hurdle by concentrating on products that the more successful competitors avoid because of low demand and shorter runs. For these types of products, product cost estimates will provide a more meaningful base for establishing prices.

CHAPTER 16

The Product Life Cycle: Its Impact on Product Cost Estimating and Pricing

The product life cycle is assumed by some to follow regularly spaced phases similar to those in the human life span, i.e., infancy, puberty, adulthood, maturity, and old age. The corresponding phases in product life cycles are often identified as development, growth, maturity, saturation, and decline. A generalized product life cycle as commonly visualized is shown graphically in Figure 16.1.

Note in the development stage that profits (shown as a dotted line) are negative. In the mid-growth stage they rise rapidly, then slow down as the product approaches maturity. When the saturation point is reached, profits begin to turn downward until the decline state is reached. At that point, the downward trend of profits get steeper.

THE DEVELOPMENT STAGE

W. W. Simmons, consultant of W. W. Simmons, Inc., made a study of the intervals between scientific discoveries and their application. In this study[1] he found that the interval between discovery and application for 11 well-known products ranged from 112 years to 2 years before people understood the technology and began to use it. (See Exhibit 16.1.) He emphasizes *people* because this is the real indicator of application. Today, communication has become so

---

[1] *How to Improve Profitability*, edited by Thomas S. Dudick, © John Wiley & Sons, 1975, p. 20.

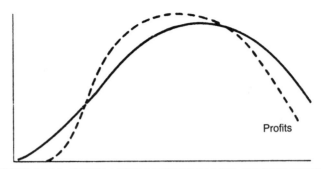

FIGURE 16.1 GENERALIZED PRODUCT LIFE CYCLE PATTERN

rapid that when something new is discovered, it almost immediately becomes a saleable product. Before proceeding further, it may be useful to review the product life cycle of a well-known product—the automobile.

The development stage in the automobile took 26 years, from 1862 to 1888. This falls between the 31-year development period for the vacuum tube and the 18-year period required for the X-ray tube.

The first motor car with an internal combustion engine was built by a Belgian engineer named Lenoir in 1862.[2] It was some time before Lenoir had sufficient confidence in his new vehicle to drive it on the public highway. In September of the following year, he drove the car about six miles to a nearby city. The journey there and back took a driving time of three hours—the average running speed approximated four miles per hour.

EXHIBIT 16.1

**INTERVAL BETWEEN SCIENTIFIC DISCOVERIES
AND THEIR APPLICATION**

Solar Battery	1953–1955	2 years
Transistor	1948–1951	3 years
Nuclear Reactors	1932–1942	10 years
Television	1922–1934	12 years
Radar	1925–1940	15 years
X-ray Tubes	1895–1913	18 years
Vacuum Tube	1884–1915	31 years
Radio	1867–1902	35 years
Telephone	1820–1876	56 years
Electric Motor	1821–1886	65 years
Photography	1727–1839	112 years

[2] Robertson, Patrick. *Book of Firsts,* Clarkson M. Potter/Publishers, 1982, p. 184.

GROWTH STAGE OF THE U.S AUTO INDUSTRY

The close interrelationship of selling price, cost, and volume was recognized by Henry Ford, an elementary school dropout, remembered for his introduction of assembly line production of the Model T. Inasmuch as the auto industry was then in the early growth stage of its life cycle, it was obvious to Ford that he must capture a large share of the market to reduce costs and ensure profitability. When he sized up the productivity of his competitors, who were still in the handcrafting stage, he recognized the need for improved manufacturing technology.

Ford set the selling price for the Model T at half the price of the four-cylinder Chevrolet. He dismissed the conventional method of first determining the cost because he felt that no one could ascertain what the real cost would be. Further, he felt there was little point in being told that production costs would exceed the selling price (which can be expected during the early period of setting up the new manufacturing procedures). His reasoning was that if he set the price low, everyone would have to dig for profits and thus achieve the necessary cost reductions.

During this period, General Motors was producing a rounded line of cars that included not only the four-cylinder Chevrolet, but the larger, premium-priced cars such as the six-cylinder Buick and the eight-cylinder Cadillac. General Motors was obviously preparing to meet competition head-on; not only through adoption of assembly line production, but through other improvements such as the closed body, self-starter, and regular body design changes.

Because Henry Ford froze the open body design of the Model T, he fell far behind General Motors in volume since the light chassis of the Model T was not suited to the heavier, all-weather, closed body which competitors were promoting. General Motors soon closed the gap and attained first place, leaving Ford behind as the number two producer. Ford then belatedly recognized the need to make changes.

MATURITY STAGE OF THE U.S. AUTO INDUSTRY

The auto industry is now in the maturity stage of the industry life cycle. It is ironic that foreign car imports have made the same inroads on U.S. car manufacturers as General Motors made on Ford after the demise of his Model T. It is worthy of note that stiff competition from foreign imports reversed the complacency of U.S. car manufacturers, forcing them to further improve manufacturing technology and to meet the quality standards of overseas competitors.

This example illustrates the characteristics of two phases of the automobile product life cycle—growth and maturity. Ford's introduction of moving assembly line production at greatly reduced prices and General Motors' introduction of a rounded line with improved design features enhanced growth. The growth phase entered maturity after the last of the more than 100 different U.S. car manufacturers disappeared from the scene, leaving the market to the big three and their foreign competitors. Price cutting took the form of reduced rates of interest on car loans or rebates in periods of slumping sales.

SATURATION AND DECLINE

Our discussion of the product life cycle to this point has been limited to the entire auto industry, rather than to individual companies. The industry has not reached saturation because of the continuing changes in design and other conveniences that keep customers interested in buying new models. American Motors, which was acquired by Chrysler, is an example of a company within the industry that went through all phases of the product life cycle and could no longer remain an active competitor.

Radio production, like the automobile, has not attained the saturation or decline stage in that industry's life cycle. Production of radios started in the early 1900s. When it appeared that radio production had reached its peak, auto radios came on the scene. Portable radios followed in the late 1930s, and clock radios were introduced in the early 1950s. The FM feature was then added to both home and auto radios. Later, stereo was introduced, further extending the life of this industry. More recently, the tape and CD features were added. Here, as in the auto industry, many companies succumbed to the intense price competition. Formerly well-known names such as Atwater Kent and Philco no longer exist.

LIFE CYCLES AS THEY RELATE TO CONSUMER PRODUCTS

Sonia Yuspeh, senior vice-president of J. Walter Thompson, points out that the world of biology and world of product marketing are vastly different:[3]

> "There is considerable appeal in thinking about the product life cycle in terms borrowed from the biological sciences. But the world of biology and the world of product marketing are vastly different—far too different to draw easy parallels.

[3] *Handbook of Business Planning*, edited by Thomas S. Dudick, Van Nostrand Reinhold, 1983.

Fundamentally, the life cycles of living organizisms are characterized by two conditions:

1. The length of each stage is fixed at fairly precise terms.
2. The sequence of each stage is fixed: each stage follows the next in an immutable, irreversible sequence.''

Variations in the Length of Consumer Product Life Cycles

Neither of the two conditions is characteristic of the marketing world. The length of the so-called life cycle stages can vary enormously from one product to the next. Examples come readily to mind. Compare the development and marketing of hair coloring with that of color television. Hair coloring products have been available for many generations, but only in recent years have they developed a substantial level of consumer acceptance. And there is still ample room for growth, especially among men. In contrast, the pattern for color television is radically different. The product is an infant compared to hair coloring. It has only been available since the early 1970s and, despite initial technical problems and high unit pricing, the acceptance of the product far exceeds that for hair coloring in a far shorter period of time. This is a dramatic contrast used simply to make a point, but if we look over the vast array of marketing case histories, we will find it impossible to make any generalizations about the length of the different stages in the purported life cycle of products.

What about the sequence of the stages? Here, too, it is impossible to make generalizations. There is no reversal of direction or skipping of stages in nature, but not so in the world of marketing, which can have a great influence on the life cycle of products. The patterns are enormously variable. One life cycle advocate attempts to put this maze of variability into some semblances of order by postulating six different life cycle curves. Another authority has developed as many as nine variants. The nine curves (noted by a broken line) and a brief description of each are shown in Exhibit 16.2. Each curve varies in a different way from the generalized pattern (noted by a solid line).

Even without defining these nine patterns of sales performance fully, they are generally recognizable. This seems to be an exercise in semantics. Certainly, it amounts to an admission that the generalized life cycle model, identified earlier in Figure 16.1, is an inadequate and misleading representation of the marketing of products.

In reviewing the literature on the product life cycle concept, not only is the life cycle issue highly variable, but the same can be said for the term *product*. The concept has been applied to product classes (cigarettes, for ex-

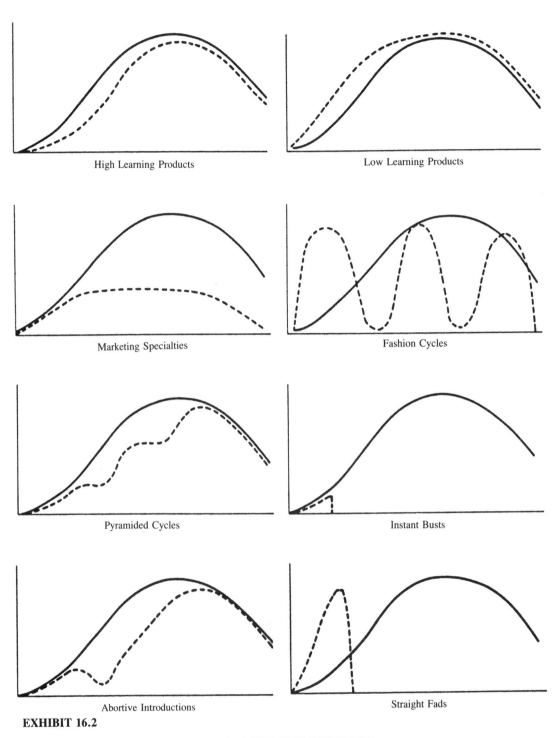

High Learning Products

Low Learning Products

Marketing Specialties

Fashion Cycles

Pyramided Cycles

Instant Busts

Abortive Introductions

Straight Fads

EXHIBIT 16.2

PRODUCT LIFE CYCLE PATTERNS

EXHIBIT 16.2 (cont'd)

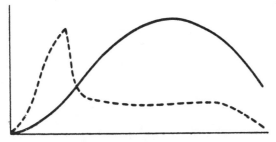

Fads with Significant Market Residual

ample), to product forms (filter cigarettes, for example), and to specific brands (Winston filter, for example). But whatever the level of aggregation—whether class, form, or brand—the utility of the life cycle concept is questionable.

Broadness of Product Class Determines Stability

Although marketers may differ in their definitions of what constitutes a class of products, it is generally recognized that the broader the classification, the more stable it is. Many product classes have enjoyed and probably will continue to enjoy a long and prosperous maturity stage, far more than human life expectancy. Examples are Scotch whisky and French perfume. Their life span can be measured not in decades but in centuries. Almost as durable are such other products as automobiles and radios, both of which were discussed earlier, soft drinks, cough remedies, face cream, and so on. In fact, broad product classes can be expected to maintain a healthy, vigorous life so long as they continue to satisfy some basic human need such as transportation, entertainment, health, nourishment, or the desire to be attractive.

What about product form? Certainly, product forms exhibit less stability than product classes. Form is what many authorities have in mind when they speak of a generalized life cycle pattern for a product. Here, too, the model is not subject to precise formulation. Presumably, there should be some guidelines indicating the movement of a product form from one stage to another. However, exceptions to generalized guidelines are not hard to find. One example is toilet tissue forms. Graph A, in Exhibit 16.3, shows the sales patterns for one-ply and two-ply toilet tissues from 1960 to 1973. The sales have been adjusted to a common base to remove such extraneous forces as population growth and inflationary pressures.

Looking at the one-ply pattern in Graph A, believers of the product life cycle concept would certainly have concluded by 1965 that one-plies were in

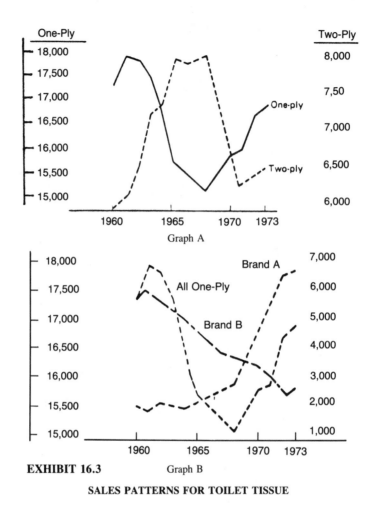

EXHIBIT 16.3   Graph B

SALES PATTERNS FOR TOILET TISSUE

a decline stage. But true to their disbelief in the product life cycle concept, Proctor and Gamble did not view the decline as inevitable. They gave strong support to a one-ply brand (Charmin®), imbued it with a two-ply image (softness), and within a few years, sales for one-plies bounced back dramatically. Graph B in the same exhibit tracks the sales performance for the two leading one-ply brands over this same period of time. Looking at the pattern for brand A and brand B, it is not difficult to figure out which one is Charmin.

Association of Life Cycle with Brands

When it comes to brands, the concept of a product life cycle is all but meaningless. Yet there are companies who guide their management of brands based on a belief in the product life cycle shown in Figure 16.1. In cases where they believe their brand is in a decline stage, they pull out all support for the brand. Then, when the brand's sales plummet further for lack of support, they nod with satisfaction about how right they were. They are, in effect, making self-fulfilling prophecies.

One of the most thorough attempts to validate the product life cycle concept was carried out a few years ago by the Marketing Science Institute. The authors examined over 100 product categories in the food, health, and personal care fields. They measured the number of observations that did not follow the theorized sequence of development, growth, maturity, saturation, and decline. They compared these actual observations with simulated sequences of equal length generated with the aid of random numbers, their purpose being to see whether the product life cycle model could explain sales behavior better than a chance model could. They concluded:

> We must register strong reservations about the general validity of the product life cycle model, even stated in its weakest, most flexible form. In tests of the model against real sales data, it has not performed uniformly well against objective standards across a wide range of frequently purchased products.

Some supporters of the product life cycle contend that its main value is not as a predictive tool. Instead, they focus on a set of marketing guidelines that are considered to be appropriate for each stage of the cycle. Exhibit 16.4 (to be discussed later) represents a summary of the competitive picture, profitability, and pricing at various stages of the product life cycle. While there may not be unanimity among advocates of the concept on the details of this summary, the basic relationship has been described repeatedly by authorities. In reviewing the guidelines for each of the elements shown, one can easily find exceptions to the recommended actions.

Camel® and Pall Mall® Cigarettes. Even in a case where a product form has had a prolonged and severe decline (such as nonfiltered cigarettes), it is questionable if a brand should follow the recommended guidelines for the decline stage. Although all the nonfilter brands have had drastic sales losses in the past 20 years, such brands as Camel and Pall Mall continue to be profitable because of their appeal to a hard-core group of committed users. Had the price been lowered as advised by the guidelines, the brands would obviously not have been as profitable.

Budweiser® Beer. This brand has been in the maturity stage for many years. According to the guidelines for this stage, its advertising weight should be moderate because most buyers are aware of the brand's characteristics. Indeed, a widely heralded experimental program undertaken by Anheuser-Busch in the 1960s demonstrated that the brand was heavily overspending in advertising—that it could halve its advertising budget without any loss in sales. In recent years, however, Budweiser has dramatically escalated its advertising weight because of the aggressive marketing of Miller Highlife® and Miller Lite®. Had it maintained the moderate spending levels recommended by the product life cycle proponents, it is highly doubtful that it could have retained its leading share position.

Considering the pitfalls of the product life cycle concept, one might well ask why it has appeal in some circles. Perhaps the answer lies, in part, with the "romance" of new products.

In the rush to enter the new products arena that characterized the 1960s, there was a tendency in some companies to ignore the old standby brands and lavish time and money on the "new babies" in the house. How comforting it is in such cases to find a rationale for doing this by citing the product life cycle concept.

But the demise of old brands is by no means inevitable. It is easy to cite many examples of old brands that have retained their vitality: Budweiser®, Coca-Cola®, Colgate®, Crisco®, Kelloggs®, and Jell-O®, to mention a few.

In contrast to these thriving old brands, the annals of business are full of records of once strong and prosperous brands that have died because of neglect and diversion of attention to new brands. A good example is the case of Ipana®. This toothpaste was marketed by a leading packaged goods company until 1968, when it was abandoned in favor of launching new brands. In 1969, two Minnesota businessmen picked up the Ipana name, developed a new formula, but left the package unchanged. With hardly any promotion, the petrified demand for Ipana turned out to be 250,000 in the first seven months of operation. In 1973, a survey conducted by Target Group Index showed that, despite poor distribution, this toothpaste was still being used by 1,520,000 adults. Considering the limited resources of the current owners, the brand would probably have been in an even stronger position had it been retained and given appropriate marketing support by its original parent company.

Prolonging the life of existing brands through effective marketing will contribute to greater stability in the cost estimating and pricing of products. So long as a product class, form, or brand satisfies consumer needs, the product should prosper for many years, as has been the case with products mentioned earlier. Coca Cola's unsuccessful attempt to change the formula of an old established drink is a case in point.

The Critical Early Growth Stage

Exhibit 16.4, referred to earlier, summarizes the impact of the five stages of the product life cycle on profitability, pricing, and the related competitive pressures. Although all five stages affect product costs and prices, the early years of growth can be the most critical. These years are critical because successful launching of new products is dependent on the degree of public acceptance. If acceptance fails, a substantial amount of development cost may never be recovered. In launching a new product, prices must be high enough to recover development costs plus some profit. However, if prices are too high, competitors who have incurred little, if any, development cost will look on this as an opportunity to undercut their prices and compete for market share.

EXHIBIT 16.4

IMPACT OF PRODUCT LIFE CYCLE ON PRODUCT COSTING AND PRICING

Stage of Product Life Cycle	Competitive Pressures	Profitability	Prices
Development	Pressure on prices not applicable to products in development stage.	Since products in development not on sale, profits not available.	Not applicable at this point.
Growth	Potential copycats in the wings ready to pounce.	Profits low in early stage of growth pending volume increase.	Prices are high to recover development costs.
Maturity	Competition builds up in this period.	Increasing competition results in price squeeze and reduced profits.	Do not hold umbrella over competition with high prices.
Saturation	Competition intensifies.	Further pressures on profits because of intensification of competition.	Competitive pressures force prices downward.
Decline	Competitors begin to drop out.	Profits decline in this period but may stabilize as more competitors drop out.	Prices may attain stability as more competitors drop out.

CASE 16.1: THE EARLY GROWTH STAGE OF TWO PRODUCTS

The first of these two products is phosphors and related chemicals. After a period of testing several formulas, the product was put into production. Product costs and profitability were monitored over a seven-year period.

The second product line consisted of three electronic components which were put into production in alternate years. The development and design period was therefore stretched out rather than being incurred at one time. The product cost and profitability were monitored over a nine-year period.

The seven-year period for the phosphors and the nine-year period for the electronic components include the early stage of the growth period.

Phosphors and Other Chemicals. Exhibit 16.5 shows the financial picture for phosphors and other chemicals. Note that this product line was in a heavy loss position for four years before costs were materially reduced. The losses were due not only to the development costs, but to equipment installation, debugging, and marketing costs. Established competitors were already producing similar products; therefore, prices were based on what the competitors charged.

In the first four years, total product cost was well above the "Gross Sales = 100%" line. The total product cost percentages for these years were 129.6% of sales, 136.3%, 123.8%, and 112.1%, respectively. The corresponding cost of sales (manufacturing cost) percentages were 129.4% of sales, 132.9%, 111.3%, and 97.4%, respectively. Year 5, with a total product cost of 98.2% of sales, and year 7, with a total product cost percentage of 100.3%, can be considered to be break-even. Year 6, with a total product cost percentage of 86.8% of sales, shows a profit of 13.2%—an indication that the critical stage of growth has been successfully dealt with.

Electronic Components. Exhibit 16.6 shows the financial overview for the three electronic components which were introduced in years 1, 3, and 5. The total product costs as a percentage of sales were 123.1% of sales, 110.3%, and 111.0%, respectively. Years 2, 4, and 6 were very close to break-even—the percentages being 103.5%, 101.0%, and 103.1% of sales, respectively. Years 7, 8, and 9 were profitable—showing profits of 6.2%, 20.1%, and 17.8% of sales, respectively—indicating that the critical stage has passed.

Some companies are overly optimistic in their expectation that a new product will be profitable in the second or third year after launching. Experience shows that a five-year period has been more realistic. For this reason, when

EXHIBIT 16.5

PHOSPHORS AND OTHER CHEMICALS

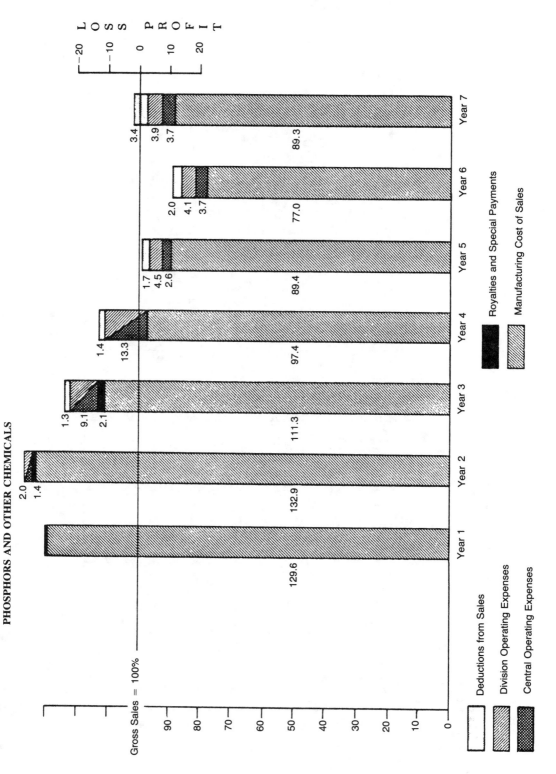

EXHIBIT 16.6

ELECTRONIC COMPONENTS

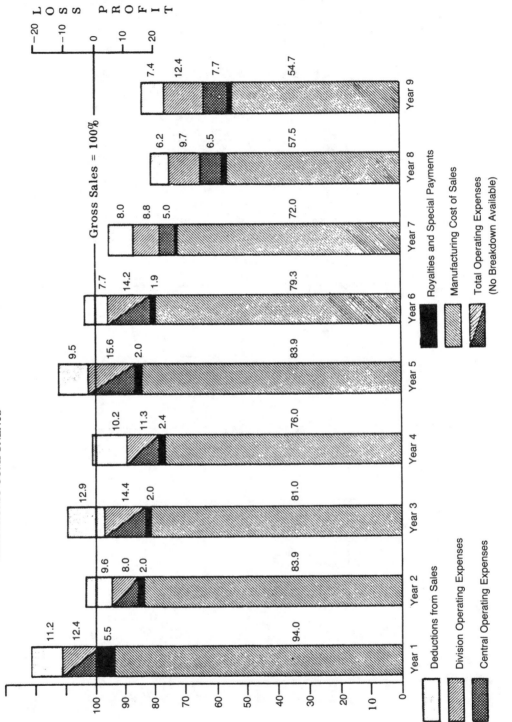

prices are established, they should allow a reasonable period for recovery of development and other startup costs.

What is a Reasonable Period? The rapid growth of technology and global competition has resulted in a substantial reduction in development and production time for many products. This is discussed in greater detail in chapter 20. See section titled Internal Factors.

CHAPTER 17

Increased Product Costs Due to JIT Are Often Overlooked

More and more customers are demanding just-in-time (JIT) delivery from their suppliers. The objective is to reduce their investment in inventory. Other advantages include reduction of storage space and material handling costs—which are automatically transferred to the supplier company.

Chapter 13 discussed several types of markup factors and their use. Case 13.2 showed how the transformer division of ElectroMag established markup factors to deal with the additional costs of making shipments under JIT. The ElectroMag management was aware of the impact of JIT on costs. This chapter deals with JIT from another perspective. It discusses the case history of a company that failed to adjust its pricing to compensate for the additional costs and the increased investment required in making JIT deliveries. In this company, and too many others, the marketing department preferred not to ''rock the boat.'' As a result, management was not aware of the large increase in product costs until a study was made. The results of the study are shown in the case which follows.

CASE 17.1: METALLAB, INC.

An analysis of 298 orders was made at Metallab, Inc. These orders were broken down into the eight product lines which accounted for the bulk of the sales. The first step was to segregate the large and small orders, as shown in

Exhibit 17.1. The tabulation shown in this exhibit indicates that 59% of the 298 orders were in the category of small orders, amounting to less than $300 but not necessarily unprofitable. While $300 was considered as the breakpoint between large and small orders, this figure would vary by company and by the nature of the product.

EXHIBIT 17.1

**BREAKDOWN OF 298 CUSTOMER ORDERS
BY LARGE AND SMALL ORDERS**

	Total Orders	Large Orders	Small Orders	Small Orders % of Total
Product line A	18	15	3	17%
Product line B	12	6	6	50
Product line C	29	10	19	66
Product line D	132	41	91	69
Product line E	22	9	13	59
Product line F	19	13	6	32
Product line G	41	13	28	68
Product line H	25	15	10	40
Total	298	122	176	59%

Further analysis of the 298 orders showed that large orders did not necessarily mean large shipments even if the entire order were fabricated at one time. This is illustrated in the analysis of the number of shipments for the large and the small orders shown in Exhibit 17.2. Note that under the large order category, 122 orders were shipped in 223 installments—a ratio of 1.8 shipments per order. The comparable ratio for small orders is 1.1 shipments per order. The ratio for all orders is 1.4 shipments per order.

Because the high ratio of 1.8 shipments per large order had the effect of almost doubling the number of shipments, the need for further analysis was indicated. Therefore, three individual orders were analyzed; one for 20,000 units selling for an average price of $62.80 per thousand units; a second for 40,000 units selling for $9.60 per 1,000 units; and a third for 14,100 units selling for $4.18 per 1,000. A breakdown of these three orders is shown in Exhibit 17.3.

Note in this exhibit that the $1,256 order—the largest of the 298 studied—contained only two shipments amounting to more than the $300 breakpoint between a large and a small order. The $384 order, which is a little above the breakpoint value of $300, required five shipments, all of which are less than $88—well below the breakpoint of $300. The $59 order required eight shipments, the highest of which had a sales value of only $22.

EXHIBIT 17.2

NUMBER OF SHIPMENTS PER ORDER FOR LARGE AND FOR SMALL ORDERS

	Large Orders			Small Orders		
	No. of Orders	No. of Shipments	Ratio of Shipments to Orders	No. of Orders	No. of Shipments	Ratio of Shipments to Orders
Product line A	15	28		3	4	
Product line B	6	9		6	7	
Product line C	10	18		19	20	
Product line D	41	76		91	107	
Product line E	9	13		13	13	
Product line F	13	21		6	6	
Product line G	13	23		28	30	
Product line H	15	35		10	11	
Total	122	223	1.8	176	198	1.1

(Large Orders over $300; Small Orders under $300)

NUMBER OF SHIPMENTS PER ORDER FOR ALL ORDERS

	No. of Orders	No. of Shipments	Ratio of Shipments to Orders
Large Orders	122	223	1.8
Small Orders	176	198	1.1
Total All Orders	298	421	1.4

EXHIBIT 17.3

**BREAKDOWN OF SHIPMENTS
FOR THREE ORDERS**

$1,256 Order—Six Shipments

	Units	Sales Value
1/20	1,200	$ 75
2/3	3,500	220
2/10	5,000	314
2/17	6,000	377
2/24	3,000	188
3/1	1,300	82
	20,000	$1,256

$384 Order—Five Shipments

	Units	Sales Value
12/20	4,000	$ 38
1/3	9,000	86
1/10	9,000	87
1/17	9,000	86
1/24	9,000	87
	40,000	$ 384

$59 Order—Eight Shipments

	Units	Sales Value
1/3	5,000	$ 22
1/10	800	3
1/17	800	3
1/24	800	3
1/31	4,900	21
2/28	800	3
3/7	800	3
3/14	200	1
	14,100	$ 59

No superior analytical skills are required to recognize that splintering of orders can be costly—if not through short runs, then through extra handling costs of the more numerous shipments. The worst offenders were found to be two sister divisions within the company. Although customers outside the company, who accounted for about half the sales, ordered according to the same type of just-in-time schedule, the dollar value of the releases was greater than those of the sister divisions.

Management recognized from this study that JIT shipments, whether made to external or internal customers, were incurring additional handling costs, storage, and paperwork in addition to requiring a larger investment in finished goods inventory. Obviously, agreement to make JIT deliveries without increasing prices is tantamount to a price reduction.

The typical salesperson who receives an order requiring frequent releases is not likely to press for a higher price. This is due partly to lack of knowledge on the part of the salesperson as to what additional costs are being incurred and partly because they do not want to risk losing the sale. Responding to management's question as to how this problem can be monitored, a recommendation was made to utilize a functional income statement in which the statement would be broken down by manufacturing and marketing.

THE FUNCTIONAL INCOME STATEMENT

The format of the external income statement intermingles manufacturing and marketing costs, making it difficult to hold the heads of these two functions accountable for their respective contribution to profits. This section describes the format of an internal income statement that establishes manufacturing and marketing as two separate businesses with their own income statements. Manufacturing sells to marketing at an agreed-on price. Manufacturing is responsible for the size of investment in raw material and work-in-process inventories as well as net fixed assets, while marketing is held responsible for the finished goods inventory and receivables. Both are charged an interest rate based on the value of the assets in their charge. The total interest charge made to each becomes the allocation to cover corporate office costs.

The use of a functional income statement minimizes the adversarial relationship that frequently develops between manufacturing and marketing, each pointing the finger at the other. When company profits decline, management becomes more confused than enlightened and must spend valuable time sorting out and evaluating the arguments advanced by both sides to determine the reasons for profit deterioration. While this adversarial relationship can never be completely eliminated, it can be somewhat diminished by establishing separate income statements wherein both functions become individual profit centers—each responsible for costs that it can control.

Developing the Functional Income Statement

Under the functional responsibility, there is a complete separation of the manufacturing and sales functions.

This permits the manufacturing executive to concentrate entirely on the manufacturing operation. It likewise permits a strong marketing executive to focus heavily on the selling effort. The relationship between the two functions would be that of seller and buyer, with the buyer having the option of purchasing from a competitor if need be. The effectiveness of both would be reflected in the individual returns on investment.

Manufacturing as the Seller. Manufacturing would sell finished products to marketing at an agreed-on price. This price, in addition to covering the cost of material, direct labor, and overhead, would include a surcharge to cover the interest on the factory investment. The items considered as factory investment would consist of net fixed assets, raw material, and work-in-process inventories. Since these items are readily available from the books of account, there should be no problem in obtaining the information. The sales figure for manufacturing would be based on the total costs of manufacturing plus the interest on investment plus the agreed-on markup on costs.

Marketing as the Buyer. The marketing income statement, in addition to showing the actual sales for the period, would base its cost of sales on the agreed-on transfer price from manufacturing adjusted by the cost of any finished goods losses and write-offs due to obsolescence. Below the cost of sales line, the statement would list the usual selling expenses, commissions, advertising, freight, warehousing costs, bad debt expense, and the like. Charges from engineering for product development would also be included on a separate line. Marketing, like manufacturing, would be charged an interest rate on its investment in finished goods inventory and receivables.

Establishing the Transfer Price. Establishing an agreed-on transfer price can present problems. It is only natural that the marketing department will exert pressure to obtain lower prices than manufacturing is willing to accept. One way to keep such problems at a minimum is to mandate that transfer prices will be set at the competitive price less selling and advertising expenses. This is logical inasmuch as the marketing department incurs the required selling and advertising expenses for sales made on the outside. Sales made between divisions of the company do not incur selling or advertising costs.

Charging Interest on Investment by Function. The rate of interest charged to manufacturing and marketing would be based on the anticipated investment for the year divided by the budgeted corporate general and administrative expenses. These would be the residual expenses after all direct charges have been made to manufacturing and marketing for specific services rendered. The aggregate of the interest charges made to both the functions would then be compared with the actual corporate expenses incurred. This comparison would serve as a measure of budget attainment by the general and administrative function.

Format of the Functional Income Statement

The two income statements are placed side by side as shown in the first two columns of Exhibit 17.4. "Intracompany Elimination," the third column, eliminates the duplication of figures in the first two columns. The items eliminated are the manufacturing net sales, cost of sales, and resulting profit. The net sales shown for manufacturing consist of the material, direct labor, and overhead cost, while the profit that is eliminated is the difference between the two.

Over- or Underabsorption of Overhead. Had there been sufficient production volume to absorb all the overhead incurred, the manufacturing income column

EXHIBIT 17.4

FUNCTIONAL INCOME STATEMENT

	Manu- facturing	Marketing	Intra- company Elimination	Combined Results
Gross Sales	$	2,000,000		2,000,000
Less Returns		60,000		60,000
Net Sales	1,500,000	1,940,000	1,500,000	1,940,000
Cost of Sales				
Material	940,000	960,000	940,000	960,000
Direct Labor	100,000	120,000	100,000	120,000
Overhead	360,000	370,000	360,000	370,000
Total Cost of Sales	1,400,000	1,450,000	1,400,000	1,450,000
Overhead Incurred	360,000			360,000
Overhead Absorbed	300,000			300,000
Overhead (Over) or Underabsorbed	60,000			60,000
Distribution Costs				
Selling Expenses		90,000		90,000
Advertising Expenses		10,000		10,000
Commissions		50,000		50,000
Freight		20,000		20,000
Warehousing		10,000		10,000
Bad Debts		5,000		5,000
Total Distribution Costs		185,000		185,000
Product Development		120,000		120,000
Operating Profit	40,000	185,000	100,000	125,000
Interest on Investment	50,000	80,000		130,000
Company Profit or (Loss)	$ (10,000)	105,000	100,000	(5,000)

would have shown a $50,000 profit rather than a $10,000 loss. The combined results would have shown a $55,000 profit rather than a $5,000 loss. Over- or underabsorption of overhead is usually correlatable with the level of order intake and is normally considered to be controllable by marketing. However, the $60,000 underabsorption is shown in manufacturing because it relates directly to the manufacturing overhead—and is carried over to the "Combined Results" column. It is analyzed to determine the cause of the shortfall in production volume. Order intake would be reviewed first to ascertain if there was a decline in the incoming orders. If the order receipts are found to be at the budgeted level, then factory efficiency would be suspect. However, finding the right direction in which to point the finger is not easy. If marketing could prove that its volume of order intake met the budgeted dollar volume, manufacturing could counter by pointing out that the orders contained many short runs which consumed more than the normal amount of setup time—thus reducing machine utilization. Such differences of opinion, though sometimes difficult to resolve to the complete satisfaction of one side or the other, usually have a salutory effect.

THE BUDGETING PROCESS

In making up the budget for the coming year, manufacturing, marketing, and the corporate office should initially prepare annual figures only. Working with annual figures at first eliminates the time-consuming monthly detail. Once the annual figures have been approved, the month-by-month breakdown can be made.

Sale Projections: The Starting Point

Each product manager in marketing should prepare as realistic an estimate of anticipated sales as possible. The need for realism is important because an overoptimistic forecast bears the penalty of a corresponding amount of underabsorbed overhead if the sales fall below the amount that was forecasted. Overoptimism could also mean an excessive inventory of finished products. This would result in a higher interest charge because the investment in inventory would be higher. It could also mean later obsolescence of some of the inventory as well as higher warehousing costs. On the other hand, too low an estimate would cause the overhead rates used for calculating the transfer prices to be too high.

The Manufacturing Budget

When the approved sales forecast is received by manufacturing, it is adjusted by the amount of inventory on hand to produce a production schedule. From this schedule, the material control department can determine the material requirements, and manufacturing engineering can project the required production hours.

Breaking Down the Material and Direct Labor by Month. Since material must be ordered to meet customer shipping dates, this provides the basis for breaking down the material requirements by months. The direct labor requirements would likewise be linked to the production schedule. Production hours would be denominated in terms of direct labor if the operation is labor paced, or in machine hours if machine paced.

Budgeting the Overhead by Month. Flexible budgets provide a more meaningful measure of overhead requirements than conventional budgets. Exhibit 17.5 shows the flexible budget formula for the manufacturing operation, in which each overhead expense is broken down into its fixed and variable segments, as was discussed in chapter 4. Each variable cost is then divided by the related production hours to arrive at a variable cost per production hour. The production hours used to make this calculation were based on the production schedule requirements for the year divided by 12 months. The budget formula in this exhibit was used to make the calculations shown in the columnar budget for various activity levels in Exhibit 17.6. The budget formula used to arrive at these figures as follows for the total budgeted costs at the 35,970 production hour level.

$$35,970 \text{ hours} \times \$5,187 \text{ per hour} = \$186,624$$

$186,624 (total variable allowance)
$225,747 (total fixed cost)
$412,371 (total overhead allowance)

The same type of calculation would be made for each month's actual level of activity, showing the budgeted overhead expenses compared with the actual expenses incurred—not only for the current month but for the year-to-date as well. Material and direct labor costs would be controlled by standard or estimated costs that are extended by the production hours and compared with the actual costs.

EXHIBIT 17.5

MANUFACTURING FLEXIBLE BUDGET FORMULA

	Total Monthly Fixed and Variable	Total Fixed Cost	Total Variable Cost	Variable Cost per Prod'n. Hour*
Production Departments				
Fabrication	$ 14,395	11,905	2,490	.069
Assembly	38,024	25,418	12,606	.350
Service Departments				
Manufacturing Administration	20,640	20,640	—	—
Industrial Relations	14,666	10,994	3,672	.102
Cost Accounting	16,024	11,214	4,810	.134
Material Control	35,308	16,882	18,426	.512
Manufacturing Engineering	18,469	12,064	6,405	.178
Quality Assurance	29,876	20,174	9,702	.270
Purchasing	10,864	6,264	4,600	.128
Maintenance	48,344	29,479	18,865	.524
Receiving and Incoming Inspection	24,987	10,643	14,344	.399
Total Production & Service Dept. Payroll	$271,597	175,677	95,920	2.666
Nonpayroll Expenses				
Disability Payments	920	600	320	.009
Payroll Taxes	8,510	5,550	2,960	.082
Compensation Insurance	506	330	176	.005
Employee Benefits	3,588	2,340	1,248	.035
Factory Supplies	200	200	—	—
Office Supplies and Forms	7,500	7,500	—	—
Other Purchased Supplies	500	500	—	—
Postage	50	50	—	—
Depreciation	1,500	1,500	—	—
Freight-in	68,000	—	68,000	1.890
Dues and Subscriptions	150	150	—	—
Purchased Services	150	150	—	—
Fire Insurance	1,000	1,000	—	—
Travel	18,200	10,200	8,000	.222
Telephone	30,000	20,000	10,000	.278
Total Nonpayroll Expenses	$140,774	50,070	90,704	2.521
Total Manufacturing Overhead	$412,371	225,747	186,624	5.187

* Total variable cost divided by 35,970 budgeted production hours.

The Marketing Budget

The fixed and variable costs in marketing would be identified by cost behavior, as was done for manufacturing. The base for denominating the variable costs

EXHIBIT 17.6

MANUFACTURING OVERHEAD

Monthly Budget Allowance for Various Activity Levels

Production Hours Per Month	31,970	32,970	33,970	34,970	35,970	36,970	37,970	38,970	39,970
Production Departments:									
Fabrication	$ 14,119	14,188	14,257	14,326	14,395	14,464	14,533	14,602	14,671
Assembly	36,624	36,974	37,324	37,674	38,024	38,374	38,724	39,074	39,424
Service Departments:									
Manufacturing Administration	20,640	20,640	20,640	20,640	20,640	20,640	20,640	20,640	20,640
Industrial Relations	14,258	14,360	14,462	14,564	14,666	14,768	14,870	14,972	15,074
Cost Accounting	15,488	15,622	15,756	15,890	16,024	16,158	16,292	16,426	16,560
Material Control	33,260	33,772	34,284	34,796	35,308	35,820	36,332	36,844	37,356
Manufacturing Engineering	17,757	17,935	18,113	18,291	18,469	18,647	18,825	19,003	19,181
Quality Assurance	28,796	29,066	29,336	29,606	29,876	30,146	30,416	30,686	30,956
Purchasing	10,352	10,480	10,608	10,736	10,864	10,992	11,120	11,248	11,376
Maintenance	46,248	46,772	47,296	47,820	48,344	48,868	49,392	49,916	50,440
Receiving and Incoming Inspection	23,391	23,790	24,189	24,588	24,987	25,386	25,785	26,184	26,583
Total Production & Service Payroll	$260,933	263,599	266,265	268,931	271,597	274,263	276,929	279,595	282,261
Nonpayroll Expenses:									
Disability Payments	884	893	902	911	920	929	938	947	956
Payroll Taxes	8,182	8,264	8,346	8,428	8,510	8,592	8,674	8,756	8,838
Compensation Insurance	486	491	496	501	506	511	516	521	526
Employee Benefits	3,448	3,483	3,518	3,553	3,588	3,623	3,658	3,693	3,728
Factory Supplies	200	200	200	200	200	200	200	200	200
Office Supplies and Forms	1,500	1,500	1,500	1,500	1,500	1,500	1,500	1,500	1,500
Other Purchased Supplies	500	500	500	500	500	500	500	500	500
Postage	50	50	50	50	50	50	50	50	50
Depreciation	7,500	7,500	7,500	7,500	7,500	7,500	7,500	7,500	7,500
Freight-in	60,440	62,330	64,220	66,110	68,000	69,890	71,780	73,670	75,560
Dues and Subscriptions	150	150	150	150	150	150	150	150	150
Purchased Services	150	150	150	150	150	150	150	150	150
Fire Insurance	1,000	1,000	1,000	1,000	1,000	1,000	1,000	1,000	1,000
Travel	17,312	17,534	17,756	17,978	18,200	18,422	18,644	18,866	19,088
Telephone	28,888	29,166	29,444	29,722	30,000	30,278	30,556	30,834	31,112
Total Nonpayroll Expenses	$130,690	133,211	135,732	138,253	140,774	143,295	145,816	148,337	150,858
Total Manufacturing Overhead	$391,623	396,810	401,997	407,184	412,371	417,558	422,745	427,932	433,119

would not be production hours but either sales, cost of sales, or conversion costs.

Sales. If the products are fairly homogeneous, with material, direct labor, overhead, and markup bearing about the same percentage of sales for all products, the variable costs can be determined as a percentage of sales dollars.

Cost of Sales. Use of cost of sales will eliminate any inaccuracies because of wide variations in the markup factors used for establishing the prices of the various products.

Conversion Costs. The advantage of conversion costs (direct labor plus overhead) over sales and cost of sales is that distortions due to large variations in the material content and in the markup factors are avoided.

General and Administrative Expenses. These residual corporate headquarters expenses, after chargeouts for specific services rendered to manufacturing and marketing, are usually highly fixed. For this reason, flexible budgets will show a lower variability in such costs.

ADVANTAGES OF THE FUNCTIONAL INCOME STATEMENT

The functional income statement is a more sophisticated tool than the conventional statement used for outside reporting. The following are some of the advantages:

1. The size of the finished goods inventory becomes the responsibility of the marketing function. This is logical, since marketing is responsible for the forecasts that generate the production of finished products.

2. Using total assets as the distribution base for corporate expenses provides a more stable basis for allocating general and administrative expenses in the form of an interest rate.

3. Since both manufacturing and marketing are charged an interest rate based on the size of their respective investments, this is a more compelling reason for each to monitor closely the size of the individual investments and the profit based on the return on investment.

GUIDELINES FOR USING THE FUNCTIONAL INCOME STATEMENT[1]

Although the functional statement measures the individual profit contribution of both manufacturing and marketing, it does not entirely eliminate disagree-

[1] See also Thomas S. Dudick, *Cost Controls for Industry,* 2nd edition, Prentice Hall, 1976.

ments between the two. Management must still look behind the figures for answers to questions such as the following:

1. Are some production runs too short to be produced economically? If so, transfer prices to marketing should include individual setup charges for such orders.
2. Are orders being accepted with incomplete specifications and only sketchy drawings when drawings are critical? This occurs with surprising frequency. If marketing accepts orders with incomplete specifications, these should be routed through product development prior to acceptance by manufacturing. The product development group's costs should be charged to the marketing income statement.
3. Does the manufacturing manager have the opportunity to review customer orders for new products? Selling prices are sometimes determined on the basis that the product being quoted is like another product with minor differences in manufacturing cost. Frequently, the "minor" differences result in major differences in manufacturing cost.
4. Does marketing reduce prices arbitrarily to obtain a larger share of the market? If so, the reduced profit should be reflected in the marketing income statement unless manufacturing agrees, in the interest of increasing its own production volume, to reduce the transfer price.

The procedures outlined here can be applied to almost any corporate entity making and marketing a commercial product or performing a service. The key to success in any type of control is management follow-up. Inasmuch as the income statement is the focal point of control, the degree to which profit responsibility can be assigned by function determines the degree of follow-up that is available to management.

CHAPTER 18

Various Formats for Estimating Product Costs

Chapter 6 explained the difference between customized and standardized products, both of which utilized a different format for product cost estimating. Because customized products are manufactured to specifications developed by the customer, each order is unique and could therefore result in many different formats for cost estimating. This is in contrast to standardized products, whose prices are often contained in published price lists. However, this does not rule out variations in product cost estimating formats, as will be shown in this chapter.

A major difference between customized and standardized products is cost classification. As was pointed out in the earlier chapters, many costs that are treated as indirect for standard products are categorized as direct charges in customized orders. These differences were discussed at length in chapters 7 and 8. Since cost estimating for customized products has been covered in some depth, this chapter will concentrate more heavily on standardized products, the pricing of which is generally more highly competitive than for customized products.

COST ESTIMATING IN TRANSITION

Chapter 1, in discussing product cost deficiencies, pointed out that manufacturing operations in some companies are highly labor paced and can, in many cases, be expected to remain so for the foreseeable future.

This was the case with one of the two plants in the JVK division of a *Fortune* 500 company. One of the plants manufactures the parts which are assembled into subassemblies and finished products in a second plant. This plant, which is highly labor paced, is located in a semirural area in which labor rates are relatively low—low enough to more than offset shipping and handling costs between the two locations.

As time went on, the volume of some of the products increased sufficiently to warrant some automation. However, product cost estimating procedures remained unchanged; the cost estimator continued to use a single plantwide overhead rate based on direct labor. When automation was introduced for the video camera subassemblies, labor costs were greatly reduced because most of the operations were transferred to automatic and semiautomatic equipment. Since direct labor remained the allocation base for overhead, product costs were greatly understated—leading the sales manager to propose a fairly large price reduction.

The general manager of the division, in reviewing the proposed reduction in price, questioned the validity of the costs on which the reduced price was based. In response to the general manager's request, a comparative study was made of the costs prior to automating and after automation. Since the material remained essentially the same, only conversion costs were considered in the study.

Conversion Costs Prior to Automation

A summary of the costs prior to automation is shown in Exhibit 18.1. The total conversion cost amounted to $37.66. This was made up of 2.65 direct labor hours at an hourly rate of $7.60, totaling $20.14. The plantwide overhead rate of 87% of direct labor was applied to the $20.14 to arrive at a total overhead cost of $17.52. This seemingly low overhead rate was due to the large labor base and relatively low overhead costs because the operations consisted of benchwork using simple tools.

EXHIBIT 18.1

VIDEO CAMERA SUBASSEMBLY PRIOR TO AUTOMATION

	Hours	Rate	Cost
Direct Labor	2.65	$7.60	$20.14
Overhead	87% of Labor		17.52
Conversion Cost			$37.66

Conversion Costs After Automation

Exhibit 18.2 shows that automation reduced direct labor by two-thirds, from $20.14 to $6.84. The labor-related overhead consists of such items as unemployment insurance, vacation and holiday pay, hospitalization, and cafeteria subsidization. The overhead related to automatic and semiautomatic equipment, which was based on machine hours, totalled $23.38, one-third higher than the $17.52 prior to automation. Although the overhead cost increased by $5.86 ($23.38 − $17.52), this increase was more than offset by the reduced direct labor cost of $13.30 ($20.14 minus $6.84). Typically, in cost reductions achieved through automation, it can be expected that savings in labor will be partly offset by higher overhead, as was the case for this product.

EXHIBIT 18.2

VIDEO CAMERA SUBASSEMBLY
AFTER AUTOMATION

	Hours	Rate	Cost
Direct Labor	.90	$ 7.60	$ 6.84
Overhead			
Labor-related	.90	2.50	2.25
Auto Assembly	.77	14.50	11.17
Semiautomatic	1.88	5.30	9.96
Conversion Cost			$30.22

Manufacture of the Tubular Assembly

Exhibits 11.7 and 11.8 in chapter 11 show the breakdown of material, direct labor, and overhead by department (production cost center). The first of these two exhibits accumulates total material, direct labor, and overhead for the first department and transfers the total of the three elements to the next department as material. The next department adds its own material plus direct labor and overhead to the material received from the preceding department and transfers the total to the next department as material cost, and so on. The second of these exhibits retains the purity of each of the three elements throughout the entire manufacturing process.

Exhibit 18.3 in this chapter utilizes both methods in developing the total product cost. Note in the first group of operations, for example, that the 6.5 pounds of resin plus a 5% loss allowance shows a standard usage of 6.83 pounds. At a rate of $.134 per pound, the standard material cost for tubing comes to $.92. The extrusion and end cutting labor totals $1.08, while the

EXHIBIT 18.3

PRODUCT COST ESTIMATE FOR TUBULAR ASSEMBLY

Material/Operation	Qty.	% Loss	Usage	Unit	Standard Material		Standard Labor		Standard Overhead		Total Cost
					Rate	Cost	Rate	Cost	Rate	Cost	
#876 Resin	6.5	5	6.83	lb.	.134	.92					.92
Extrusion			.2271	hr.			4.36	.49	11.10	2.52	2.52
Extruder Process			.1135	hr.					6.32	.72	1.21
End Cutting			.2271	hr.			2.58	.59	6.32	1.44	2.03
						.92		1.08		4.68	6.68
Tubing	1,000	2	1,020	M	6.68	6.81					6.81
Stretch & Center Cut			.2000	hr.			2.58	.52	6.32	1.26	1.78
						6.81		.52		1.26	8.59
Tubing	1,000	2	1,020	M	8.59	8.76					8.76
Print			.1429	hr.			3.36	.48	6.32	.90	1.38
						8.76		.48		.90	10.14
Tubing	1,000	4	1,040	M	10.14	10.55					10.55
Plug			.1912	hr.			2.58	.49	6.32	1.21	1.70
						10.55		.49		1.21	12.25
Tubing	1,000	1	1,010	M	12.25	12.37					12.37
Carton	1	5	1.05	ea.	.15	.16					.16
Liner	1	5	1.05	ea.	.01	.01					.01
Bag	40	5	37	ea.	.02	.74					.74
Misc. Packaging		5				.03					.03
Bag, Seal, & Pack			.2999	hr.			2.58	.77	6.32	1.90	2.67
Make & Seal Carton			.0271	hr.			2.58	.10	6.32	.23	.33
						13.31		.87		2.13	16.31
To Finished Goods	1,000	1	1,010	M	16.31	16.47					16.47
Standard Cost by Element						1.86		3.44		10.18	
Scrap by Element						.73		.07		.19	
Actual Product Cost by Element						2.59		3.51		10.37	16.47

related overhead amounts to $4.68. The total of the three elements aggregates $6.68. This total is transferred to the stretch and center cut operation as material. Since this operation provides for a 2% loss, meaning that 1,020 units are needed to produce 1,000 good units, the $6.68 is factored upward to $6.81 ($6.68 + 2% = $6.81). The total accumulated material, direct labor, and overhead in the stretch and center cut operation, amounting to $8.59, becomes the starting material cost in the tubing/print cost center.

The transfer of the cumulative material, direct labor, and overhead costs continues on until the final cost center operation, in which the total manufacturing cost amounts to $16.31. This becomes the cost of the finished product transferred to finished goods inventory. Since losses can occur while products are in storage, a 1% allowance for such losses is provided. Thus, the $16.31 transfer price becomes $16.47 after the provision for losses.

The bottom three lines of the exhibit summarize the three cost elements as they were incurred individually throughout the manufacturing process. The total pure material cost, for example, was determined by adding the $.92 for resin to the carton, liner, bag, and miscellaneous packaging material to arrive at the total pure material cost of $1.86. To the $1.86 pure material cost was added the $.73 for scrap losses that were provided for in the various operations. The same was done for direct labor and overhead.

Some companies favor the cumulative transfer valuation method because they sell products at various stages of completion. Other companies favor the pure method of costing inventories because revaluing inventories is easier when the three cost elements are dealt with individually. This company, which has a computerized cost system, prefers to use both methods, as illustrated in the exhibit.

Manufacture of Cosmetic Cases

Plastic cosmetic cases are manufactured by another plant in the same division that makes tubular assemblies discussed in the preceding section. In the tubular assembly operations, the resin was extruded into tubing which was stretched and cut, printed, plugged, and then packaged.

The cosmetic case (see Exhibit 18.4) consists of two parts, a top and bottom, each of which were molded separately, assembled, and then packed. Direct labor costs for making the top and the bottom are included in the burden rate, which is applied on machine hours.

As was the case with tubular assemblies, the total cost of the top, $7.60 per 1,000, is transferred to assembly at a cost of $7.90 after providing for a 4% loss. The same applies to the $8.12 per 1,000 cost of manufacturing the

EXHIBIT 18.4

STANDARD PRODUCT COST SHEET
PRODUCT: PLASTIC COSMETIC CASES

EFFECTIVE JAN. 1, XX

Quantity - 1000
(500 per case)

STANDARD PRODUCT COST SHEET

MATERIALS OR OPERATION DESCRIPTION	CODE NUMBER	QUANTITY SPECIFIED	% WASTE	STANDARD	UNIT OF MEASURE	MATERIAL RATE	MATERIAL COST	LABOR RATE	LABOR COST	BURDEN RATE	BURDEN COST	TOTAL COST
TOP Plastic	771	20.0	5	21.0000	lb.	.134	2.81					2.81
Molding	38			.3768	hr.					12.70	4.79	4.79
							2.81				4.79	7.60
BOTTOM Plastic	771	21.0	5	22.0500	lb.	.134	2.95					2.95
Molding	38			.4072	hr.					12.70	5.17	5.17
							2.95				5.17	8.12
ISSUE TO ASSEMBLY FLOOR												
Molded Plastic Top	151	1,000	4	1,040	M	7.600	7.90					7.90
Molded Plastic Bottom	152	1,000	4	1,040	M	8.120	8.44					8.44
Carton (holds 500)	6	2	5	2.1000	Ea.	.268	.56					.56
Bag	18	50	5	52.5000	Ea.	.031	1.63					1.63
Crate	6	2	5	2.1000	Ea.	.162	.34					.34
Assemble & Pack	64			1.0000	Hr.			2.58	2.58	6.32	6.32	8.90
							18.87		2.58		6.32	27.77
TRANSFER VALUE TO FINISHED GOODS	2131	1,000	1	1,010	M	27.77	28.06					28.06
							28.06					28.06
TOTAL COST BY ELEMENT							8.61		2.61		16.84	28.06

	$ PER CASE	%
SALES PRICE	17.35	100.0
STANDARD COST	14.03	80.8
GROSS PROFIT	3.32	19.2

bottom plate, which is also transferred to assembly. A similar 4% provision for loss is added—increasing the cost to $8.44. The $27.77 total manufacturing cost is increased by a 1% allowance, thus increasing the finished goods valuation to $28.06 per 1,000 units.

The product costing format for this product is very similar to the format used for the tubular assembly except in one respect: This format includes provision for showing the selling price, standard cost, and profit, which appear in the lower right-hand corner of the product cost estimate. Including this type of information is a desirable practice because it continually focuses on figures which are critical to the well-being of the company.

SLOTTING NEW PRODUCT COSTS INTO A FAMILY

When a company adds a new product to the line, it is not always necessary to develop a completely new product cost from the ground up. In many cases, it is possible to make cost adjustments to existing products in determining the cost of another product in the same family.

Exhibit 18.5, showing the cost of a seven-contact electrical socket of the type used for plugging in a cathode-ray tube, will be used as a base for costing a similar five-contact socket. This section will first develop the cost of the seven-contact socket, whose overall manufacturing requirements are shown in the uppermost section of the exhibit. The items referred to are as follows:

Resin required: 5.5 pounds
Resin cost: $.44 per pound
Curing cycle: 90 seconds
Cavities in mold: 30.

The Molding Operation

Under the material category, the number of pounds of resin per 1,000 sockets are multiplied by the cost per pound to arrive at the total material cost required to mold the body (insulator). Determination of the labor and overhead cost for the molding operation is based on the cycle time, which for this product is 90 seconds or 40 cycles per hour (60 minutes $\div$ $1\frac{1}{2}$ minutes $= 40$). Forty cycles multiplied by 30 cavities in the mold equals 1,200 socket bodies molded per hour. The 1,200 socket bodies at a press rate of $16.22 per hour equals $13.52 per 1,000 ($16.22 $\times$ 83.33%). The total material cost plus the molding operation, factored by a 2% allowance for spoilage, equals $16.26 per 1,000.

EXHIBIT 18.5

MANUFACTURING COST
OF SEVEN-CONTACT MOLDED SOCKET
WITH SADDLE

Material Required	5.5#
Material Cost	$.44 per pound
Curing Cycle	90 seconds
Number of Cavities	30

Cost of Molded Body

	Cost per 1.000
Material	
5.5#Powder © $.44	$ 2.42
Labor & Overhead	
Cycle Time of 90 Sec. = 40 Cycles/Hr.	
40 Cycles × 30 Cavities =	
1,200 Socket Bodies per Hour	
1,200 Socket Bodies © Press Rate of $16.22/Hr.	13.52
Other	
2% Allowance for Spoilage	.32
Total Cost per 1,000 Socket Bodies	$16.26

Cost of the Assembled Socket

	Cost per 1,000
Material	
1 Molded Body	$16.26
1 Saddle	3.00
7 Contacts	14.00
Labor & Overhead	
2,000 Assembled per Hour © 10.71/Hr.	5.35
Other	
1% Allowance for Spoilage	.39
Total Cost per 1,000 Completed Sockets	$39.00

The Assembly Operation

Material costs in the assembly operation include the $16.26 per 1,000 cost of the molded bodies, saddles $3.00, and contacts at $2.00. The labor and overhead costs for the assembly operation are based on an assembly production rate of 2,000 per hour costed at $10.71 per hour, or a total cost of $5.35 per 1,000. A 1% allowance for spoilage added to the material and conversion costs aggregates a total of $39.00 per 1,000 finished sockets.

Using the foregoing costs, the next section will illustrate how the product cost of a five-contact molded body without a saddle can be calculated by making plus-and-minus adjustments.

PRODUCT COSTING THROUGH PLUS-AND-MINUS ADJUSTING

In connection with the preceding example of the seven-contact molded socket, the company planned to produce a five-contact socket using the same molded body even though it was formed with openings to accomodate seven contacts. The plus-and-minus adjustments necessary to accomplish this are shown in Exhibit 18.6.

Column 1 lists the total costs as shown in the previous exhibit for the seven-contact version. Column 2 subtracts out the cost of two of the contacts and the saddle. It also makes an adjustment for the reduced assembly cost and the proportionate spoilage allowance. The total reduced cost amounts to $7.72. Column 3 adds cost increases due to supplier price increases. These add up to

EXHIBIT 18.6

ADJUSTING THE COST OF A SEVEN-CONTACT SOCKET
TO DETERMINE THE COST OF A FIVE-CONTACT SOCKET

	Col. 1 *Estimated* *Cost of* *Seven-Contact* *Molded Socket*	*Col. 2* *Adjustment* *to Arrive at* *Cost of* *Five-Contact* *Molded Socket* *W/O Saddle*	*Col. 3* *Adjustments* *for Price* *Changes*	*Col. 4* *Total* *Estimated* *Cost of* *Five-Contact* *Socket W/O* *Saddle*
Components				
Material	$ 2.42	$ 0	$ .12	$ 2.54
Processing	13.52	0	0	13.52
Spoilage Allowance	.32	0	0	.32
	$16.26	$ 0	$ .12	$16.38
Assembly Costs *Plus Purchased* *Components*				
Purchased Contacts	14.00	(4.00)	.50	10.50
Purchased Saddle	3.00	(3.00)	0	0
Assembly Operation	5.35	(.62)	0	4.73
Spoilage in Assembly	.39	(.10)	.02	.31
	22.74	(7.72)	.52	15.54
Manufacturing Cost	$39.00	$(7.72)	$ .64	$31.92
Cumulative Cost	$39.00	$31.28	$31.92	$31.92

$.64 per 1,000 units. Column 4 shows the net result, which amounts to $31.92 for the five-contact sockets.

This method ensures consistency in costing and pricing because the new product added to the family will be uniformly costed and priced with other members of the family. At the same time, it will call attention to any updating required to the base product from which cost data is being extracted.

A Matrix Approach to Slotting New Products into the Family

Exhibit 18.7 illustrates how three new products were slotted into an existing family of four similar products. The three new types, 43-2424, 43-2425, and 45-2507, are variations of the existing types for which product cost estimates were required.

The costs of the four preexisting types were based on optimum volume and optimum efficiencies. Management therefore felt that they represented costs that are competitive. The advantage of this method is that it provides a matrix approach in which the various material items can be readily evaluated. The top plates, bottom plates, contacts eyelets, and total material costs can be readily compared. The same applies to the assembly costs, spoilage allowances, and total manufacturing cost. (Chapter 19 will illustrate how prices were developed through a similar matrix approach.)

HOW SIMILARITIES AND DISSIMILARITIES IN COST ELEMENTS AFFECT PRODUCT COSTING

In the preceding examples, both the material content and conversion costs differed from one product to another. Often, one will find that the material content will be the same for a number of products in a family line of products but conversion costs will differ.

Figure 18.1 shows drawings of two tire valve stems in which the material content is different because one stem is longer than the other. The conversion cost is the same, however, because setup time and rate of production is the same.

The following example shows the range of difference in the material costs of two tire valve stems in which conversion costs are exactly the same:

Product Number	Conversion Cost/M	Material Cost/M	Total Cost per/M
6342	$38.97	107.37	146.34
	27%	73%	100%
9764	38.97	18.78	57.75
	67%	33%	100%

EXHIBIT 18.7

ELECTRONIC COMPONENTS
COST MATRIX FOR PRICING

Material	Two Contacts		Three Contacts		Four Contacts		Five Contacts
	42-2511	42-2440	43-2424	43-2425	44-2467	44-2447	45-2507
Top Plate							
12-2524 1/32 XP	3.60						
12-2466 1/16 XP		3.74					
12-2448 1/16 XP			5.62				
12-2460 1/32 XP				5.62			
12-2440 1/32 XP					7.50		
12-2423 1/32 XP						7.50	
12-2412 1/32 XP							9.37
Bottom Plate							
13-2524 1/16 XP	4.00						
13-2466 3/64 XP		4.24					
13-2448 3/64 XP			6.37				
13-2460 3/64 XP				6.37			
13-2440 3/64 XP					8.50		
13-2423 3/64 XP						8.50	
13-2412 3/64 XP							10.62
Contacts							
10-431	2.00						
10-562		2.00					
10-567			3.00	3.00			
10-632					4.00	4.00	
10-636							5.00
Eyelets							
46	.60	.60	.60	.60			
48					.70	.70	.70
Total Component Cost	$10.20	$10.58	$15.59	$15.59	$20.70	$20.70	$25.69
Assembly Labor and Overhead	2.00	2.00	2.20	2.20	2.40	2.40	2.40
Spoilage Allowance	.24	.25	.36	.36	.46	.46	.56
Total Cost	$12.44	$12.83	$18.15	$18.15	$23.56	$23.56	$28.65

TWO TIRE VALVE STEMS

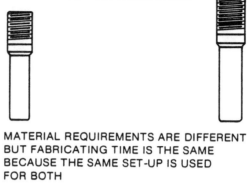

MATERIAL REQUIREMENTS ARE DIFFERENT
BUT FABRICATING TIME IS THE SAME
BECAUSE THE SAME SET-UP IS USED
FOR BOTH

FIGURE 18.1 Similarity and dissimilarity in two products.

Although the dollar cost of conversion is exactly the same for both products, the percentage conversion cost ranges from 27% of the total cost of product 6342 to 67% of the total cost for product 9764. The reverse is true for material costs, in which the percentage of total cost is 73% for the first product and 33% for the second. Similar variations would occur in products in which conversion costs vary and material costs remain the same.

Impact on Product Costing

The wide variations just cited can distort pricing if the markup factor is based on the single total manufacturing cost. This is shown in Exhibit 18.8 using the markup percentages discussed in chapter 13. Exhibit 13.10 showed the following markup factors based on factory investment as it relates to (a) material—20.3%; (b) conversion cost—67.2%; and (c) total manufacturing cost—47.5%.

It is obvious from the prices shown in Exhibit 18.8 that products with wide variations in material and conversion costs will be distorted when a single markup factor is used. Note that the price for product 6342 is understated and product 9764 overstated when the single markup factor is used. The markup percentages used in this illustrative example are not necessarily the correct ones, but they serve to illustrate the point.

CASE 18.1: PRODUCT COSTING OF JEWELRY

Midwest Jewelry Company is looked on as one of the leaders in the Midwest. Prices were determined from a total manufacturing cost base to which

EXHIBIT 18.8

SINGLE MARKUP FACTOR
47.5% OF TOTAL PRODUCT COST

	Product 6342	Product 9764
Conversion Cost	$ 38.97	38.97
Material Cost	107.37	18.78
Total Product Cost	146.34	57.75
Markup @ 47.5%	69.51	27.43
Price	$215.85	85.18

INDIVIDUAL MARKUP FACTORS
FOR MATERIAL AND CONVERSION COST

	Product 6342	Product 9764
Conversion Cost	$ 38.97	38.97
Material Cost	107.37	18.78
Total Product Cost	$146.34	57.75
Markup		
Material @ 20.3%	21.80	3.81
Conversion @ 67.2%	26.19	26.19
Total Markup	47.99	30.00
Price	$194.33	$87.75

a markup factor was applied to arrive at the selling price. The marketplace does, of course, play some part in influencing deviations from prices so determined.

The manufacturing cost base to which the markup factor is applied contains the following:

· materials which range from gold at approximately $370 per ounce to silver at $6.50 per ounce;

· internal direct labor and purchased services; and

· low overhead costs because in-house operations are labor paced and inexpensive tools are used.

A markup factor of 115% was being applied to prime cost to cover both overhead and profit. Although the management had intended that the 115% applied to prime cost would result in a 15% profit, the actual realized profit was slightly above 4%.

Probable Reasons for Reduced Profits

Use of the 115% markup factor was highly suspect. Additionally, the mix of products sold was quite different than the desired mix. Tests indicated that some products were over-costed and therefore overpriced in relation to competitive prices. Others were undercosted and therefore underpriced. As a result, the company was losing sales on items that were overpriced and was increasing its share of market on items that were underpriced. It was obvious that changes in arriving at the product cost base and markup factor were needed. Accordingly, the following more detailed review was made of the manufacturing cost elements:

1. *Material:* The range of material costs for this product line was found to be much greater than the range shown in any of the illustrative examples previously discussed. Gold at $370 per ounce, for example, is 57 times as expensive as silver.

2. *Direct labor:* What is normally considered direct labor was being combined with purchased services. The inside labor consisted of bench-type operations. Plating and punch press work, which was done outside, accounted for one-third of the total labor category and was considered part of the base for allocating overhead.

3. *Overhead:* Since the more expensive manufacturing operations such as plating and press work were being subcontracted, these purchased services were actually purchased components that should have been treated as material rather than direct labor.

On completion of the reclassification of product cost elements, it became obvious that material was the predominant cost element and that the precious metal content dictated a return on investment approach in which separate markup factors were required for material and for conversion costs. The approach taken was similar to that illustrated in Exhibit 13.10 in chapter 13.

Comparison of Selling Prices

When the markup factors for return on investment pricing were completed, they were tested on three items of jewelry: a religious figure, a pendant, and earrings. The comparison is shown in Exhibit 18.9.

The comparison shows that the religious figure and the pendant had been understated, while the earrings had been overstated by the old method. At the request of the plant manager, a more extensive test was made. This included some 34 products which accounted for 71% of the sales volume. The net change for the 34 products showed an overall increase of 6% in prices under the new method.

EXHIBIT 18.9

COMPARISON OF FACTORY SELLING PRICES
FOR THREE PRODUCTS

	Religious Figure	Pendant	Earrings
Old Method	$ 6.30	15.81	22.77
New Method	$ 7.29	17.40	21.09
Percent Change	+ 15.7%	+ 10.1%	− 7.9%

CASE 18.2: HOW A PREDOMINANT PRODUCT CAN DISTORT OTHER PRODUCT COSTS

Freeze-Dry, Inc. (name disguised) dehydrates certain fish, meats, vegetables, and fruit in a frozen state under high vacuum. This process is performed in cabinets built for this purpose. The product is contained in trays inside the cabinet. The pounds of water removed from the various products are the basis used to determine the allocation of fixed overhead as between the amount chargeable to the various products and that chargeable to "idle plant" costs. The charges are based on the relationship between the weight of water actually removed and the water removal ability of the cabinets computed at 55 pounds of water per hour of potential cabinet operations.

In principle, this is a sound basis. However, because the cabinets were designed for freeze-drying of shrimp, it was somewhat difficult, under such circumstances, to attain a water extraction rate of 55 pounds per hour in the case of certain products—particularly mushrooms. There was not sufficient tray capacity in the cabinets to hold enough mushrooms (and other products) from which to extract 55 pounds of water per hour.

Use of Cabinets for Small Lots

The cost of experimental products was being understated by use of the water extraction method of allocating fixed costs because the cabinets were frequently only partly loaded, with the result that a cabinet with, say, a 65-tray capacity may be tied up by an experimental product which would occupy one-third of the trays or less. The unused capacity through a lowered water extraction rate resulted in incorrect allocations of the fixed costs.

Other Cost Distortions

The actual cost system used by Freeze-Dry, Inc. was another reason for product cost distortion. The actual costs as recorded each month were distributed to the respective products. Since shrimp was the dominant product and because it used processing facilities not required by the other products, overhead costs peculiar to shrimp were distributed to nonshrimp products. Although these costs were relatively small per dry pound of shrimp, they loomed large in relation to the smaller volumes of other products. The figures in Exhibit 18.10 show how individual product volume fluctuations can affect product costs.

EXHIBIT 18.10

PRODUCT VOLUME FLUCTUATIONS

Products	Month of June		Month of August	
	Wet Pounds	% of Total	Wet Pounds	% of Total
Shrimp	195,325	82.8%	3,270	20.1%
Beef	22,722	9.6	—	—
Chicken	15,300	6.5	12,300	75.7
Vegetables	50	—	—	—
Mushrooms	2,515	1.1	—	—
Bananas	—	—	687	4.2
Total	235,912	100.0%	16,257	100.0%

Note that in the month of June, production of chicken was 6.5% of the total wet pounds of all production. In the month of August, although chicken production was 3,000 pounds less than in June, this smaller volume represented 75.7% of total production. The very low volume of shrimp accounted for the percentage shift. Because chicken production predominated in August, it absorbed the lion's share of the various costs incurred in that month.

Corrective Action

Since the major factor causing the product cost distortions was due to incorrect overhead distribution to products, predetermined standard overhead rates were developed. These were calculated for a sufficiently extended period to avoid the errors due to month-to-month fluctuations in the individual products. Additionally, instead of applying the overhead on the basis of wet pounds of water extracted, it was applied on the basis of dry pounds of finished product. The predetermined overhead rate per dry pound included only those overhead costs that were common to all products. It would exclude costs applicable solely to shrimp—such as thawing, grading, cooking, peeling, and deveining. For these shrimp-related costs, a separate rate was calculated. When costing shrimp, both the general predetermined rate and the differential rate were applied; for all other products, only the general (basic rate) would be applied. This approach is similar to the basic and differential rates discussed in chapter 3.

COMPUTERIZED PRODUCT COSTING FORMAT

The various product costing formats discussed to this point were being prepared manually by the various companies studied. For standardized products, particularly when the number of items and variations thereof are large, the computer can play a significant role. As in the manually prepared formats, the computerized version will vary from company to company because of differences in the product and in the nature of the manufacturing process.

For discussion purposes, the products shown in Exhibits 11.4 and 11.5 in chapter 11 will be used. Exhibit 18.11 illustrates the format of the manufacturing process sheet, which is the foundation on which the product cost estimates are constructed. This manufacturing process sheet represents level 04 in the product structure and contains the following information:

· Line 1 shows the PC (Product Code) 01, the basic product number which is 02608, the 01 suffix, and the machine code. The machine code, 0008, is the computer's identification for level 04. The product code, basic, and suffix numbers are shown on all printouts of data. These provide a more detailed description of the product features.
· Lines 2 and 3 show the name of the part, material code, kind of material, and size of the material.
· Line 4 indicates the shape of the material, which in this case is a coil, and the engineering spec number.
· Line 5 shows the unit of measure, which for this material is measured in pounds. The quantity is measured in both gross and net weight of brass per thousand pieces. The difference represents unavoidable material loss, the scrap value of which is credited to the product.
· Line 6 lists the production cost centers through which the product is routed within level 04.

The lower section of the manufacturing process sheet shows the following columns:

1. operation numbers,
2. operation description,

EXHIBIT 18.11

MANUFACTURING PROCESS SHEET

ISSUE DATE	ISSUE #	REVISED:				SHOP ORDER #
DRAWING #		LAST C.A.				DATE ISSUED

P.C. 01	BASIC 02608	SUFFIX	MACH. CODE 0008	REFERENCE		
PART NAME	STEM					QTY. TO MAKE
MTL. CODE 20-2800		KIND BRASS		SIZE .280 DIAMETER		RAW MTL. REQMT.
SHAPE COIL	SPEC. 26-4		TEMPER	HARDNESS		REQD. COMPLETION DATE
UNIT LBS.	PER/M GROSS 37.8		PER/M NET 17.0			LEVEL ④

ROUTING MACHINING, COATING, INSPECTION, COMPONENTS STOCKROOM

OPN. #	OPERATION DESCRIPTION	EQUIPMENT	DEPT.	SET-UP HRS.	LAB. GRD.	PROD. HRS./M	LAB. GRD.	NO. MACH.	NO. MEN	COST CENTER
010	CUT-OFF & HEAD	HEADER	MACHG	3.0	10	.15	5	2	1	0447
020	ROLL THREAD	ROLLING MACHINE	MACHG	2.0	10	.50	5	2	1	0450
030	HEADING	HEADER	MACHG	12.0	13	.81	12			0761
050	DEGREASE	DEGREASER	COATG			.07	4			0568
	INSPECT		QC							

PROCESSED FOR MIN/MAX RUN OF: | PCS. | PROCESS ENG'G. | STDS. ENG'G.

246

3. equipment used,

4. department (cost center) name,

5. setup hours where applicable,

6. labor grade of individuals making the setups,

7. production hours per thousand units,

8. labor grades of the machine operators,

9. number of machines used in the operation,

10. number of employees used in each operation, and

11. cost center for each of the operations.

    The manufacturing process sheet includes only the engineering and manufacturing data. Material, direct labor, and overhead costs are developed separately and listed on the cost routing sheet, which appears in the upper portion of Exhibits 11.4 and 11.5. Note that the cost routing sheet starts at level 05 and structures the costs through the finished stage in level 01. Exhibit 18.12 shows graphically the material, direct labor, and overhead cost for each of the five levels as well as the total manufacturing cost for the completed product.

    For a more detailed discussion of computerizing the cost accounting system, see *Dudick on Manufacturing Cost Controls,* by Thomas S. Dudick, Prentice Hall, 1985.

PRODUCT COST ESTIMATING MUST KEEP UP WITH THE TIMES

We are all creatures of habit. Once a routine has been established, there is a tendency to resist change. This applies to product costing and pricing as well as many other facets of business reporting. A significant change that has occurred in recent years, which affects product costing, is the requirement by many customers that deliveries of material be made according to just-in-time schedules supplied by them.

    Chapter 13, on the subject of markup factors, called attention to the additional costs incurred within ElectroMag, Inc. when one of its divisions was required to make shipments to another division on a just-in-time schedule. The general manager of the selling division, who was highly cost oriented, revised his product costing to reflect the additional cost of complying with the just-in-time delivery requirements.

    When customers introduce this requirement, the customer is, in effect, shifting inventory carrying costs to the supplier. In many cases, the supplier

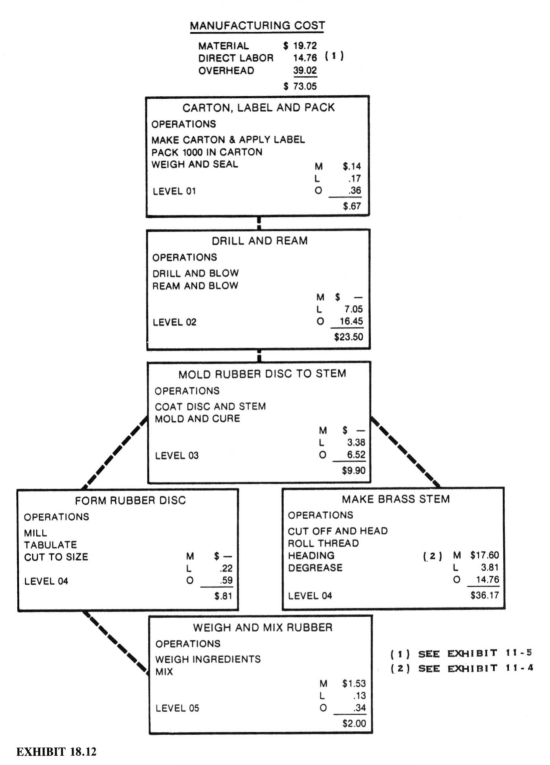

MANUFACTURING COST

MATERIAL	$ 19.72
DIRECT LABOR	14.76 (1)
OVERHEAD	39.02
	$ 73.05

CARTON, LABEL AND PACK

OPERATIONS

MAKE CARTON & APPLY LABEL
PACK 1000 IN CARTON
WEIGH AND SEAL   M $.14
                             L   .17
LEVEL 01   O   .36
                                  $.67

DRILL AND REAM

OPERATIONS

DRILL AND BLOW
REAM AND BLOW
                             M $ —
                             L   7.05
LEVEL 02   O   16.45
                                 $23.50

MOLD RUBBER DISC TO STEM

OPERATIONS

COAT DISC AND STEM
MOLD AND CURE
                             M $ —
                             L   3.38
LEVEL 03   O   6.52
                                  $9.90

FORM RUBBER DISC

OPERATIONS

MILL
TABULATE
CUT TO SIZE   M $ —
                   L   .22
LEVEL 04   O   .59
                        $.81

MAKE BRASS STEM

OPERATIONS

CUT OFF AND HEAD
ROLL THREAD
HEADING   (2) M $17.60
DEGREASE   L   3.81
                      O   14.76
LEVEL 04 $36.17

WEIGH AND MIX RUBBER

OPERATIONS

WEIGH INGREDIENTS
MIX
                   M $1.53
                   L   .13
LEVEL 05   O   .34
                        $2.00

(1) SEE EXHIBIT 11-5
(2) SEE EXHIBIT 11-4

EXHIBIT 18.12

PRODUCT COST BY MANUFACTURING LEVEL

may be required to locate warehouse space in closer proximity to the customer. The supplier should be fully aware of the magnitude of the additional inventory carrying costs even if competitive pressures limit the amount that can be recovered through price increases. Inasmuch as these costs can be in excess of 25% of the inventory dollars, it seems appropriate to spell out what these costs include. The balance of this chapter will therefore analyze the items making up this cost.

INVENTORY CARRYING COSTS

In a manufacturing plant, inventory can represent as much as 50% of the total investment—depending on the product. The floor space required for receiving, storing, and staging inventories can amount to more than 40% of total floor area at the factory location. The amount of investment and rent-equivalent costs alone provide the clue that carrying inventory is expensive.

Items Included in Inventory Carrying Costs

Terminology, as well as the nature of costs related to carrying inventories, can vary from company to company. Our discussion will be based on a composite of several companies. Differences in certain costs have been taken care of by grouping the items under a broader category. Variations in the magnitude of individual costs have been smoothed so the figures more closely approximate an average than a midpoint of extremes. The items making up these costs are broken down into the following categories:

1. Rent-equivalent costs
   a. Building maintenance services
   b. Building depreciation and/or rent
   c. Fuel oil
   d. Real estate taxes
2. Taxes and insurance
   a. Personal property taxes
   b. Liability and fire insurance
3. Operational costs
   a. Equipment depreciation
   b. Equipment maintenance
   c. Electricity
   d. Stock handling
   e. Breakage and obsolescence

4. Financing
   a. Cost of money

Often, certain extensions of the manufacturing operation are performed in a warehouse in which the manufactured product is stored. Examples of some of these operations are (a) tests made on certain pharmaceutical products after a specified holding period; (b) branding and packaging when products are sold under more than a single label; and (c) final testing and calibration of electronic equipment. In these instances, the costs are adjusted to reduce them by the amount of such expenditures attributable to the manufacturing operation.

Rent-equivalent Costs. These are the costs associated with housing the inventory. They include the building and building equipment depreciation and/or rentals; building maintenance services such as cleaning and maintenance of building structures, fuel oil, real estate taxes; and public liability insurance. These costs are applied as a cost per square foot to segregate the inventory storage costs from costs of the manufacturing operations that are performed in the warehouse.

Taxes and Insurance. Although real estate taxes are part of occupancy costs, personal property taxes are not. The latter are assessments made by municipalities, the basis being value. While some taxing authorities assess as of a certain date each year, others base the tax on the average inventory during the year. The method used in this study was based on the average inventory. Fire insurance costs follow a pattern similar to personal property taxes in that the amount of premium paid is based on the value. Public liability, on the other hand, has nothing to do with valuation placed on assets. It covers claims for injury sustained on company property. Accordingly, this cost should be considered part of the occupancy cost.

Operational Costs. These relate to the following items:

- *Equipment Depreciation and Maintenance:* This covers the amortization of equipment used for handling inventory in storage areas (see Exhibits 18.13a and 18.13b). When products in warehouses are tested, packaged, or otherwise processed prior to shipment, depreciation of such processing equipment would be considered as manufacturing cost rather than inventory carrying charges.
- *Electricity:* Electricity is used in stockrooms and warehouses for lighting, charging batteries used in lift trucks, and for automatic handling equipment used in storing the inventory.
- *Stock Handling:* Includes personnel costs of loading, unloading, stocking shelves, operating lift trucks, record keeping, payroll-related expenses, freight

EXHIBIT 18.13a

INVENTORY, SHIPPING, AND DISTRIBUTION OF PRODUCT COMPONENTS

Electronic components are stored in 19,000 bins along ten 30-foot high aisles. Permission for use of photograph granted by Arrow Electronics, Inc., Melville, NY.

EXHIBIT 18.13b

Electronic components are stocked and retrieved at the end-of-aisle computer workstations. Skilled
operators at each workstation interact with high-speed robotic cranes to process up to 2,500
customer orders every day. Permission for use of photograph granted by Arrow Electronics, Inc.,
Melville, NY.

costs, and supplies. It also includes charges for services performed by the
accounting department and the central data processing department.

· *Breakage and Obsolescence:* This category of costs includes the cost of stock
that must be written off the books because of breakage in handling. It also
includes a provision for obsolescence. This figure is based on experience
during the past five years adjusted for known conditions that might affect
historically derived information.

· *Financing Costs:* The cost of money is frequently based on the anticipated
prime rate for the coming year and is considered as part of the inventory
carrying cost.

EXHIBIT 18.14

COSTS OF CARRYING INVENTORY

	Inventory Storage Areas	Less Costs Applicable to Production	Net Inventory Carrying Cost
Rent-equivalent Costs			
Building Maintenance Services	$ 201,342	30,240	171,102
Depreciation and/or Rent	408,600	36,900	371,700
Fuel Costs	38,364	5,751	32,613
Real Estate Taxes	201,204	30,180	171,024
Taxes and Insurance			
Personal Property Taxes	261,072	19,800	241,272
Liability and Fire Insurance	25,779	3,870	21,909
Operational Costs			
Equipment Depreciation	42,300	36,180	6,120
Electricity	59,400	37,260	22,140
Stock Handling Costs	717,900	255,600	462,300
Breakage and Obsolescence	1,010,100	361,500	648,600
Cost of Money	1,691,280	165,000	1,526,280
Total Inventory Carrying Costs	$4,657,341	982,281	3,675,060

Putting It All Together

The various expenses making up the inventory carrying costs are summarized in Exhibit 18.14. The first column lists the carrying costs for the inventory storage areas. The second column shows the portion of the costs that are applicable to, and therefore chargeable to, production. The third column shows the net inventory carrying cost after deducting the charges applicable to production.

The total inventory value covered by these costs amounts to $16,912,800. The net inventory carrying cost is $3,675,060, or 21.7% of the total inventory value. Companies in which the size of inventories is increased to accomodate just-in-time requirements should be aware that the additional inventory is incurring costs that must be considered in their product cost estimates.

Some companies increase their purchases when anticipating a price increase of, say, 5%. One of the companies used in this study purchased a year's supply of one of the materials used in their product to avoid the price increase.

Had they considered only the cost of money tied up in the additional inventory, they might have had second thoughts before making the larger than normal purchase. Certain of the variable costs that fluctuate with the size of inventory, such as personal property taxes and handling costs, should also be considered before making purchases in anticipation of a price increase.

CHAPTER 19

Product Costs Must Play a Larger Role in Setting Prices

As was pointed out in chapter 1, many senior managers are surprisingly naive on the subject of product costing and its relationship to pricing products for sale.

PRODUCT COSTING DEFICIENCIES THAT DIRECTLY AFFECTED PRICES

Discovery of the product costing deficiencies discussed in the section resulted in corrections of the product costs and pricing changes in two of the companies in which these deficiencies were found.

Most product costing deficiencies occur because of failure to take into account what actually occurs on the factory floor. The following three examples pertaining to three different companies illustrate the types of costing errors that cause product cost distortions and, in some cases, incorrect pricing.

Plating Ground Rod

Ground rod is a steel rod plated with copper. This product is a type of lightning arrester to carry off excess electricity into the ground. The thickness of the

Portions of this chapter were taken from the author's article "Pricing Strategies for Manufacturers," which first appeared in the November, 1989 issue of *Management Accounting,* National Association of Accountants, Montvale, N.J.

copper plating varies with the application. The more plating that must be deposited, the slower the speed through the plating process and the less weight of finished product that will come off the plating equipment in a given time period. Platers, Inc. (name disguised) used weight of finished product as the basis for applying overhead such as depreciation of equipment, maintenance, floor space, and energy. Since the thinly plated rod moved through the plating process more rapidly, the weight of finished product accumulated faster. The more heavily plated product took longer—therefore less weight of finished ground rod was accumulated. Obviously, the use of weight as the basis for applying overhead was erroneous because it overstated the cost of the thinner gauges of copper plating that moved more rapidly through the process and understated the thicker gauges. The more suitable basis for applying the overhead would have been plating hours.

Preshrinking Costs in Garment Manufacturing

Chapter 1, which discussed numerous costing deficiences, included the case of Garment Manufacturers, Inc. The deficiency discussed concerned incorrect application of shrinking costs, which penalized fabric that was not sent out for shrinking and understated the cost of material that was actually preshrunk. Additionally, the combined overhead of the cutting plant and the garment sewing plant was applied to finished garments through a single overhead rate based on the amount of sewing labor required for the various garments. This was a second deficiency in overhead distribution because the cutting operation warranted the distribution of its own overhead based on the labor in the cutting operation. The type of material being cut made a difference in the time requirements. Cutting corduroy, for example, required more time than cutting polyester cotton—more time than the sewing labor method of allocation would provide. The cutting plant and the sewing plant should each have distributed their own overhead.

Tooling Costs

Chapter 1 also discussed improper treatment of tooling costs. Tooling can be substantially higher for some products than for others. Nonetheless, many cost systems include tooling in a pool that is allocated arbitrarily. Sewing Notions, Inc. (name disguised) was mentioned as a case in point. This manufacturer followed the practice of allocating tooling as a percentage of total manufacturing cost of each product until an operations review disclosed that the actual tooling costs for their Grommet Plier Kits were $3\frac{1}{2}$ times greater than the amount being allocated by use of the straight percentage method. Inasmuch as there were only a few items in which tooling costs were unusually large, the suggestion was made that tooling costs be directly charged to these products. The overall percentage method, exclusive of the directly charged items, would not materially distort the others.

SELLING, GENERAL, AND ADMINISTRATIVE COSTS

Chapter 2 was devoted entirely to allocation of SG&A. This below-the-line cost is often allocated on the basis of sales, or manufacturing cost. SG&A costs can vary widely in the different markets for several reasons, among which are the following:

1. Selling expenses are lower in the original equipment market (OEM) because fewer sales calls are required.
2. Warehousing and shipping costs are greater for the replacement market than OEM because orders are packaged in smaller cartons rather than being shipped in bulk. A fairly large-sized inventory must also be maintained for shipment to many retail locations.
3. Advertising and promotion costs differ by market.

The foregoing examples, and the others discussed in earlier chapters, are only a few of the many types of product cost distortions that can be found in practically every manufacturing company. Manufacturing technology is constantly changing. Surprisingly, the very executives who coordinate the efforts of the disciplines responsible for reducing costs are unaware that the product costs do not correctly reflect the improvements. True, the cost reductions are taken into account on an overall basis. However, they are not correctly shown on a product-by-product basis because of arbitrariness in the methods followed in arriving at individual product cost estimates.

The answer does not lie in seminars; it can only be found in the factory in the course of a plant tour conducted by a factory-wise foreman or industrial engineer.

ROLE OF PRODUCT COSTS IN SETTING PRICES

Too many pricing decisions are made by what is called ''feel of the market.'' It was the writer's opinion that a number of interviewees who made reference to the feel of the market were using the term as a figure of speech for ''guesstimating.'' More reliably developed product costs will facilitate the introduction of the pricing strategies discussed next.

PREMIUM PRICING

Premium pricing can be used in the growth stage of the product life cycle, as was done by General Motors some 60 years ago when the Buick and Cadillac were added to the product line. It can also be used in the maturity stage when new conveniences are added, as was the case when self-cleaning ovens were introduced and ice cubes in home refrigerators ''at the push of a lever'' were added.

Many consumer products are made in more than one model. Usually, there is a standard or basic product. In addition to the standard product, there may be one or more variations with certain decorative or convenience features. The manufacturer is entitled to charge an additional amount for the enhanced models that are described as deluxe.

Erroneous Premium Pricing

Although deluxe models are priced higher than the standard products, the writer has found instances in which the increased price resulted in a smaller profit percentage for the deluxe model than for the standard item. The KAC Company (name disguised) is a good example. Its product line included such items as mixers, blenders, skillets, rotisseries, and oven broilers.

The company made a decision to add model 1602 to the mixer line. This model had a stainless steel bowl with a nylon button on the bottom of the beater to avoid scarring. The factory selling price of the 1601 standard model was $49.54, while the price established for the 1602 was $53.50. When the two prices were compared with the cost, the gross profit for model 1601 was 35% of the selling price, while the gross profit for model 1602 was only 33%, even though this was the deluxe model.

The same kind of inconsistency was found between the 6221 and 6223 blenders. The 6223 was a deluxe model with a chrome motor cover and solid state features. The selling price of the former was $34.50, and the deluxe model was priced at $36.95. In this case, the comparison of percentage gross profit for the two showed 37% for the 6221 and 34% for the deluxe model.

It was obvious from the foregoing that establishment of selling prices for the deluxe models must go beyond increasing absolute dollars, as was done in these two cases: Percentage profit should be the price determinant.

Pricing Same Product under Different Brand Names

Although premium pricing is ordinarily associated with additional decorative or convenience features, this is not always the case. There are instances in which more than one price is charged even when the products sold are exactly the same. Vodka is a good example. U.S.-made vodkas are not very different from one company to another. Although production costs are about the same regardless of the brand name under which they are sold, prices can be quite different. Studies have shown many customers to be psychologically impelled to choose the higher priced of two or more brands because price is looked on by many as an indicator of quality. This reinforces the fact that knowledge of customer psychology is often a factor in setting prices.

Impact of Changing Trends

Making a good product at a high premium price can be highly profitable. Maytag's reputation for quality has been known for years. Its advertising features an idle repairman complaining that his idleness is due to the company's policy of making the best washing machine in the industry. The premium prices charged by Maytag have yielded the company the highest return on investment in the industry.

According to *Forbes,* May 29, 1978, page 56, two trend factors began to weaken Maytag's position:

1. Since Maytag does not sell to the large catalog chains, it lacks the aggressive marketing support of a company like Sears.
2. Real estate contractors usually do not look for the longest-lasting product on the market when they make purchases for acres of tract housing: They look for price.

The *Forbes* article suggests, "They could cut their prices closer to the levels of competitors in the washing machine segment of the market and boost volume greatly."

A recent review of tests performed by Consumer Reports on nine washing machines shows Maytag still to be number one with the best repair record. Interestingly, the two lowest-rated washers were priced higher than the Maytag.

As an alternative to the *Forbes* recommendation, the company could retain its high-quality reputation and also introduce a lower-priced private brand to broaden its market share. Marginal pricing, which follows, is the appropriate pricing strategy in this case.

MARGINAL PRICING

Marginal pricing was popularized in the mid-1950s when numerous articles and books were written on the subject of variable (direct) costing. In marginal pricing, which is an adaptation of variable costing, the fixed cost content in the selling price is reduced to make the price more attractive, thus increasing volume.

Marginal pricing is more often applicable in the growth stage when new technology provides an innovative company with an advantage over competitors. This, in effect, is the approach followed by Henry Ford when he developed the moving assembly line that gave him a great advantage over competitors. This advantage enabled him to increase his share of market so that costs per car were greatly reduced—to the point that he was able to increase wages to a then unheard of sum of five dollars per day. Marginal pricing can work to a company's benefit if the company has a significant advantage over its competitors. It is also appropriate in the maturity stage when a company making a brand name product decides to add a private brand at reduced prices.

This was not the case with a large candy manufacturing company whose controller proposed the adoption of marginal pricing. The company had purchased automatic chocolate molding equipment for Easter bunnies, Santa Clauses, and other molded figures in order to reduce the large labor costs incurred because of the labor-intensive nature of the operations. The controller, an ardent proponent of variable costing, prepared a study showing that the labor savings would bring down the total variable costs by more than half. Since this reduction would greatly increase the contribution to fixed costs and profits, he recommended that prices be dropped 5% below the prices of competitors.

What he overlooked was that the company had been losing money on its molded chocolate products. The decision to go automatic required a capital equipment investment in excess of a half-million dollars to purchase equipment similar to that already in use by competitors. Another factor that was overlooked in the controller's study (and this occurs in many such studies) was an allowance for a costly debugging period that could last as long as six months.

There is a big difference between this example and the earlier one relating to the reduced pricing of the Model T car. Ford was the innovator who introduced mass production while his competitors were struggling with other problems. In the molding of chocolate figures, competitors were already using automatic equipment and had made price reductions as a result of the cost savings.

The innovative company that is first in the introduction of better technology is in a better position to become the price leader and low-cost producer. The followers who are less innovative will remain behind the leader unless they become even more innovative or the leader becomes complacent.

BREAK-EVEN TEST FOR PRICING

When a new product is introduced, management is faced with the age-old question: "What price should we charge?" This question was raised by the KAC Company when it decided to produce the model 7420 20" fan. A common practice in many companies is to calculate the total cost of making a specific quantity and then to apply a percentage markup in obtaining a selling price. If the price at this specific level appears to be too high in relation to competitors' prices, arbitrary adjustments are frequently made to the markup factor and/or manufacturing cost to arrive at a price that will be more competitive.

This method has a major weakness because it is based on figures that relate to only one volume level. It does not take into account that the price leader who "sets" the market price may be basing the price at a different volume level. This is where the break-even test, illustrated in Exhibit 19.1, can be employed. In this approach, the break-even cost per fan has been calculated for five production levels within the normal operating range. A markup was added to these five levels to arrive at the selling prices. The figures for columns A through E are as follows:

EXHIBIT 19.1

BREAK-EVEN COST PER FAN AT FIVE VOLUME LEVELS
WITHIN THE NORMAL RANGE OF OPERATIONS

Col. A No. of Fans in Normal Range of Operations	Nonvariable Costs		Col. D Variable Cost per Fan	Col. E Break-even Cost per Fan
	Col. B Dollars	Col. C Per Fan		
12,000	226,560	$18.88	$9.92	$28.80
14,000	226,560	16.18	9.92	26.10
16,000	226,560	14.16	9.92	24.08
18,000	226,560	12.59	9.92	22.51
20,000	226,560	11.33	9.92	21.25

1. *Column A:* This column shows the number of fans produced at five different levels of production within the normal operating range.

2. *Column B:* The total nonvariable dollars ($226,560) is the total of all costs that remain constant within the normal operating range. These include such items as equipment depreciation, building depreciation, real estate taxes, insurance, and supervision.

3. *Column C:* This column shows the nonvariable cost on a per-fan basis for each of the five production levels. These figures were calculated by dividing the $226,560 by each of the five production levels shown in column A.

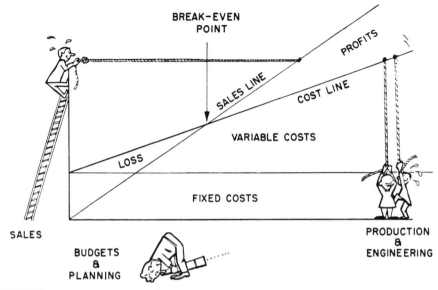

EXHIBIT 19.2

FINDING THE RIGHT BREAK-EVEN POINT

The cost line is made up of fixed and variable costs. The point at which the sales line crosses the cost line is the breakeven point—which means neither profit nor loss. The breakeven point can be lowered by:
Increasing sales through:

1. Selective selling
2. Raising prices (easier said than done)

   Reducing costs through:

1. More efficient material utilization
2. Greater labor efficiency
3. Higher machine utilization
4. Smaller overhead organization
5. Redesign of products to reduce costs

4. *Column D:* The variable cost, which remains constant per fan, is made up of the following variable costs:

a. Material/fan	$4.76
b. Direct labor/fan	1,39
c. Variable overhead/fan	3.77
d. Total variable cost/fan	$9.92

5. *Column E:* Since this column shows the total cost per fan with no markup for profit, it represents the break-even cost for each of the five levels of production.

Once the markup has been applied to the five levels, the logical question is "Should we set the selling price higher to recover our product development costs sooner, or should we set it low to discourage competitors?" The KAC Company decided initially to introduce a deluxe model at a higher price and then to follow it up with a standard model. As volume increased, prices were progressively reduced to make competition less inviting.

PRICING WITHIN A FAMILY OF PRODUCTS

The word *family,* as it relates to products, indicates similarity, such as the function performed. Electrical connectors are illustrative of a family. The manufacturing process and the materials used are similar. The differences are in number of electronic contacts, contact arrangement, and alternate insert positions. When new products are added to a family, it is important that there be a consistency in costing and pricing all family members.

Exhibit 18.7 in chapter 18 illustrated a matrix approach to show how new products added to the line can be slotted within a family to ensure a consistently developed product cost base for pricing new products.

Exhibit 19.3 goes on to the next step—determining selling prices for the three new products added to the line. The exhibit shows the costs of seven electronic connectors, three of which are new products. Four of the types have been in the line for some time, but three types, 43-2424, 43-2425, and 45-2507, are new types for which selling prices had to be established.

All costs are based on reasonably attainable standards which are competitive. To arrive at selling prices for the three new types, the percentage of cost to selling price was first calculated for the existing types. The percentages showed that product 42-2511 has a cost to selling price ratio of 79%; this ratio for 42-2440 is 80%; it is 76% for both 44-2467 and 44-2447. The selling prices for these items are based on known competitive prices.

In the case of 43-2424 and 43-2425, it was felt that the 76% ratio that applies to the 44-2467 and 42-2447 should also apply to these because of similarity in volume and manufacturing. The 76% was then divided into the manufacturing cost of $18.15 to arrive at a selling price of $24. For the 45-2507, the industry volume was anticipated to be somewhat lower than the rest of the line because the number of applications of this item is small.

While a 72% or 73% ratio would have been desirable for this new five-

EXHIBIT 19.3

ELECTRONIC COMPONENTS PRICING MATRIX

Material	Two Contacts		Three Contacts		Four Contacts		Five Contacts
Top Plate	*42-2511*	*42-2440*	*43-2424*	*43-2425*	*44-2467*	*44-2447*	*45-2507*
12-2524 1/32 XP	3.60						
12-2466 1/16 XP		3.74					
12-2448 1/16 XP			5.62				
12-2460 1/32 XP				5.62			
12-2440 1/32 XP					7.50		
12-2423 1/32 XP						7.50	
12-2412 1/32 XP							9.37
Bottom Plate							
13-2524 1/16 XP	4.00						
13-2466 3/64 XP		4.24					
13-2448 3/64 XP			6.37				
13-2460 3/64 XP				6.37			
13-2440 3/64 XP					8.50		
13-2423 3/64 XP						8.50	
13-2412 3/64 XP							10.62
Contacts							
10-431	2.00	2.00					
10-562			3.00				
10-567				3.00			
10-632					4.00	4.00	
10-636							5.00
Eyelets							
46	.60	.60	.60	.60			
48					.70	.70	.70
Total Component Cost	$10.20	$10.58	$15.59	$15.59	$20.70	$2.070	$25.69
Assembly Labor and Overhead	2.00	2.00	2.20	2.20	2.40	2.40	2.40
Spoilage Allowance	.24	.25	.36	.36	.46	.46	.56
Total Cost	$12.44	$12.83	$18.15	$18.15	$23.56	$23.56	$28.65
Selling Price	15.75	16.00	24.00*	24.00*	31.00	31.00	38.75*
% Cost to Selling Price	79%	80%	76%*	76%*	76%	76%	74%*

Note: Selling prices rounded off to nearest $0.25.

* New types.

contact unit, this would have resulted in a selling price that would have exceeded the price of a two-contact plus a three-contact unit; therefore, a 74% ratio was used.

This method of pricing products within a family rather than using a stand-alone approach when new items are added has the advantage of ensuring that there will be a consistency within the family for both costing and pricing.

Consistency of costing and pricing within a family was carried to an extreme by a former cost estimator. This individual's approach was to determine the low and high points of a range of costs and prices within the family and to extrapolate the intermediate values by reading them from the straight line connecting the low and high points.

Exhibit 19.4 illustrates this graphically using the data shown in Exhibit 19.3. The upper chart shows the costs and prices for the seven products based on extrapolation of the values from the straight line. The lower chart shows the product-specific values discussed earlier. A comparison of the two charts shows the fallacy of assuming that costs and prices within a family have a linear relationship.

UNDERPRICED REPLACEMENT PARTS

The writer has found a surprising number of companies that underprice replacement parts, even though they are not proponents of marginal pricing. Underpricing, in many cases, is due to failure to take into account the cost of maintaining an inventory of such parts for 10 or more years after production of a product or model has been discontinued.

Doral Electronics (name disguised) is a case in point. Although Doral does not consciously use marginal pricing, the net effect of the method it does use is the same. The sales price for replacement parts was set to yield an 18% profit, which the company felt was quite adequate. A study showed that the inventory carrying costs alone amount to 23.8% of inventory value. The items included in the inventory carrying costs are similar to those discussed in chapter 18. Cost of money is the largest item in the 23.8% inventory carrying cost. Since the cost of money, as well as other costs, can vary depending on economic conditions, inventory carrying costs must be monitored closely to ensure that costs affected by interest rates and inflation are taken into account.

SUBSTITUTE MATERIAL

The preceding sections of this chapter have focused mainly on competition within a single industry. Competitive pressures and the resulting struggle for share of market often cross industry lines.

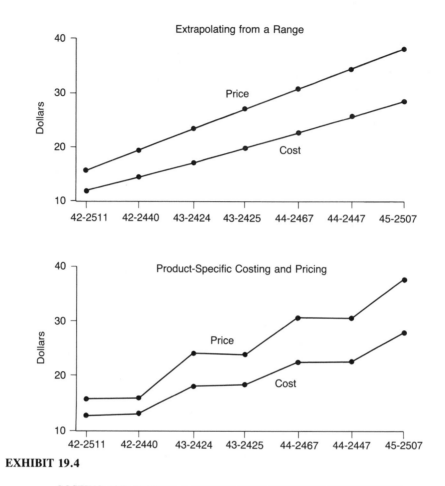

EXHIBIT 19.4

COSTING AND PRICING A FAMILY OF ELECTRONIC COMPONENTS

Illustrative of this are materials used in the construction of residential homes. Many tract housing developers, in the interest of lowering costs, have shifted away from wood siding to aluminum. By using aluminum siding with its baked-on finish, the builder eliminates the cost of exterior painting. Not to be outdone, the plastics industry introduced vinyl siding which, like aluminum, eliminates the need for painting. Another feature of vinyl is that it is available with an embossed grain similar to that of wood. Manufacturers of wood siding have lost their share of the market to the aluminum and plastic industries.

Use of substitute material does not always result in reduced costs. On the contrary, the substitute material may be more costly. In the manufacture of metal garbage cans, for example, the sheet metal accounts for 21.4% of the manufacturer's selling price. The plastic material used in making the plastic version accounts for 41.2% of the manufacturer's selling price (see *Creative Pricing,* by E. Marting, AMA, 1968, page 36).

The higher price for the plastic item does not necessarily mean that buyers will favor the lower-priced product. Plastic garbage containers have certain advantages over their metal counterparts. These include resistance to denting, reduction in noise, less weight, and freedom from rusting. The typical user of the plastic garbage container feels that the higher price of the plastic product is more than offset by these advantages.

PRICING DIFFERENCES IN JOINT PRODUCTS

Flexibility in pricing joint products can vary widely. Oil refining and meat packing are good examples.

The Oil Refining Process

Exxon USA describes the refining process in the following words:

> "Wielding sledgehammers of heat and pressure, and the magic wand of catalysts, refineries can take the hydrocarbon molecules apart, clean them of impurities and put them together again as fuels such as gasoline and diesel oil; lubricants such as oil and grease; and chemical feedstock—the building blocks for countless plastics, elastics and much more."

Exhibit 19.5 illustrates the downstream products which will vary according to the type of crude oils, refinery configuration, petrochemical process, and processing methods employed. The change in demand for the various products will result in variations in products and pricing.

Meat Packing

A Conference Board Study on the subject of "Prices: Policies and Practices" made an interesting comparison between oil refining and pork products. The study quotes an executive of a meat packing company as follows:

> "The total supply of livestock coming to market is predetermined by decisions farmers made a considerable time before the livestock arrive at the packing plant. Thus, though we know what we paid for a hog, we don't know the exact cost of a ham from a hog, as opposed to a loin or side of bacon. Unlike the oil industry, our product mix is largely predetermined.

EXHIBIT 19.5

BREAKDOWN OF PRODUCTS MANFUACTURED FROM 100 GALLONS OF CRUDE OIL

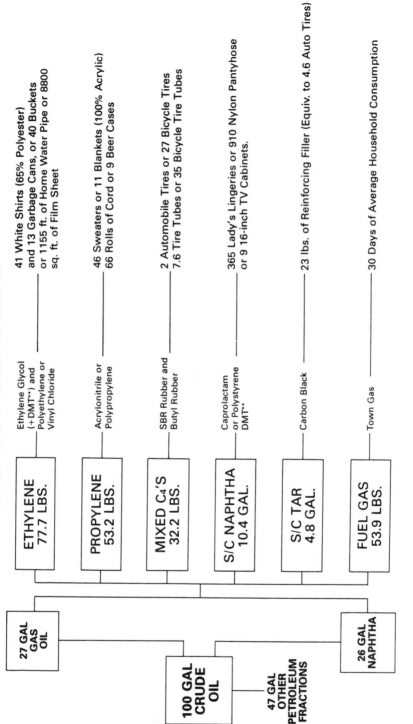

Ethylene Glycol (+DMT**) and Polyethylene or Vinyl Chloride — 41 White Shirts (65% Polyester) and 13 Garbage Cans, or 40 Buckets or 1155 ft. of Home Water Pipe or 8800 sq. ft. of Film Sheet

Acrylonitrile or Polypropylene — 46 Sweaters or 11 Blankets (100% Acrylic) 66 Rolls of Cord or 9 Beer Cases

SBR Rubber and Butyl Rubber — 2 Automobile Tires or 27 Bicycle Tires 7.6 Tire Tubes or 35 Bicycle Tire Tubes

Caprolactam or Polystyrene DMT** — 365 Lady's Lingeries or 910 Nylon Pantyhose or 9 16-inch TV Cabinets.

Carbon Black — 23 lbs. of Reinforcing Filler (Equiv. to 4.6 Auto Tires)

Town Gas — 30 Days of Average Household Consumption

ETHYLENE 77.7 LBS.

PROPYLENE 53.2 LBS.

MIXED C₄'S 32.2 LBS.

S/C NAPHTHA 10.4 GAL.

S/C TAR 4.8 GAL.

FUEL GAS 53.9 LBS.

27 GAL GAS OIL

100 GAL CRUDE OIL

47 GAL OTHER PETROLEUM FRACTIONS

26 GAL NAPHTHA

Hypothetical situation: actual mix of downstream products will vary according to type of crude oil, refinery configuration, petrochemical process, and fabrication method employed.

**Dimethyl Terephthalate

BY PERMISSION OF EXXON CHEMICAL COMPANY U.S.A.

The oil industry can make more gasoline and less fuel oil. However, each hog comes with two hams and it is difficult to make more. Since we have no control over our supply, we don't know what each cut really costs and cannot alter the product mix. It is obviously necessary for us to find our prices rather than set them. The price we try to find are those that will move our particular assortment of products promptly before they spoil and leave us ready to handle the next day's receipt of livestock."

Gasoline was once a waste product and pollutant. But with the development and growth of the auto industry, this waste product became a highly competitive commodity. The product mix in meat packing, on the other hand, is not interchangeable as it is in the case of crude oil products. The mix is constant and the product is highly perishable. It becomes obvious from this example that there can be no one-size-fits-all formula for pricing joint products. Differences such as the aforementioned must be taken into account. Judgment in such cases becomes an important factor in price determination.

STANDARD AND CUSTOMIZED PRODUCTS IN THE SAME PLANT

There is a natural tendency when new products are added to a line to treat them in the same manner as the existing products. If the existing products are considered to be in the standardized commercial category, and standard costing procedures are followed, the costing for any new version of the same product is likely to be the same. Selling prices are also likely to be geared to the commercially oriented pricing strategies.

This is precisely what happened to nuclear components ordered by nuclear power plants in the 1970s. Even though the Atomic Energy Commission (AEC) required all manufacturers of such nuclear components as valves, pumps, pressure vessels, reactor vessels, safety valves, and piping to adhere to highly engineered specifications, there were companies that continued to cost and price the nuclear components as if they were to be used for the less restrictive applications. As the percentage of nuclear business increased and profitable companies started to show reduced profits, and even losses, many managers only then began to question the selling prices being received for the nuclear part of the business.

A study of several companies producing both the commercial and nuclear components revealed that costs such as engineering, drafting, quality, rework, factory supplies, and shipping costs were substantially greater for the nuclear components. Nonetheless, the standard cost systems in use allocated these costs through an overhead rate(s) based on production hours. In view of the highly engineered and customized nature of the nuclear components, such costs should have been charged directly to the individual jobs on a direct-charge basis. The following examples are discussed at greater length in chapter 7.

Engineering. Engineering effort expended on nuclear components can be expected to be double or triple the amount of effort that is required for the commercial types.

Quality Assurance. With the more demanding requirements, quality assurance must relate to the total controlled manufacturing system. This encompasses the following:

· audit and control of internal departments and suppliers to ensure conformance to code and contract requirements;
· internal training of inspection personnel;
· development and monitoring of programs for calibration of measuring equipment; and
· control of internal quality standards and quality documentation.

Inspection. The cost of inspection for nuclear components (in this case, nuclear valves) is more than double that required for the commercial types. There can be more than 900 inspection, hold, witness, approval, and verification points by the manufacturer, Atomic Energy Commission, and the utility company.

Rework. Rework costs are relatively small for commercial valves because the presence of sand holes in the casting is not as serious a defect as it might be in a casting used in a nuclear component. In the event that a defect is found in such a casting, the following corrective operations are required:

1. gouging out the defect;
2. welding the hole(s);
3. grinding the weld;
4. hand dressing;
5. X-ray;
6. heat treat; and
7. remachine and inspect.

The cost of supplies, shipping expenses, tools, and fixtures, likewise, are substantially greater for the nuclear components than for the commercial types.

There was no doubt, on completion of the writer's study, that selling prices for the nuclear components had to be cost based. In preparing the cost estimates, it is necessary to identify correctly the costs applicable to nuclear components as a basis for establishing the selling price. This is no different than is being done on defense contracts and for products that are unique to one customer. (See chapter 8, "Cost-based Pricing: Commercial.")

In the implementation of the required job costing system, proper reporting of labor by individual customers can be troublesome because of resistance by many salaried professionals who are not accustomed to accounting for their time. Frequently such individuals will wait until the end of an accounting period, at which time they will "guesstimate" how their time was utilized during the period. Management must therefore explain the significance of reporting by job and emphasize the importance of accurate and timely reporting.

MONITORING THE YIELD ON PRICE QUOTATIONS

Since the goal of pricing strategy is to maximize profits, management should regularly monitor the effectiveness of price quotations. Checking the bottom line on the income statement is too broad a measure. The company should therefore review the number of quotation requests received during the period, the number that resulted in firm orders (success ratio), and the breakdown of these orders by gross profit percentages. This is shown in Exhibit 19.6. Note

EXHIBIT 19.6

EFFECTIVENESS OF PRICE QUOTATIONS

Gross Profit Range	Number of Requests	Breakdown of Firm Orders	% Firm Orders by Profit Range
40% and above	63	—	—
35% to 39%	114	3	2.6%
30 to 34%	126	6	4.8%
25% to 29%	288	30	10.4%
5% to 24%	252	42	16.7%
Total	843	81	9.6%
Recapitulation of the Foregoing			
Above 30%	303	9	3.0%
5% to 29%	540	72	13.3%
Total	843	81	9.6%

that of a total of 843 requests for price information received, 81, or 9.6%, resulted in firm orders. This raises the question as to whether a 9.6% success ratio is adequate. Unfortunately, there are no industry figures available to check this out. However, each period's success ratio percentage can be compared with subsequent periods.

Monitoring the success ratio percentages by the five individual profit percent ranges can also be quite useful. Note in the recapitulation in Exhibit 19.6 that the percent success ratio for the first three lines averages 3%, while the last two average 13.3%. When this was discussed with the controller, he agreed that the success ratio was skewed too heavily toward the orders on the last two lines, which show the lowest profitability.

This raised the question as to whether the costs of the items on the first three lines were excessive—thus overstating the price and reducing the sales. A list of the products in question was therefore given to the product development group to evaluate the cost reduction possibilities. On completion of the analysis, the product development manager advised that almost half the items on the list contained fabricated parts that were being purchased on the outside. He recommended that the company purchase the necessary equipment to expand its own capacity rather than having the work done on the outside.

An earlier effort to obtain this equipment had been turned down, but when the foregoing facts were presented to the general manager, he was able to obtain capital expenditure authorization to purchase the necessary equipment—illustrating the importance of good documentation support.

During a review with the general manager, his attention was focused on the recapitulation section of Exhibit 19.6. When he saw that only 9 of the 81 firm orders yielded a gross profit above 30%, he requested a sales analysis for each customer showing the breakdown of orders by size.

A total of 934 recent orders were broken down into 11 selling price ranges as shown in Exhibit 19.7. The "All Customers" column indicated that 32% of the customers were below $99. Of the 57 orders placed by customer A, 54 of the orders, or 94%, were below the selling price of $99, with only 6% in the higher price category.

Inasmuch as customer A manufactured a product that required much more than 6% of the higher-priced items, the question arose as to whether this customer, and others, were attracted to the lower-priced items because the selling prices for this group of products were below the prices charged by competitors. This raised the further question as to whether the company's higher-priced orders were priced too high and therefore discouraged sales of the higher-priced and potentially more profitable items.

A number of other "customer A types" were found whose purchases of

EXHIBIT 19.7

BREAKDOWN OF 934 CUSTOMER ORDERS BY DOLLAR VALUE

Selling Price Range	All Customers		Customer A	
	Orders	% of Total	Orders	% of Total
Below $49	147	16%⎫ 32%	32	56%⎫ 94%
50 to 99	150	16 ⎭	22	38 ⎭
100 to 499	418	45	3	6
500 to 999	120	13		
1,000 to 1,499	47	5		
1,500 to 1,999	22	2		
2,000 to 2,499	10	1		
2,500 to 2,999	5	.4		
3,000 to 3,499	4	.4		
3,500 to 3,999	2	.2		
4,000 and over	9	1		
Total	934	100%	57	100%

products at $99 and below accounted for the bulk of their purchases. The general manager requested his sales manager to look into this matter further to determine why the order size was so greatly skewed toward the less profitable products.

Many companies analyze total sales to individual customers. A more detailed breakdown by profitability range could be highly informative.

SUMMARY

Increasing the share of market is a popular battle cry in many companies. But in too many instances, the strategy followed by the marketing department to achieve higher volume sometimes includes arbitrary price cutting. The company management is often unaware of this until there is a sharp decline in profits and a shakeout in the industry. Each company affected by the resulting profit squeeze then points an accusing finger at price-cutting competitors.

Management would be better advised if the emphasis were placed on profitability rather than volume of sales dollars. A good first step in reducing the practice of arbitrary price cutting would be to adjust sales compensation so a greater portion of the paycheck would be based on profitability of the orders rather than volume at any price.

An important second step would be to ascertain if the applicable pricing strategies are being properly applied. The following summary of guidelines should be helpful in that respect.

Premium Pricing. In setting a premium price for a deluxe model, do not merely add a flat dollar amount, as was done by the KAC Company. Make certain that the premium price results in a higher percentage return than the return on the standard model.

Marginal Pricing. Marginal pricing is appropriate when a company has an advantage over its competitors such as (a) application of a new manufacturing technology that materially reduces costs; and (b) adding a private brand in addition to its existing name-brand product. The fixed cost content of the private brand's selling price can be reduced, but the brand name should continue to carry its full measure of fixed costs.

Break-even Test for Pricing. Most companies have been found to develop the selling price for a new product at only a single volume level, which may be quite different than the level used by the price leader. Therefore, when pricing a new product, first determine the break-even cost at four or five volume levels within the normal operating range. Then apply the markup factor to determine which of the four or five prices comes closest to the competitive market price. Using this strategy will help management determine whether it has the necessary capacity to meet the required production level and whether its marketing organization is sufficiently broad to attract the required volume.

Pricing within a Family of Products. When a new product fits into a family of similar products, do not reinvent the wheel. Fit the newcomer into its proper position within the family to ensure a consistent relationship to the other members of the family.

Underpricing Replacement Parts. When pricing replacement parts for discontinued products or for models no longer in production, do not overlook changes in inventory carrying costs of replacement parts for a probable 10-year period. Carrying costs, particularly the cost of money, will increase when interest rates rise. Other costs can also be affected in inflationary periods.

Substitute Materials. Contrary to common belief, substitute materials are not always cheaper. But there is nothing wrong with increasing the price when the advantages of using the more expensive material outweigh the increased price.

Cost-based Pricing. Customized products made to a customer's unique specifications should use the cost-based pricing strategy to account properly for a number of overhead costs which are normally allocated to standard products through an overhead rate. Some of the overhead costs, such as engineering, drafting, quality control, and rework, are usually much higher for customized products than for the standard products that are built to inventory. Such costs should be charged directly to the job as if they were direct labor and/or material.

In light of the topics discussed in this chapter, is there a place for "feel of the market," mentioned earlier? Yes, but only after the appropriate pricing strategy has first been applied and the results carefully evaluated.

CHAPTER 20

External and Internal Factors Affecting Product Costing and Pricing

The objective of pricing products for sale is to maximize the return on investment (equity). As was explained in chapter 13, return on investment is calculated by multiplying the return on sales by the annual turns of investment as related to sales (see Exhibit 13.6). Return on investment (ROI) therefore takes volume into account. Exhibit 13.10 and the related text explains how the ROI markup factors provide the mechanics for pricing.

Management's responsibility does not end with the determination of the markup factors—it must continually monitor external and internal factors that can influence the company's competitive position. The external factors will be discussed first.

EXTERNAL FACTORS

Innovation and Coping with Competition

Market acceptance of products is important for the obvious reason that non-acceptance or slow acceptance of a product means loss of the investment made in new product development. Exhibit 16.2 in chapter 16 illustrates various product life cycle patterns. The "instant bust" pattern occurs when an entire investment is lost because of nonacceptance of the product in the marketplace. The "straight fad" pattern shows some recovery of the investment of a product that was accepted only as a fad. The other patterns in this exhibit show varying degrees of acceptance.

Market acceptance of a new product is difficult to predict with accuracy. Automobiles and airplanes, in their first 20 years, had quite different degrees of public acceptance. The first acceptable auto was made in 1903 and was recognized as a standard road vehicle of the twentieth century in 1910. The airplane, on the other hand, had a great deal of difficulty with acceptance. Even those responsible for designing and building airplanes were found to be reluctant to fly.

Product quality can be a significant factor affecting acceptance. Westclox, for example, was established in the late 1800s by a highly skilled clockmaker who had a good reputation for making a quality product. The greed of the company's stockholders, who wanted quick profits, resulted in downgrading of quality. The deterioration of quality was disastrous to the company. In 1889, five years after establishment of the company, the assets and controlling interest were purchased by a smart businessman. He simplified the operations as well as the number of styles and varieties of watch and clock products, with the result that the company prospered. This is an example in which the product already had acceptance but lost it because of deterioration of quality in the interest of earning "a fast buck." The new owner had to make a further investment in the business to improve the operations and renew the marketing effort.

H. H. Timken recognized the need for a new type of bearing when he observed that trains in the 1880s made horrible noises in rounding curves and riding on rough roadbeds. This resulted in a high degree of wear and tear to axles and other train parts. The existing ball bearings and straight bearings did not solve the problem. Continued experimentation resulted in the tapered bearing. Since the tapered bearing also had good application in the manufacture of carriages in those pre-auto days, Timken, in addition to expanding his operations to accommodate the new type bearings, also provided capacity to build carriages. This example illustrates how investing in an improved product can be carried over to another product to provide a broader base for yielding a higher return on investment.

With rapid changes in technology, products can be quickly obsoleted by competitors with a different manufacturing expertise. This was the case when the hand-held electronic calculator was introduced by Texas Instruments in 1972. This product contained fewer than 100 parts and listed for about $150, compared with the electro-mechanical Fridens, Marchants, and Monroes containing hundreds of parts and selling at prices approximating $1,000. With continued improvements in technology, a comparable calculator today sells for less than $10. Such is the power of microelectronics technology.

The January, 1986 issue of *Planning Review* points up the case of NCR, which for years had the best and the least expensive mechanical cash register on the market. Then Burroughs developed a fully integrated electronic cash register and shifted the demand away from the NCR product.

The typewriter provides another example of product improvements versus technological shifts. Over the years, improvements to the mechanical typewriter reduced its size and weight, made it more sensitive to the touch, and permitted faster operator performance with less fatigue. Underwood failed to realize that further improvement meant another type of technology. It was IBM that pioneered the electric typewriter, which permitted use of different typing elements facilitating use of a variety of typefaces as well as a lift-off tape for correcting errors. Surprisingly, IBM had continually improved its electric typewriter but did not see the word processing revolution coming. Wang's word processor dominated the word processing market and IBM, the electronic giant, was caught off guard.

There is a human side to innovation. Managers, engineers, manufacturing executives, and sales personnel tend to become dedicated to existing technology. This often means that they are not the best suited for developing and implementing innovative production methods.

State of the Economy

Business moves in cycles between periods of overproduction and underproduction. Amax, Inc., in a leaflet dated April 1, 1982 entitled "Meeting the Economic Challenge," commented on recessions with regard to its own situation:

> In most business cycles, the rebound in demand for metals and minerals comes some months after the general economy turns up. The strong demand at the upturn comes mainly from the need to increase inventories at all levels in the producer-to-end-customer chain. The odds favor the present recession in the minerals business ending in the same way, with faster recovery in areas where our customers are carrying bare minimum working inventories.

The impact of a recession on profits can vary from industry to industry, as was indicated in chapter 13 from figures taken from annual reports of six companies.

Profits peaked during the sharp recession of 1973–1975 for Dow Chemical, Allied, Republic Steel, and Bethlehem Steel—and declined for Goodyear Tire and Firestone.

Inflation

The economy in the 1970s was affected adversely by inflation, which reached record proportions. When prices rise rapidly, one can expect demands for higher wages from employees as well as higher prices for materials purchased from suppliers. Because of the loud public outcry, government price controls were instituted. The excerpts from annual reports for the six companies referred to in chapter 13 include complaints because of the limitation of price increases. It is interesting to note in Exhibit 14.5 in chapter 14 that television set prices remained fairly constant during the 1970s, while U.S. goods and services more than doubled. This was undoubtedly due to downward pressure on prices because of cheaper foreign imports.

INTERNAL FACTORS

It is sometimes difficult to segregate external and internal factors that affect pricing. The product life cycle, for instance, can be shown to be an external factor sometimes and internal in other cases. In discussing it as an external influence, it is assumed that the company is affected by trends in the industry—market acceptance, for example. As an internal strategy, the company must recognize that its pricing cannot be based on a consistent relationship between cost and selling price.

The February 13, 1989 issue of *Fortune* lists several companies that have substantially reduced the amount of time required to develop new products. The article also lists companies that have successfully reduced the order-to-finished-goods time. See Exhibit 20.1.

Reducing Development Time

The *Fortune* article cites as an example Hewlett Packard's success in reducing development of computer printers from 4.5 years to 22 months. The company, not satisfied with this, has announced a companywide program called BET (break-even time) in which the employees were challenged to cut by half the interval between new product conception and profitability. To accomplish this, workers are required to begin pulling in the same direction and deciding co-operatively what steps need to be taken. Contrary to expectations that employees

EXHIBIT 20.1

DEVELOPMENT INNOVATORS

Company	Product	Old Time	New Time
Honda	Cars	5 Years	3 Years
AT&T	Phones	2 Years	1 Year
Navistar	Trucks	5 Years	2.5 Years
Hewlett-Packard	Computer Printers	4.5 Years	22 Months

PRODUCTION INNOVATORS

Company	Product	Old Time	New Time
General Electric	Circuit Breaker Boxes	3 Weeks	2 Hours
Motorola	Pagers	3 Weeks	2 Hours
Hewlett-Packard	Electronic Testing Equip.	4 Weeks	5 Days
Brunswick	Fishing Reels	3 Weeks	1 Week

would feel strained, the company indicates that the workers like the challenge and feeling of accomplishment.

Reducing Order-to-Finished Goods Time

The article also suggests that companies should take a hard look at the number of times a product or service requires internal approval before reaching the customer. It points out further that manufacturing typically takes only 5% to 10% of the total time between receipt of the order and getting the product to the customer—the rest of the time being taken by administration and the related paperwork compliance.

Monitoring the Backlog of Orders

With competition as fierce as it is, modern industry must constantly have its finger on the pulse of customer requirements. A clue to these requirements is available through a study of the trend of new orders. The company which can move quickly and ship these orders promptly is the company which will be remembered by the customer when subsequent new orders are placed. This monitoring method is helpful for determining capacity utilization. Many companies prepare a daily or weekly report showing the new orders received, shipments, and the resulting backlog. The backlog is a residual figure which can be used as an indicator as to whether incoming orders are on the increase or decrease. Exhibit 20.2 illustrates such a report. A new week is added to the preceding weeks so that prior reports need not be filed or consulted. Exhibit 20.3 plots the figures to show graphically the status of the backlog as well as the trend of new orders and shipments.

EXHIBIT 20.2

ORDER INTAKE VERSUS SHIPMENTS AND BACKLOG

Weeks	New Orders	Shipments	Backlog
1	$26,310	$11,415	$120,065
2	15,960	16,205	119,820
3	12,100	12,402	119,518
4	12,350	12,075	119,793
5	21,100	10,779	130,714
6	13,965	11,905	132,774
7	17,014	9,642	140,146
8	22,212	18,060	144,298
9	16,126	13,782	146,642
10	17,130	18,392	145,380
11	21,324	23,062	143,642
12	19,134	26,436	136,340
13	16,031	37,345	115,026
14	11,213	13,619	112,620
15	11,962	19,947	104,635
16	13,402	14,696	103,341
17	12,111	13,390	102,062
18	10,320	12,165	100,217
19	10,721	20,736	90,202
20	11,420	23,580	78,042
21	11,306	15,046	74,302
22	11,904	13,225	72,981
23	13,416	17,731	68,666
24	13,333	15,738	66,261
25	12,620	14,781	64,100
26	11,220	12,270	63,050
27	11,350	12,300	62,100
28	11,441	11,561	61,980
29	16,688	15,643	63,025
30	15,843	14,878	63,990
31	14,400	14,328	64,062
32	13,926	15,946	62,042
33	14,667	13,062	63,647
34	16,660	16,591	63,716
35	18,899	18,417	64,198
36	25,554	14,360	75,392
37	20,002	18,349	77,045
38	18,309	14,738	80,616
39	14,445	14,023	81,038
40	13,212	12,053	82,197
41	13,196	12,057	83,336
42	11,778	16,198	78,916
43	11,662	10,470	80,108

EXHIBIT 20.2 (cont'd)

ORDER INTAKE VERSUS SHIPMENTS AND BACKLOG

Weeks	New Orders	Shipments	Backlog
44	15,925	18,261	77,772
45	20,669	27,403	71,038
46	12,210	13,031	70,217
47	13,312	18,030	65,499
48	14,121	18,503	61,117
49	14,365	17,426	58,061
50	20,259	30,103	48,217

The line showing the backlog is calculated by adding new orders and subtracting shipments from the prior week's backlog. This line indicates a steady down-trend. This is an important trend to watch because some companies use it as a precursor to changes in selling price. A falling backlog could be an indication of a faltering economy, which might result in falling prices. A rising backlog, on the other hand, could be an indicator of business recovery and rising prices.

The controller of one company carried the analysis of his backlog a step further. His approach and reasoning was stated as follows: ''After we calculate our overall backlog each week, we break it down by production work centers.

EXHIBIT 20.3

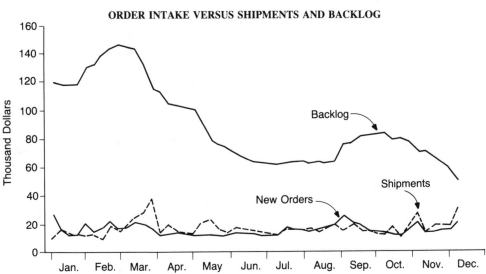

ORDER INTAKE VERSUS SHIPMENTS AND BACKLOG

This tells us which work centers will be overloaded and which will be underutilized.'' This suggests the following steps:

1. *Overloaded work centers:* Adjust schedules to permit longer production runs. This permits scheduling on a more logical basis. The company not only gains by scheduling longer runs; it is also able to schedule in a manner in which the changeovers from one machine to another are sequenced to avoid having a radical changeover for one run and then immediately tearing down the entire setup for the next run. Another saving is that the company has fewer changeovers and therefore spends less time setting up the equipment and more time manufacturing the product at reduced costs.

2. *Underutilized work centers:* When the company finds that some work centers will be underutilized, it determines which items in its product line will bring back additional volume for the underutilized centers. This information is communicated to the marketing department. The company also looks into the possibility of soliciting work from other manufacturers whose facilities might not be adequate for their needs. The aforementioned controller's company recently purchased some computer-controlled equipment which is not fully utilized. Its marketing department contacted two companies in the area who were only too happy to purchase part of the unused time on this equipment.

Balancing Development and Production Contracts

Trends are often monitored graphically because changes in direction or slope of a line can be more easily discerned than poring over statistical data. Ethcos Company (name disguised) received both development and production contracts from the government. Development contracts usually, but not always, led to follow-on production contracts. Management was aware that maintaining factory operations at a reasonable level of capacity required a sufficient backlog of development contracts. In view of this, the graph shown in Exhibit 20.4 was prepared. The general manager monitored the trend in the first few months of the first year and then relegated the responsibility to one of the staff members, who did the updating but did not get deeply enough involved to recognize potential problems.

When the staff member saw the sharp upward trend in the backlog of development contracts in August of the first year, he assumed that sooner or later, factory activity would catch up as a result of follow-on production contracts. Had he become more familiar with the content of later development contracts and their impact on production, he would have learned that most of

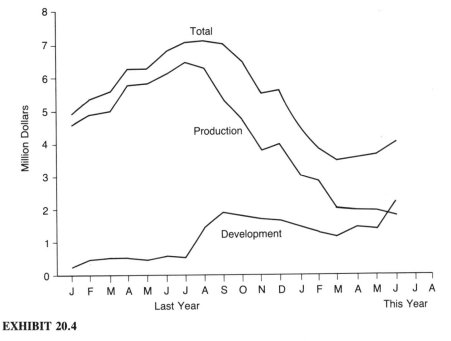

EXHIBIT 20.4

TOTAL BACKLOG OF CONTRACTS SHOWING BREAKDOWN BETWEEN DEVELOPMENT AND PRODUCTION

the upswing in development work was based on a different type of development for which there would be no production follow-on work. Fortunately, the general manager had become aware of the declining backlog of production contracts and had already taken steps to bring in other work. If the staff member had been more analytical, the corrective action could have been taken sooner.

Customer-related Pricing Strategy

In one of the management meetings of key executives at Halco, Inc. (name disguised) held each month, it was the purchasing manager's turn to make a presentation on profit improvement suggestions. He started by pointing out that practically all of the companies with which he was familiar identified their inventory by A, B, C, and, in some cases, D items. The A and B items usually account for the bulk of the dollars (65% to 85%) but only 15% to 20% of the number of items. The C and D items, on the other hand, represented a minor portion of the dollars but the bulk of the number of items (60% to 80%).

Because of the lower dollars tied up in C and D items, the buyers for these companies did not pay as much attention to prices paid for these as to the A and B items that were more costly. Therefore, the pricing of the C and D items need not be "shaved" as closely as pricing of the A and B category.

The sales manager challenged this suggestion; he asked how one could possibly know which items the customer classified as A, B, C, or D. The materials manager responded by pointing out that the nature of the customer's product was a good indicator of the items that constituted the various categories. This information could be highlighted on the incoming requests for quotation by the engineer who edited the incoming quotation requests. The controller, who was responsible for cost estimating, argued that companies sending in requests for quotation indicated, by so doing, that they were seeking competitive bids regardless of how they categorized the individual items. The division manager reminded the controller that there were C and D items built for stock and listed in the catalogs. He stated that these items were often discounted further by the salespeople. Here is where the purchasing manager's recommendation regarding items sold out of stock might apply. The customer's C and D items may well be A or B items to the manufacturer. The general manager closed with the request that this matter be given serious consideration.

Estimating Manufacturing Costs of Competitors

It is not unusual for companies to disassemble competitor's products to estimate their manufacturing costs. Material, which is a fair-sized item, can be discussed with the company purchasing manager. Production time can be determined by the industrial engineer. These two cost elements (prime cost) can be compared with the company's own prime cost. The comparison can be quite revealing. The engineering department can also analyze the disassembled product to take note of the design features—as the Japanese have been doing for years. This practice was followed by U.S. television manufacturers in the 1950s.

New Product Innovativeness

Sales personnel working in the field have direct contact with customers. They have the opportunity of knowing a good deal about the customer's product line and the applications that are made of the products. They also know the customer's problems and needs. One innovative salesman was responsible for creation of a new product that he sold to a cathode-ray tube manufacturer who was having problems with bent pins in the picture tube bases. In the process of packing and shipping this product, many of the pins in the base were bent. Straightening the pins in a completed cathode-ray tube was not always a practical solution. When the salesman returned to his office, he mentioned this problem to one of the engineers. The engineer designed a plastic plug that could be slipped over the pins of the completed cathode-ray tubes. This product could be made cheaply because it could be molded from excess "regrind" plastic material. The reground material was obtained from the runners that were cut off after plastic parts were molded or from improperly molded parts. Frequently, there was an accumulation of the reground material of various colors that could not be used. Since the color of the protective plug did not matter, any color or mixture of colors could be used. The company made some samples that were given to the customer for trial. The customer immediately placed an order for a large quantity. Not only did the innovative company benefit from reuse of the large excess of reground material; it could produce this new product continuously on automatic equipment that required only minimal operator supervision. Availability of this product provided an entree to other cathode-ray tube manufacturers.

Lending Assistance to the Customer

The engineer responsible for editing incoming requests for quotation is in a good position to evaluate the design of the customer's product. He can familiarize the customer with certain new material that could be substituted for ensuring better performance or reducing costs. Suggestions such as these are helpful in cementing relations with customers and encouraging more business.

The engineer of one company, in editing a customer request for quotation, noted that the request specifications called for use of numerous screws in the chassis of a new type of electronic measuring equipment. He suggested that screws be used in only certain key points in the event that disassembly is required at some future time, but that spot welding be substituted in those areas in which fastening of two pieces of sheet metal was to be the only function served by the screws. As simple as this suggestion was, the customer had not thought of it. The suggestion was adopted, and the prospective customer submitting the quotation request increased the volume of business with this company by 30%.

Quality Assurance

One of the major responsibilities of the quality control function is to assure that the product being manufactured meets the requirements called for in the specifications. Monitoring quality starts with the inspection of material in the receiving department; it includes first-piece checks of machined parts, subassembly inspection at various stages of production, and final inspection. Many quality assurance departments prepare statistics on defects to be distributed to the various department heads and the plant manager, to alert them to problem areas. Many of these reports are overly detailed. This is particularly true of reports that have been computerized. The new quality control manager of one company described his philosophy for reporting defects in a simpler and more effective manner.

In spite of the availability of highly detailed reports listing production defects, the Duralex Company (name disguised) was plagued with a high percentage of customer returns because of product defects in the field. Because the quality control manager did not have the management's confidence, a replacement was hired. The new manager advised that the basic information which was available on the computer was of value but, because of excessive detail, none of the recipients of the reports could make effective use of the information. The new quality control manager described his philosophy of reporting and control as follows:

> "Department heads are too busy to pore over page after page of lists of defects. This data must be presented in a digest that points out the key items that can be handled promptly. My approach is to select those key items that need immediate attention and to present these as a daily spoilage report for each area. The report is issued each morning for the previous day. Each of the reports, by area, is summarized on a weekly basis by type of unit and defect causing the rejection. Dollar values are then calculated and a listing made in order of dollar magnitude of spoilage with the highest cost items appearing at the top of the list. The part number rejected is shown as well as the final product in which the part is used. The week's scheduled production is also shown in order that a relationship can be made to show the magnitude of the rejects. [A variation of such a report excluding dollar values is shown in Exhibit 1.6 in chapter 1.] The report is closed out at the close of business on Tuesday and issued Wednesday morning, at which time a meeting of the quality control representative and production foremen discuss the causes of spoilage and remedies for correction."

Simplifying the Manufacturing Process

Industrial engineers (sometimes referred to as manufacturing engineers), in their work in establishing the operational sequences through which a product passes, are in a position to make changes to accommodate the introduction of a new process or a new machine. Through such changes, savings can often be made. In one company the industrial engineer, in reviewing the routing shown on the manufacturing process sheet, noted that a part went through a heading machine, then degreasing, threading, and another degreasing operation before drilling a hole to complete the part. Although this had been a standard procedure for years, the industrial engineer could see no reason for degreasing between the heading and threading operation. His recommendation for eliminating the superfluous operation was adopted.

The industrial engineer is usually responsible for making recommendations with regard to tool design. If the quantity of production justifies it, the company can save money in metal stamping through use of a sectional die. This permits replacement of individual parts of the die with minimum maintenance time. In the case of molding, the volume of production of a particular part will determine the optimum number of cavities.

Material Costs

The responsibility of the purchasing department to obtain the lowest possible price from suppliers can be affected by the lead time allowed in making the purchase. If the lead time is too short, it may be necessary to obtain the required material without obtaining competitive bids—or, it may be necessary to request the supplier to use air freight, and thus add substantially to the cost.

The buyers in purchasing are in a position to suggest which parts might be standardized to reduce the number of similar types carried in stock. This will not only reduce the size of the inventory but will facilitate the ordering of a greater quantity of the standardized part at lower prices. The purchasing department head in one company discovered that different engineers making up the parts lists for various products favored certain brands of 21 components, small motors, for example. A check with the stockroom showed that there were four different brands of motors in stock. When this was pointed out to the plant manager, he asked the stockroom supervisor to make up a list of the various other items that were stocked in more than one brand. When the list was completed, a review was made with the engineering department with the recommendation that the number of different brands be reduced to a minimum. When the work was completed, the stockroom supervisor estimated that 65 feet of shelf space would be made available by elimination of multibrand purchases. All decisions with regard to standardizing parts should, of course, be cleared with the engineering department because there may be a good reason for using a certain brand for a particular application.

Allocating Overhead to the Products

The manner in which indirect costs are applied to products can be quite important in product costing. This applies to the method for accounting for production losses as well. The provision for losses cannot be made arbitrarily any more than allocating overhead on an across-the-board basis. (This was covered in chapters 1–4.)

Qualifications of Cost Estimators

The cost estimator must be factory-wise, must feel comfortable in a factory atmosphere, and must be able to associate factory processes with the costs of performing the various operations in making the product. In addition to these qualifications, he or she must have good personality traits. The latter is important because of the need to deal with different individuals within the company and the need to use diplomacy when challenging data they supply.

To Whom Should the Cost Estimator Report? The lines of organization, insofar as the cost estimator is concerned, vary from company to company. The advantages and disadvantages of three reporting relationships are shown in Exhibit 20.5. However, the determination as to whom the cost estimating function should report cannot be dogmatically stated through a judgment based purely on the advantages and disadvantages shown in the exhibit.

Qualifying Cost Estimators by Type of Products. Chapter 6 refers to two general types of products—those that are customized to each customer's specifications, and those that are standardized according to the manufacturer's specifications.

In the first case, requests for product cost quotations are received con-

EXHIBIT 20.5

TO WHOM SHOULD THE COST ESTIMATOR REPORT?

Reporting Relationship	Advantages	Disadvantages
Reports to sales.	Sales department exerts pressure to keep costs low.	Undue pressure may be exerted on the estimator to understate estimated product costs. Pressure to get out quotations might result in shortcutting.
Reports to plant manager.	Estimator more likely to be up to date on changes in manufacturing.	Sense of urgency in getting out quotations may not be sufficient.
Reports to accounting.	Estimates more likely to be mathematically correct.	Approach to estimating could become too mechanical. Emphasis on clerical accuracy and detail, rather than production considerations, could lead to unrealistic estimates.

tinuously—each requiring a detailed analysis and review with one or more department heads. The cost estimator in this case must be very familiar with manufacturing processes and problems. He or she must, therefore, be physically located in the factory rather than in the sales or accounting departments.

In the second case, when the products are standardized, product costs are developed at the beginning of the year for inventory valuation purposes. For cost/selling price comparisons and interim product cost estimating, the standards must be adjusted to current costs. This information can be made available by maintaining a file of updated standards. The cost estimator in this case would be a member of the accounting department with knowledge of the factory operations.

Sales and Accounting Coordination is Important

Carter Brass Company has recently broken down its sales organization into four groups, each headed by a product manager. It also changed its method of sales compensation. The new method of payment included base pay plus a percentage of the profit on the products sold. Previously, the percentage had been based on volume of sales dollars. The product managers were advised that they had every right to question any product costs that they thought were too high to be competitive.

The intent, of course, was to encourage closer collaboration between the two departments. The general manager felt that this would bring both groups closer to the realities of the real world of manufacturing and selling.

About a month later, the four product managers had accumulated 68 questions, which were submitted to the company controller. Seven of the more representative questions and responses are summarized here.

Question: Why is the cost of product 5168A5 so much greater than product 5168A6 when both products are identical?

5168A5	Factory Cost	$444.03/M
5168A6	Factory Cost	251.97/M

Response: The cap on the first product is machined from brass rod, while the cap on the second product is stamped from brass sheet.

Comment: This question and response was helpful to the product manager because previously, he was not aware that the cap on the more expensive product was machined rather than being stamped out of sheet brass.

Question: Why is product 8556A6 half the cost of the first product when both are so much alike?

8446A6   Factory Cost $251.67/M
8556A6   Factory Cost   126.06/M

Response: Bill of Material file lacks costs for component 41680B2, thus understating the cost of product 8556A6 as well as several other products using this same component.

Comment: This admission of an error is embarrassing and will result in greater care in costing.

Question: Since product 248K834 is the same as 248K198, except for the addition of a cap, does this mean that the cap costs $252.90/M?

248K198   Factory Cost $186.00/M
248K834   Factory Cost   438.90/M

Response: The difference in cost is due to the individual packaging of each of the 1,000 parts which the customer requested.

Comment: Prior to the raising of the question, no one was aware of the amount of packaging cost required for individual packaging. The general manager asked the industrial engineer to determine if the packaging cost could be reduced. As a result of the review, the packaging costs were cut by 30%.

Question: Why is the factory cost of product 1498A6 so great when the selling price is only $179.35?

1498A6   Factory Cost $207.82

Response: This product is purchased from a sister plant at its factory cost plus a sizeable markup.

Comment: This was called to the attention of the general manager, who met with his counterpart in the supplier plant to discuss the matter of transfer prices. As a result, the markup was reduced to a more reasonable level.

Question: Why is the factory cost of product IAP004 so high and the selling price is only $106.50?

1AP004   Factory Cost $104.31

Response: This cost was developed when we did not yet have the automated equipment; the cost is based on the semiautomatic equipment.

Comment: This was another embarrassment to the accounting department because the factory cost had not been updated.

Question: Why is the factory cost so high when the selling price is only $344.10?

7-782-52   Factory Cost $839.16

Response: This item was molded with a six-cavity mold requiring 22.5 production hours. A higher volume of sales would justify building a mold with more than six cavities for the larger press.

Comment: This response impressed the product manager with the impact that volume can have on the factory cost.

Question: Since the products 332-001 and 332-008 are quite similar, why is there such a wide spread in the factory costs?

332-001	Factory Cost	$407.65
332-008	Factory Cost	326.82

Response: Because of the low volume, the first item was made on a hand screw machine, while much higher volume of the second item made it feasible to use the Brown and Sharp.

Comment: This provided another example of the need for volume to reduce factory costs.

The general manager's action in bringing about greater collaboration between sales and accounting worked out well. At first, more heat was generated than light. But after several questions had been discussed, both sides recognized the need for closer coordination.

The product managers became more aware of the importance of reducing product costs because this would increase profitability and increase the profit base on which part of their compensation would be based.

The general manager, who sat through one of the meetings, became aware of the "highballing" of intracompany transfer prices by the selling plant. He also became aware of the high packaging costs, which he was able to reduce.

The controller, who in the course of obtaining answers to the questions had to consult factory personnel, became far more familiar with the manufacturing processes and problems.

CHAPTER 21

The Integrated Cost System: Its Role in Product Costing and Pricing

In many companies that have implemented Computer Aided Manufacturing (CAM), computer integrated cost systems have been found to lag.

Progressive manufacturing companies have discarded drafting tables in favor of Computer Aided Design (CAD). The computerized design specifications are translated into engineering/manufacturing bills of material. With computerized bills of material, this manually posted Kardex® files have followed the drafting tables into oblivion. The resulting network of subsystems furnishes production time data by operation, provides the ability to track units of production through every operation, and provides the production control and scheduling department with inventory status reports for every item in inventory at the various stages of production.

With the availability of computerized bills of material that have been structured operation-by-operation and level-by-level, it is only logical that the cost accounting system be integrated with CAM. The Manufacturing Process Sheet (Exhibit 21.1) would provide accounting with the same data used by manufacturing. Using the Manufacturing Process Sheet, shown in structured form in Exhibits 11.3 and 11.6 in chapter 11, the computer would develop the standard material, direct labor, and overhead costs for the various fabricated parts, subassemblies, and finished products.

EXHIBIT 21.1

MANUFACTURING PROCESS SHEET

ISSUE DATE	ISSUE #	REVISED:	P.C. 01	BASIC 02608	SUFFIX 1	MACH. CODE 0008	REFERENCE		SHOP ORDER #
DRAWING #		LAST C.A.	PART NAME STEM						DATE ISSUED
			MTL. CODE 20-2800	KIND BRASS		SIZE .280 DIAMETER			QTY. TO MAKE
			SHAPE COIL	SPEC. 26-4	TEMPER	HARDNESS			RAW MTL. REQMT.
			UNIT LBS.	PER/M GROSS 37.8	PER/M NET 17.0				REQD COMPLETION DATE

ROUTING   MACHINING, COATING, INSPECTION, COMPONENTS STOCKROOM   LEVEL (04)

OPN. #	OPERATION DESCRIPTION	EQUIPMENT	DEPT.	SET-UP HRS.	LAB. GRD.	PROD. HRS./M	LAB. GRD.	NO. MACH.	NO. MEN	COST CENTER
010	CUT-OFF & HEAD	HEADER	MACHG	3.0	10	.15	5	2	1	0447
020	ROLL THREAD	ROLLING MACHINE	MACHG	2.0	10	.50	5	2	1	0450
030	HEADING	HEADER	MACHG	12.0	13	.81	12			0761
050	DEGREASE	DEGREASER	COATG			.07	4			0568
	INSPECT		QC							

INTEGRATING THE COST SYSTEM MUST GO BEYOND CAM

Let us assume that the material type and quantity, direct labor grades, and production rates for making the various products have already been programmed into the cost system. The next step is to develop the standard costs of material, direct labor, and overhead. Before this can be done, the following additional steps are required:

1. A realistic financial plan is needed as a basis for determining the capacity level required for the coming year.
2. Realistic allowances for unavoidable losses in fabrication of components must be made.
3. Provision must also be made to update the standard costs during the year in a separate file.

Importance of a Realistic Financial Plan

The annual financial plan is an important management tool that serves as a blueprint for achieving optimum utilization of resources and a desirable return on investment. Its development requires an integrated effort on the part of the sales department, production/scheduling, and the cost department (see Exhibit 21.2). The first step is development of a reasonably attainable sales forecast. This is an important step because the resulting production volume determines the level of plant and equipment utilization.

EXHIBIT 21.2

ANNUAL FINANCIAL PLAN

Sales Department
Sales Forecast by Products

Production Control/Scheduling
Sales Forecast
+ Backlog
− Inventory
Production Plan

Controller's Department
Manufacturing Cost Breakdown
Material
Direct Labor
Overhead

The Starting Point: A Sales Forecast. Many financial plans run aground at the sales forecasting stage. A surprising number of sales executives shy away from making forecasts for individual products. Whenever they can—and this is a frequent occurrence—they will forecast sales in the aggregate. The writer is aware of numerous instances in which the sales manager merely advised the controller to add a factor of X percent to the current year's annualized sales and use this as the sale forecast in the following year's financial plan.

The Controller's Responsibility. Because of year-end pressures, many controllers will accept the "quick and dirty" forecast based on an aggregate figure with no breakdown by products. This immediately flaws the next step, which is the determination of the production plan. The breakdown of manufacturing costs must then be based on broad averages rather than using the computerized bills of material to determine the manufacturing cost breakdown on a product-by-product basis. In carrying out his or her duties, the controller has a responsibility to see that the information input into the financial plan is properly developed, must reject any hastily made forecasts, and should insist that the forecasted sales be shown by individual products. Accuracy is admittedly difficult to achieve, but this is not a justifiable excuse for going to the other extreme.

Production Control/Scheduling. Another weakness in financial planning is that production control/scheduling is not consulted. Because this group is responsible for scheduling and tracking production through the plant, it is intimately familiar with potential bottlenecks in the manufacturing process. It is therefore in a position to point out that an increase in certain products would require additional equipment or the addition of another shift or partial shift in the bottleneck operations.

In most companies, preparation of the annual financial plan is a stand-alone project in which too little effort is expended in coming up with a breakdown of sales by products and quantities. As a result, when actual sales, manufacturing costs, and profits are compared with the annual plan, the differences can be substantial and difficult to explain. These unreconcilable differences can be highly frustrating to management, with the result that credibility of the cost system is impugned.

Realistic Allowances for Unavoidable Losses

Production losses can be classified into two types: (a) subassemblies, assemblies, and finished products; and (b) losses in fabrication, which are difficult to account for.

Losses incurred in subassemblies, assemblies, and finished products can be accounted for with a reasonable degree of accuracy because formalized inspection procedures are used. Part of this inspection procedure is to record the number of rejects and the reason for rejection (or necessity for rework). This type of inspection can be justified because of the cost and importance of these units in the finished product.

Fabricating losses, on the other hand, are highly elusive. They occur in such operations as molding, metal forming, die casting, painting, plating, and wire drawing. Some illustrative examples follow.

Molding. During a plant tour, the plant manager of a plastics molding operation explained the difficulty of measuring production losses of molded plastic parts:

> As a mold gets more and more use, cavities can develop defects that result in malformed parts. Troublesome cavities are frequently blocked to minimize the number of such defects. Production readings are taken off the counters on each press. This shows the number of cycles that the machine has completed. The number of cycles multiplied by the number of cavities in the mold shows the estimated production so that I can see how close we are coming to completion of the production run. Accounting likes to use this figure because it provides ''documentation'' of what was produced. I explained to them that this is only an estimate. They think that they will receive a scrap report showing how many units were scrapped. There just isn't such a report. Most of the defects and runners are reground and remolded so there is very little loss of material. There is some excess machine time and related cost but it wouldn't pay to make such calculations on the factory floor. The stockroom counts the good parts and inputs the number into the computer terminal. If Accounting used this figure, then the losses would be automatically excluded from good production. With this information, they should be able to determine the excess cost without requiring a lot of clerical work on the production floor. We do lose material when we purge presses at the end of the run. The presses have to be purged whenever a different material is to be used. When the change is from a dark to a light color, the purging loss is greater than if the dark color followed the lighter one. . . . The purged material, which is quite hot, is moved out of the way; it cannot be re-used; this is an unavoidable loss.

Metal Forming. When the question of reporting excess usage of material was brought up in the metal forming plant of another company, the manufacturing superintendent pointed to a bank of machines, each of which was producing approximately 12,000 rolled pins per hour.

> We use air pressure to blow the pins out of the way before the next pin is formed. Some of the parts are bound to fall on the floor and into the oil

under the machines. It isn't economical for us to expend labor to collect and count these pins. If it were, we would collect and clean them and there wouldn't be any scrap to report. The coiled sheet stock in our other metal forming section is purchased in standard widths to eliminate the need for slitting. If we run a part requiring stock $1\frac{7}{8}$ inches wide, we use two-inch wide stock. This will result in a loss of $\frac{1}{8}$ inch. It's not economical for us to expend the time and labor required to account for the total cost of such losses for the various types of metals we use.

What Is the Answer to Fabrication Losses? The plant manager of the plastics plant and the manufacturing superintendent of the metal forming plant made some points that the texts on cost accounting overlook. To find the solution, the cost accountant should review the production control procedures followed in arriving at the quantities shown in the inventory status reports. These reports base their figures on only the good units accepted into the fabricated stock areas. Additionally, the stockroom personnel regularly check the physical quantity in stock with the number shown on the inventory status reports. The accounting department's inventory value in many companies is less accurate because the typical cost system includes all material, labor, and overhead costs incurred in production and relies on scrap reports to back out the excess costs incurred. If the cost system were integrated so that only good units were recognized as production, most of the phantom inventory and overreporting of profits could be avoided.

Limitations of Frozen Standards

Many companies that use frozen standards for valuing inventory do not maintain a computerized file of updated standards for use in determining the current manufacturing cost of the various products. An updated file should be maintained because it can be used to show the current manufacturing cost of the various products so that current gross margins for the individual products can be monitored. In addition, at the end of the year, when standards are due for revision, the frozen standards can be updated with a minimum of delay. Without the updated file, it would be necessary for the cost department to expend a substantial amount of time at year end, when time is at a premium.

CHAPTER 22

Summing Up:
Ten Commandments for More
Realistic Costing and Pricing

Pricing is a function that has a direct impact on company profits and therefore warrants high-level management attention. Competition, no matter what the language, is the limiting factor if prices are set too high; product costs, when properly developed, set the lower limit. The following commandments apply:

1. *Sales forecasts must be improved:* Don't lump sales forecasts for the coming year into a single dollar figure based on X percent of the previous year's total sales. List the products and quantities.

2. *The sales forecast and the financial plan:* Convert the sales forecast to a production forecast of the products and quantities to be manufactured. (See Exhibit 21.2.) Once the manufacturing breakdown by products is developed, you can start preparing the financial plan.

3. *Standard (normal) volume of production:* Compare the normal volume of production with the forecasted production volume. Remember that prices cannot be based on idle capacity.

4. *Building reliability into product costs:* Review chapters 1 through 5 to ensure that product costs do not contain any of the deficiencies.

5. *Use the cost system that fits the product:* Remember that specifications for customized products are determined by the customer (and are unique to each customer). The manufacturer determines the specifications for standard

products. If your company makes customized products read chapters 6 through 8. For standard products read chapter 11.

6. *Integrate the cost system with the manufacturing operations:* If your company has implemented computer aided manufacturing (CAM), it is logical that your cost system would profit by being computerized because of the advantage of using a common data base.

7. *Real-world problems in customer orders that Marketing should monitor:* Marketing must monitor all incoming requests for quotations to ensure that all drawings and specifications are clear.

8. *Markup factors in pricing:* Review chapter 13 to ensure that markup factors used in establishing prices are not arbitrary.

9. *Impact of product life cycle on costing and pricing:* Remember to take into account the product life cycle when costing and pricing products. See chapter 16.

10. *Product costs must play a larger role in pricing:* Too often, prices are set by intuition or "feel for the market." Chapter 19 discussed a number of pricing strategies in which product costs are taken into account before finalizing the selling price.

If these ten commandments are used as a frame of reference, they will aid immeasurably in providing more realistic product costs and prices—as well as increased profitability as a natural byproduct.

Index